Writers & Society in Contemporary Italy
A COLLECTION OF ESSAYS

Writers & Society
in
Contemporary Italy

A COLLECTION OF ESSAYS

EDITED BY

Michael Caesar

AND

Peter Hainsworth

ST. MARTIN'S PRESS
NEW YORK

All rights reserved. For information, write:
St. Martin's Press, Inc., 175 Fifth Avenue, New York, NY10010
Printed in Great Britain
First published in the United States of America in 1984

Paperback edition 1986

Library of Congress Cataloging in Publication Data
Main entry under title:

Writers & society in contemporary Italy.

  Includes bibliographies and index.
  Contents: The transformation of post-war Italy/
Michael Caesar, Peter Hainsworth—The neo-avantgarde/
Christopher Wagstaff—Umberto Eco/David Robey—
[etc.]
    1. Italian literature—20th century—History and criticism
—Addresses, essays, lectures.   2. Italy—Civilization
—1945 –   —Addresses, essays, lectures.   I. Caesar,
Michael.   II. Hainsworth, Peter.   III. Title: Writers and
society in contemporary Italy.

PQ4088.W75   1984   850'.9'00914   83 – 40503
ISBN 0 – 312 – 89350 – 7
ISBN 0 – 312 – 89351 – 5 (pbk.)

Contents

Editors' Preface

Although the editors bear the final responsibility for any shortcomings of this book, its making has required a more than usual degree of collaboration between all the contributors. Once the general shape of the volume had been agreed between us, the contributors came together on two occasions during the writing of it. The first meeting was devoted to an early draft of Chapter 1 and led to numerous modifications being incorporated into the final version printed here. The second was an opportunity for us to discuss in detail the first draft of each of the remaining chapters. The book is therefore not so much the result of two editors soliticing individual pieces as the product of a common effort.

Between us, we would have so many people to thank, for reading, listening, arguing, suggesting, informing and correcting, that we hope they will all recognize themselves as included in our thanks and not be offended if none is mentioned by name. But we owe a special debt of gratitude to the two people who between them produced at very short notice a great deal of the final typescript, Jane Stowell at Oxford and Sue Macdonald at Canterbury. We should also like to thank Elena Jeronomidis and Diego Zancani for their work in the early stages of the project; the authorities of the Italian Institute, London, and Bedford College, London, for making rooms available for meetings; and Peter Armour of Bedford College in particular for unlocking the door on chilly Saturday mornings. We should like to acknowledge, finally, the invaluable encouragement given us at a critical moment by Professor Cecil Grayson.

A note on Bibliographies, References and Quotations

Bibliographies are appended to each chapter. Each is intended to be useful rather than comprehensive and is divided into three sections: the first gives the principal works of the author who is the subject of the chapter, the second works cited in the course of the chapter and the third suggestions for further reading. An asterisk indicates the work which contains the fullest further bibliography. The bibliographies to Chapters 1 and 2 are organised along slightly different lines in view of the somewhat different material covered in them.

References to the bibliographies in the text follow the Author-Date system. As regards the works of the author in question, unless otherwise indicated the date given in brackets in the text is the date of publication of the first Italian edition. If, for reasons of convenience, references and quotations relate to a later edition, then the edition used is indicated in the bibliography as 'ed. cited'. English versions of titles given in the text are, unless otherwise indicated, titles of published English or American translations, of which details are given in the bibliographies. Where no published translations exist, the titles have been translated by the author of the chapter, as have all passages quoted.

Quotations from fiction and poetry have generally been given in Italian with English translations. In some cases, for reasons of length, only the English has been given. Quotations from essays, articles and critical works have normally been given in English only.

Notes on the Editors and Contributors

MICHAEL CAESAR (Lecturer in Italian, Kent University) has published articles on Leopardi, Manzoni and on modern Italian writing. He has translated Galvano della Volpe's *Critica del gusto* (New Left Books, London, 1978).

PETER HAINSWORTH (University Lecturer in Italian, Oxford University and Fellow of Lady Margaret Hall) has published articles on early Italian poetry and on Zanzotto, and has edited (with T. Gwynfor Griffith) *Petrarch: Selected Poems* (Manchester University Press, Manchester, 1972).

RICHARD ANDREWS (Senior Lecturer in Italian, Kent University) has published articles on Ariosto and on Italian Renaissance comedy. He has also published a critical edition of a fourteenth century text on Italian metrics by Antonio da Tempo.

DAVID FORGACS (Lecturer in Italian Studies, Sussex University) has published articles on modern criticism, education and political theory. He has recently contributed to *Modern Literary Theory* (edited by Ann Jefferson and David Robey, Batsford, London, 1982) and has edited (with Geoffrey Nowell Smith) *Antonio Gramsci, Selected Cultural Writings* (Lawrence and Wishart, London, due 1984).

JOHN GATT-RUTTER (formerly Senior Lecturer in Italian, Hull University) has published articles on modern Italian fiction and is the author of *Writers and Politics in Modern Italy* (Hodder and Stoughton, London, 1978).

VERINA JONES (Senior Lecturer in Italian, Reading University) has published articles on Manzoni and on Croce.

LINO PERTILE (Reader in Italian Studies, Sussex University) has published articles on Dante, Montaigne, Leopardi, Pavese and on contemporary Italian writing. He has translated Dario Fo's *Non si paga, non si paga* (*Can't pay! Won't pay!* Pluto Press, London, 1978).

JUDY RAWSON (Senior Lecturer in Italian, Warwick University) has published articles on Italian fiction and has edited Ignazio Silone's *Fontamara* (Manchester University Press, Manchester, 1977).

DAVID ROBEY (University Lecturer in Italian, Oxford University and Fellow of Wolfson College) has published articles on Renaissance literature. He is the editor of *Structuralism: An Introduction* (Clarendon Press, Oxford, 1973) and (with Ann Jefferson) of *Modern Literary Theory: A Comparative Introduction*, (Batsford, London, 1982).

CHRISTOPHER WAGSTAFF (Lecturer in Italian, Reading University) has published articles on Italian Futurism and on the Italian cinema.

Michael Caesar
Peter Hainsworth

1 The Transformation of Post-war Italy

In 1962, introducing Sergio Pacifici's valuable *Guide to Contemporary Italian Literature,* Thomas G. Bergin located the book in a historical context marked deeply by the experience of the Second World War and its aftermath. 'Ever since the Fascist wall was breached some two decades ago', Bergin wrote, 'the American public has given a good deal of attention to the Italian cultural scene and Italian writers have been translated, Italian films have been imported – even Italian fashions have infiltrated American life to a degree previously unheard of.' Italian culture was presenting a newly interesting and acceptable face to the rest of the Western world and preparing to enter (or re-enter) modernity. Now, twenty years on, we seem to be witnessing a revival of interest in the country's writers similar to that shown in the late 1950s and early 1960s. Montale's Nobel Prize in 1975, the translations of his work and of the work of other poets, the growing reputation of Italo Calvino, the recent successes of Dario Fo, the impact of the ideas of Gramsci and his post-war successors on questions of culture and politics, and the reception of Umberto Eco's outstanding work in semiotics are some indication of this Italian presence in the Anglo-Saxon literary and intellectual culture.

But the historical questions to be asked are necessarily different from those of twenty years ago. The moment at which Bergin and Pacifici were writing has itself become a fundamental point of reference for this book. In the early 1980s we are less immediately concerned with the problem of the rehabilitation or revival of Italian culture after Fascism. Instead, the historical point to which everyone involved in writing this book has constantly had recourse is the period of profound change which since 1956 has affected all levels of Italian life – economic, social and political, as well as cultural. We say 'since 1956', though in fact it is difficult to give precise dates to this period. The bases of economic expansion were laid in the late 1940s, the 'boom' itself was short and sharp (a mere five years between 1959 and 1963), and its consequences and implications are still working themselves out today. The transformations which the country underwent during these years occurred more rapidly and in more concentrated a form probably than in any other Western European nation, though many Third World countries have experienced an even more dizzying rate of industrialization and 'modernization'. The combination of this almost colonial rate of expansion and a highly sophisticated and articulate intellectual culture with deep roots in the European past produces a tension which is one of the distinguishing features of recent Italian writing.

Not all the writers discussed in this book concern them-selves with explicitly social issues. But they are all, in different ways, writers of modern Italy, of an Italy that has been transformed from the relatively poor, traditionalist, largely agrarian country of the mid-1950s into one of the world's ten largest industrial powers, with a consumer economy, with new and complex social and political problems and of course with strong residues of its past jostling, fusing or more commonly clashing with the energies of the present. These are some of the writers of that transformation. All began to write before the 'economic miracle' of the late 1950s, and some had even had work published before the war. But their careers as mature writers extend from the 1950s to the present. In their work, from different and changing perspectives, what has been happening in the country is articulated, interpreted and in some cases resisted and denounced. To read them is both to see rapid changes in the society, culture and economy of the country reflected, more or less directly, in writing, and it is also to see how those changes might be given form and significance in words, to gain some idea of what they might mean in other terms than those of statistics, sociological analysis or political economy. And despite the particularity of the Italian situation, their interest is not purely local: for in their work the general problems of literature and of articulate understanding in advanced capitalist society in general achieve intense, sometimes brilliant formulation.

Two criteria have operated in the selection of the authors

discussed in this book. On the one hand, we are interested in 'writing' in a familiar literary sense of the word. Buzzati, Sciascia, Calvino and Morante are primarily novelists or short-story writers, and it is on this aspect of their work that the respective chapters focus; similarly it is Zanzotto as a poet who commands our attention here. But others are not writers in this sense at all. One, Dario Fo, does not write books, but rather scripts, for performance by himself and others, and can only be said to be a writer in the sense that texts of his plays have been published. Eco has recently written a successful novel, but his major work is as a semiologist and cultural theorist. Fortini is a poet, but he is also and more importantly a cultural and political critic and theorist, and it is as such that he is discussed here. The reason for their inclusion in this volume is not only that they are acute observers of the contemporary scene, but also that in their practice they are constantly presenting challenges to the notion of literature, rubbing out its boundaries, and upsetting its assumptions. We do not mean to set up any kind of theoretical opposition between the literary and the non-literary. Rather, the presence of both kinds of voice is an acknowledgement of the fact that creative writing in Italy has historically gone hand-in-hand with analytical reflection on the nature of literature and its social status. Often, of course, as the chapters on the Neo-avantgarde and on Pasolini make clear, the roles of creative writer, literary theorist and cultural critic are combined in the same person.

At one level, then, this book acknowledges and derives from the widespread sense that the boundaries of literature are shifting, that new demarcations are in the process of being drawn between literature and history, between literature and ideas, between one form of writing and another. If we do not address this issue systematically, it is because our aim was not completeness. Other writers might well have been chosen than those on whom we do concentrate. The decision to devote the major part of the book to a fairly detailed presentation of a dozen or so individuals itself precluded any summary or synthetic treatment of the period as a whole, except briefly in this introduction. That decision was, we believe, justified if the book was to be anything other than a catalogue of titles and trends; and we hope that a small number of writers, of substantial reputation and achievement, will reveal more about their society and times than would a hundred names.

The pages that immediately follow are intended to establish the general context within which the individual writers that we look at are to be seen. The first section summarises the main economic, social and political changes of the past thirty years. The second surveys the effects that these have had in terms of publishing, of readership and of the role of literary and intellectual culture in Italian society. And the third passes from the sociology of that culture to developments within it, and is a short survey of the major currents, issues and figures since the mid-1950s.

(a) The Economic Miracle and After

The economic and social changes that Italy has undergone in the past thirty years have been unprecedented in the country's history in their size and scope. No Italian has been able to ignore them, for their effects have been tangible in all aspects of life.

The impetus to change came in the 1950s from the economy. A number of factors contributed to a steady recovery after the devastation of the war, and then to a period of rapid and sustained growth which lasted from 1951 to 1963, with a particularly dramatic expansion towards its end, 1959–1963 being the years of the so-called 'boom' or 'economic miracle'. The removal of the protective tariff-barriers which had surrounded the country's economy since Unification, the injection of substantial amounts of U.S. aid, the use of credit restrictions to encourage competitiveness, the stability of the banking system and the relative stability of the prices of raw materials (important in a country like Italy which is lacking in minerals and sources of energy) all contributed to create a climate of opportunity and entrepreneurial confidence. In addition, the unions were divided and weak and labour was cheap. Public investment in the South of Italy helped to create for the first time a large national market for consumer durables . Productivity increased as equipment became more standardized, while industrialists could draw on technical know-how imported from abroad without having to bear the costs of research and development. Investment was high (in 1961 investment had grown to one-and-a-half times what it was in 1954), and so were profits.

The main expansion occurred in manufacturing industry. Its share of the GNP rose by 10% between 1950 and 1960. By 1962, the four essential sectors of an industrial economy – steel, chemicals, engineering and electricity – represented 16.1% of the economy (compared with 19.3% in France). But the most visible effect of this expansion was in the labour market, where within ten years the traditional preponderance of agricultural employment had been reversed. Where in 1951 just over 40% of the active labour force had been working on the land, in 1961 the figure had fallen to 25%, (and it has continued to decline steadily ever since, to an estimated 13% of the active labour force in 1980). By no means all of this labour released from the land went straight into the factories. A proportion of it moved into the more slowly growing service sector. A further, and significant, portion was forced to leave the labour market altogether, particularly women who had contributed to the rural economy, but for whom there was no, or less, room in the towns. But while the percentage of the workforce employed in industry remained steady at around 36%, the absolute numbers increased by over a million in ten years, from just over 7 mill. in 1951 to 8.25 mill. in 1961.

The boom of 1959-63 was led by exports, which, from 1955 on, accounted for an increasing share of the rise in aggregate production. These were the years in which Italian brand-names like FIAT, Olivetti, Pirelli, Zanussi began to sound familiar to foreigners. The money was in cars, domestic appliances, office equipment – mass-produced goods not requiring unusually sophisticated technology. While exports surged ahead, the domestic market expanded more slowly. Both prices and wages remained depressed throughout the 1950s, and then accelerated somewhat during the boom itself. But it was not until 1965 that the rate of growth of private consumption began to outstrip that of the GNP as the new purchasing power went in search of cars, televisions, better furniture and food and less tangible goods such as travel and entertainment. Within a few years, and on the crest of a 'renewed but uneasy expansion' (Podbielski 1974, 16) following a short recession in 1963-65, Italy's 'consumer society' was born.

The remarkable expansion of the industrial economy between the 1950s and the 1960s was undoubtedly a tribute to the inventiveness and adaptability of Italian workers and managers. It also led unquestionably to a significant improvement in the material quality of life for very many people. By the late 1960s Italy had come a long way from the situation described by a Parliamentary Commission on Poverty which as recently as 1953 had reported that 24% of Italian households were either 'destitute' (*miseri*) or 'in hardship' (*disagiati*), that there was 'overcrowding' (i.e. more than two people to a room) in 21% of dwellings, and that 52% of homes in the South were without running drinking-water, while only 57% had a lavatory (Moss and Rogers 1980, 164-5). But the economic miracle was not pure uninterrupted progress and it became clear in the course of the 1960s that behind it lay major problems.

In the first place it seemed that industry was developing in a dangerously unbalanced way, and that export-led growth was resulting in a splitting of the economy. On the one hand there was a competitive, efficient, technologically progressive industrial sector which, however, provided only a limited expansion of employment opportunities, e.g. in industries using metals and chemicals. On the other hand there was a sheltered home-market sector, with predominantly backward and inefficient methods of production and only slowly rising productivity but with a large capacity for absorbing labour (Podbielski 1974, 21). Much more obvious was a worsening of the imbalance between regions as a result of the boom. Modern industry was becoming more and more concentrated in the North, especially in the 'industrial triangle' formed by Turin, Milan and Genoa. But the richer regions were failing to act as a locomotive for the poorer ones, and the result was what Moss and Rogers in 1980 describe as 'the persisting inequalities in life-chances, on almost any indicator, between those born in the south and those born in the north' (167). A third problem consisted in the fact that while industry expanded and modernized, agriculture became steadily more inefficient and unproductive. An unsuccessful land-reform in the early 1950s had been followed by mass migration, and what chances there were for a correction of this trend – for example through the use of funds provided by the *Cassa per il Mezzogiorno* (Southern Development Fund) or those earmarked for agricultural subsidy or regional development by the EEC – were constantly hampered by the fourth major obstacle: an overgrown, inefficient and frequently corrupt public administration, whose own shortcomings caused dysfunctions throughout the system.

Such problems were rooted in the very structure of Italian industry and society. They were exacerbated by others of a more immediate nature that were sparked off by the size and speed of the boom itself. By far the more serious of those was the situation created by the physical movement of hundreds of thousands of people from one part of the country to another. Official figures speak of some one million Southerners moving North between 1959 and 1963; in the peak year of emigration, 1961, a total of 292,000 people went North. Since there were many reasons for migrants either not wanting or not bothering to register with the authorities, these are certainly underestimates, representing perhaps no more than half the real figure. Southern rural areas like Basilicata, the Abruzzi, Molise and Calabria recorded a lower population in the 1961 and 1971 censuses than in 1951. Correspondingly, the population of the host cities of the North grew at a dizzying rate: between 1955 and 1961, 50–90,000 people were added to the population of Milan annually, while the number of people living in Turin rose by more than 50% in the 1950s, mainly in the latter half of the decade. As the immigrants arrived with the promise or the hope of a job, they found themselves in cities that were completely unprepared for them, with nothing like enough housing, health facilities, schools or transport. Immigrant ghettoes rapidly developed, either in decaying city-centres or more frequently in slum-dwellings and shanty-towns on the outskirts. Their inhabitants were faced by exceedingly unpleasant living-conditions, unfamiliar and demanding patterns of work, and frequent displays of racism on the part of the host population. Nevertheless, there seems a case for arguing that, for a time at least, the traditional patriarchal structure of the emigrant family survived and helped the first wave of immigrants to make the transition from rural labourers to semi-skilled factory workers. What no doubt also helped was a perception, shared by employers and employees alike, of a common interest and a common ethic based on notions of hard work, good pay and the building up of capital. The transition was less easy for the second generation of Southern immigrants who began to arrive as the economy turned up again in 1966–67. By this time consumerism was in full swing, while the traditional peasant attitudes of self-sacrifice and respect for authority had lost much of their attraction and apparent sense. But the conditions these new immigrants encountered were not much improved on those of eight or ten years before. Indeed, if one thing was clear, it was that the politicians did not know how to begin coping with a range of social pressures that by the end of the 1960s were reaching crisis proportions.

In fact, the politicians had not kept pace either with economic development or with the social evolution (and problems) which had followed in its wake. Nobody doubted, at least in public, the necessity and urgency of reforms: the problem was which reforms, and how to put them into practice in the face not only of the immobility of the state administration, but also of the entrenched interests of the political parties, in particular the Christian

Democrats (DC). The DC under the leadership of Alcide De Gasperi had won 48% of the vote in the elections of April 1948 and during the 1950s it reinforced its position of pre-eminence, making the most of the advantages accruing from its commitment to the aims of Western policy within the context of the cold war. Economically, it had, as the main party of government, helped to smoothe the way for the miracle, by its direction of state funds and by its hostility to the unions. It should be noted, however, that the entrepreneurial élite of the country did not necessarily identify with the DC, which was intent on building itself as a mass party. Ideologically, it based its appeal on four principal themes: the rights of property, the neutrality of the state, the values of the family, and anti-communism. It therefore straddled, in a conservative rather than specifically Catholic way, the twin and sometimes conflicting demands of free enterprise and moral propriety. In the early 1960s the Christian Democrats could boast of putting a TV in every Italian living-room, but they reserved the right to control what could be seen on it, just as they reserved the right to censor magazines and films.

Both the economic leverage and the ideological appeal of the DC were reinforced at the political level by the construction of a network of client-relationships throughout the administrative structure and the institutions of the state. These in particular made any far-reaching reform difficult to enact, since it was always possible for one interest group or another to bring pressure to block what was proposed or to divert finance once the reform had been approved. Nor did the transition from centre-right to centre-left government alter the situation very much. When, in December 1963, after several years of delicate manoeuvring, Aldo Moro was finally able to form a government which included ministers from the Socialist Party (PSI), the institutions of administration and government had been too deeply infiltrated for there to be much prospect of significant change. This is not to say that the case for reform was not put strongly, or that certain important measures were not in fact carried out – the nationalization of the electricity supply industry in 1962, the raising of the school-leaving age to 14, and the abolition of *mezzadria* (sharecropping) are three important examples – but they occurred against a background in which few voters put much trust in the ability of politicians to improve their conditions of life.

On the left, throughout the 1950s and 1960s, the Communist Party (PCI) established and consolidated its role as the main voice of opposition (it polled 22.6% of the vote in the 1953 elections, 22.7% in 1958, and then rose to 25.3% in 1963). Its darkest years had been from 1948 to 1953 when the combined effects of electoral defeat, rising unemployment, police harassment, and identification with the cold-war enemy, the Soviet Union, had isolated it on the Italian political scene and driven it to adopt a defensive, inward-looking posture. At the same time, however, it built up its membership, which reached a peak of 2,145,317 in 1953, of whom about 60% were working-class (Acquaviva and Santuccio 1976, 189). The great majority of these members were schooled in the idea of a highly disciplined party which took its orders from above. For such a party, the slight thaw that began to make itself felt in 1953 and, most dramatically, the succession of events which threw the communist world into disarray in 1956 were to provide a severe test. An estimated 300,000 members, many of them intellectuals, left the party altogether after the suppression of the Hungarian uprising (Mammarella 1978, 320) while reports of Khruschev's secret denunciation of Stalin at the Twentieth Congress of the CPSU caused consternation amongst the rank-and-file. In the new atmosphere of relative liberalism, the party secretary, Palmiro Togliatti, needed all his considerable diplomatic skills to explore a 'national road to socialism' that would mark the PCI's distance from the Soviet Union without antagonizing the latter, and to undo the bureaucratic rigidity into which the party had fallen without upsetting the veteran militants upon whose loyal work the party's solid mass-support depended.

By the time of Togliatti's death in 1964, the PCI had managed by and large to shake off its Stalinist past and had augmented its electoral strength. But membership, and in particular working-class membership, was declining. The party had been slow to recognize that the capitalist world, of which Italy was after all a part, had changed at least as much as the communist one. The young people in the factories knew it, however, and they were beginning to develop forms of stuggle which the party-dominated unions were not willing to endorse. Although still on a very limited scale, there was also coming from these same workers a form of syndicalism which proclaimed the factory itself as the principal site of confrontation with the ruling class – thus throwing the leading role of the party into doubt. It was not until 1961 that the PCI addressed itself to an analysis of neo-capitalism, but when it did, there began to emerge, for the first time since the war, quite divergent strains of thought within it, between those who were prepared to go a long way towards recognizing the special role of union activity in propelling the party forward politically and those, on the contrary, who wanted to keep union activity as an important but limited part of a much broader programme of social reform initiated by the party. This debate continued through most of the 1960s. While the 'new left', much of it outside the PCI, sometimes mythicized the absolute power of the new forms of capital, it was only slowly that the party was weaning itself from the image of a largely agrarian and impoverished Italy with a small but highly skilled and specialized proletariat and recognizing the reality of a semi-skilled industrial mass participating, or more often not participating, in an increasingly prosperous and expectant society. But the gradual definition of the new reality made it no easier for the PCI than for the other political forces to understand, still less to dominate, the social unrest that gathered momentum in the closing years of the 1960s.

The years 1968–69 were the years of *contestazione*, protest against the system. In the early 1960s access to education at both secondary and tertiary levels had been much extended, but inadequate provision was made to enable the educational system to renew itself in order to deal with the new influx of students. Starting off from what were often localised issues within the universities, the student movement spread rapidly downwards into the schools (thus ensuring for a period at least its own continuation) and, more importantly, sideways into the factories. There the newest immigrants were less ready than their predecessors to accept either the conditions imposed by the bosses or the cautious stance favoured by the official unions. At the same time protest fed on international figures and events, in particular the Vietnam war which served the dual function of focussing in symbolic form the protest of the young against the evils of their *own* society at the same time as lending that protest the exhilarating security of a sense of international, cross-cultural, human solidarity. 1968 was the year of the students, during which the universities were regularly occupied and, for the first time in Italian academic history, the police were called in to clear them. The following year saw major confrontations on the industrial front in view of the triennial contracts to be negotiated for 1970–72. 302 mill. hours were lost through strikes in 1969 (as against 74 mill. the previous year), mainly concentrated in what was called the 'hot autumn' (*l'autunno caldo*). In many cases these strikes were organized by the rank and file against the union leadership and used methods condemned by the latter, including violence and industrial sabotage. But for the most part the unions were able to ride the tiger. The strikes of 1969 secured wage-rises of 21.6% for 1970, whereas the average annual increase during the boom had been less than a third of this figure. Beyond that, the *autunno caldo* ushered in a period of enhanced union militancy which reached far beyond the usual targets of pay and conditions. The early 1970s saw coming from the unions a consistent resistance to speed-ups on the production-line, denunciations of poor housing, transport and social services, demands for more facilities for professional training, and generally demands for a greater say in many issues of social and economic planning. The success of this militancy was reflected in the agreements secured in the 1972–73 round of negotiations.

The economic and social gains secured by industrial workers were for the most part sustained for much of the 1970s, until the recession began to force the unions once again onto the defensive. But the political impetus of the students' and workers' movement came to an abrupt halt on 12 December 1969 when a bomb exploded in a Milanese bank located in the central Piazza Fontana, killing sixteen people and injuring nearly ninety others. The attack, though in fact mounted by the extreme right, was immediately attributed by the authorities to anarchists and, in the aftermath of outrage and horror at the massacre, it was depicted as an example of what lawlessnes and carnage the protest movement in the schools and factories would lead to. The unions quickly settled on the new contracts, and directives to observe social peace and good order went out from the main left-wing parties. Piazza Fontana, as it turned out, was only one of the first of an almost uninterrupted series of terrorist actions that were to punctuate Italy's political life for the next ten years. Over 400 people lost their lives in the attacks, the highest death-toll being that caused by the Neo-fascist bombing of the waiting-room at Bologna station in August 1980.

Two distinct strategies were clearly operating under the general heading of political terrorism. Up until the autumn of 1974, most of the incidents took the form of indisciminate bomb attacks and were the work of extreme right-wing groups enjoying the complicity and protection of certain sectors of the intelligence services and the armed forces. They were part of a 'strategy of tension' (*strategia della tensione*) designed to push a frightened and disorientated public opinion to the right, not necessarily to accept an overtly fascist government but at least to recognize the need for a strengthening of the state. But then a good deal of confusion was engendered when self-proclaimed *leftist* terrorists appeared on the scene. At first dismissing these people as provocateurs, the official left had to come to terms with the fact that there was an autonomous armed movement on its own flank which saw itself as a vanguard of the working class in the factories promoting a struggle of resistance against the counter-revolutionary and reformist policies of the PCI. The targets of the principal groups involved (notably the Red Brigades) were less anonymous crowds than individuals, who were chosen for kneecapping, assassination or abduction on the basis of their 'exemplary' role in the productive or political process. First lower-echelon bosses in the factories were singled out, then state personnel, then local Christian Democrat politicians and some Communist officials and shop-stewards, national newspaper editors and journalists (Allum 1978, 7). In the person of Aldo Moro who was kidnapped on 16 May 1978 and killed fifty-five days later, the Red Brigades struck at the most representative figure imaginable, the man who had been in the forefront of DC and national politics for over twenty years and who would almost certainly have become the next President of the Republic, someone therefore very close to the 'heart of the state' which it was the Brigades' declared intention to attack. Above all, he was the architect of the understanding with the Communist Party which was to be sealed the very morning of his abduction by the swearing-in of a minority DC government supported by the PCI.

A parliamentary arrangement of this kind (which was to be ended by the PCI's return to opposition in January 1979) was the outcome of a strategy which the Communist Party had been pursuing for some years, that of the 'historic compromise' (*compromesso storico*). In a series of articles reflecting on the lessons to be learned from the downfall of the Allende government in Chile, published in the autumn of 1973, the Party Secretary Enrico Berlinguer had argued:

> The seriousness of the problems facing the country, the ever-present threat of reactionary adventures, and the need at last to open to the nation a secure path to economic development, social renewal and democratic progress, make it increasingly urgent and timely that we reach what might be called the new

great 'historic compromise' between those forces that encompass and represent the great majority of the Italian people. (Berlinguer 1975, 638-9)

Those forces included of course the Christian Democrats and the compromise proposed was not so much 'new' as a re-issue of the old one that had held together the anti-Fascist parties in the leadership of the Resistance (1943-45) and the first post-war government of reconstruction (1945-47). At the same time as laying claim to the moral and political leadership of the struggle against the strategy of tension, the PCI was also tacitly admitting that a government of the left parties alone was no longer on the agenda. Berlinguer's proposal was not welcomed with much enthusiasm by many members of his own party, especially as it was made at a moment of ideological tension with the Catholic party, in the run-up to the referendum on the divorce law which was to be held the following year. But a string of impressive election results reinforced the Communist claim to a privileged relationship with the government party. The retention of divorce after a hard-fought compaign in which the PCI was at the forefront of 'lay' opinion, together with Communist successes in the provincial elections of 1975 (33.4%) and the general elections of the following year (34.4%), ensured that it was in a sense impossible for the Christian Democrats actually to govern without the Communists. That is, they had either to take account of PCI views and policies in forming their own, as they did, to a lesser extent, of those of the other lay parties, or they had to put up with the return to outright opposition of a party whose vote was almost as large as their own, the DC having polled 38.7% of the vote in the 1976 elections. But the fact that the United States, NATO, and a large swathe of conservative Italian opinion would not tolerate the thought of Communists actually entering the government itself meant that, at least in a symbolic sense, it was also impossible to govern with them. Thus the relationship between the two major parties, far from being the progressive 'compromise' which Berlinguer had envisaged in 1973, was in danger, five years later, of becoming stalemate, the epitome of that 'ungovernability' of the country which it had been designed to overcome. The PCI's withdrawal from this unofficial grand coalition was prompted in part by the realization that it was not wringing enough concessions from the government to be able to justify its continuing support to its own voters. At the same time the hard line it took over law and order and the defence of the status quo at the time of the Moro affair, anticipated in the stance it had adopted a year earlier during student disturbances in March 1977 in Bologna and Rome, did not sufficiently reassure those who believed the PCI was a more or less willing agent of the Russians. The party's fears were realized in the elections of June 1979 when the Communist share of the vote fell to 30.4% while that of the Christian Democrats remained steady. In 1983, however, it was the turn of the DC to suffer a humiliating electoral defeat (its share of the vote fell to less than a third) while the PCI consolidated and in some of the large cities improved its position, and the PSI and the smaller centre parties also gained.

The strategy of tension, fears of a coup, left-wing terrorism, the question of political violence, the search for an historic compromise, a grand coalition, a new formula for governing the country, were the dominant themes of Italian politics in the 1970s and reflected the country's radical instability in the wake of the upheavals of the late 1960s. One factor that was perhaps contributing to the instability was the changing social structure of the country and the challenge that this posed to the political parties seeking to represent society. More than 50% of the country was estimated to be 'middle class' in 1974 (Sylos Labini 1975), a calculation which reflected the steady growth in the service sector of the economy (from 27.6% in 1961 to 38.2% in 1971 and an estimated 44.6% in 1980). A major part in this expansion is accounted for by a disproportionate growth in the public administration, estimated recently to have grown by 31.6% in the past ten years and currently employing nearly 4 mill. people (CENSIS 1982).

This shift into the service sector has been accompanied in recent years by a marked withdrawal from party politics, though it is difficult to see whether there is any necessary connection between the two phenomena. Caught between sawn-off shotguns and parliamentary minuets, people have chosen to profess contempt and indifference for the political process and to withdraw into privacy. At the same time, however, new and untraditional politics have been emerging, whether in the flamboyant style of the issues-oriented Radical Party or in the mobilization achieved by the women's movement on such key questions as abortion (overwhelmingly endorsed by popular referendum in May 1981). The sense of a gap and one that is widening, between the 'real' country and the 'legal' or 'official' country is one that is frequently expressed. It is not just that no-one trusts the politicians and no-one believes the statistics; it is that there is little or no perceptible relation between what is happening and what is said to be happening. Nowhere is this more evident than at the level of the economy. Italy has been both suffering the worst effects of the recession, with inflation averaging around 20% per annum, high unemployment, especially among the young, shutdowns of industrial plant and so on. But, apparently, at the same time the country has been thriving off a black economy, the exact details and extent of which are not readily available to the taxman. The undoubted prosperity of significant sectors of the population cannot, however, disguise the fact that under the pressure of the recession, in Italy as in Britain, the gap between the rich and the poor in the early 80s is widening, as it is between the employed and the unemployed, between those who are educated and those who are not, between those who can find their way around the bureaucracy and those who are destined always to be its victims, between those who can command specially fitted prison cells to serve their fifteen days for tax-evasion and those who, fifteen years after their homes were destroyed by earthquake, are still living in tents.

(b) The Reading Public and Literary Culture

The social, economic and political changes we have discussed in the previous section have had profound effects on every aspect of literary culture in Italy. It is not simply that what has been written has been directly or indirectly concerned with them and affected by them. Everything surrounding the actual literary texts has been affected too – production, distribution, sales and, above all, the reading public. Changes in all these areas in turn have had their effects on writing itself, on its general role and status in society and on the role of those who write. At the same time traditional practices and long-standing social factors have continued to play an important part, exerting a conservative, braking pressure on the drive towards innovation and expansion.

In the nineteenth century the printed word was the province of a small minority of the population, the literate few in a society that mostly consisted of dialect-speaking illiterate peasants. In 1861 78% of the population were illiterate, and less than 5% spoke Italian, though undoubtedly some dialects (that is, regional or local languages, overlapping with the national language but largely independent of it) were more mutually intelligible and more intelligible to Italian speakers than has sometimes been suggested (De Mauro 1976). But the fact remains that political disunity (until 1861) meant that there was no strong central force at work to impose a national language and with it a national culture on the country as a whole. There was also an exiguous bourgeoisie. Hence, even apart from linguistic factors, there was not the economic and social underpinning for the development of a strong bourgeois literary culture, and in particular for the development of its cornerstone, the realist novel. In spite of heroic efforts and some remarkable achievements, literature teetered on the margins of Italian life, arcane and archaic in its language and style, unrelated to the administration of power, the reserve of a vociferous, educated but largely impotent élite.

What was a historical reality has survived as something of an incubus haunting literary culture up to and including the present day. In the decade following the end of the Second World War it was still uncomfortably close to the truth, even though very large improvements had taken place since unification. In the mid-1950s the national culture in its most evident form, language, was still not well-established. According to recent estimates, only 18% of Italians habitually (but not all of these all the time) spoke Italian and about 20% spoke only dialect (De Mauro 1978, 9). Illiteracy was still widespread: the census of 1951 revealed that 12.9% of Italians over the age of six were illiterate, the figure rising to 24% in the South. There had been a greatly increased demand for books in the euphoric period immediately following liberation, a demand that seems to have come from the working class as much as from any other section of the population, and initially this demand had created some response. But there were material difficulties, such as the shortage and cost of paper: the publishing houses were not geared to large-scale production: and much that was actually written and published was still uncompromisingly literary. Not surprisingly by the early 1950s it seems that the reading public was once more the traditional one of the cultivated middle classes, intellectuals and students. In 1948–49 there were some 168,000 university students *in toto*: in 1956–57 the figure had risen only to 212,000 (*Aspetti*, 73). In 1956 a mere 5,623 books were published, including original works, translations, new editions and re-prints, that is less than in 1948, when the total was 8,343 (Cadioli 1981, 18 and 35). And in 1957 40.8% of Italian families, according to official figures, did not habitually read printed matter of any kind (*Aspetti*, 67).

There had, however, been one substantial development since Unification which it is worth stressing. It may still have been difficult for Italians to produce realist fiction that convinced at a representational level even in the 1950s, since peasants and workers and, in some measure, other classes too, habitually spoke dialects that could not be easily and conventionally rendered in an adapted form of the national language – in contrast, for example, with the situation of D.H. Lawrence or John Steinbeck writing about English or American workers. All the same an appetite for fiction has shown itself to exist throughout the century. From 1945 to the present fiction has taken up between 15 and 20% of all books printed, with literature as a whole (as opposed to books on politics, religion, social science etc.) taking up around 35% of the total (Cadioli 1981). In the late 1940s and for much of the 1950s the novelists who sold best were often foreigners. A.J. Cronin in particular enjoyed a success which he has never had in Britain. Of Italian writers only Giovanni Guareschi, the author of the Don Camillo stories, and Alberto Moravia, with his sensational version of existential anguish, came at all close to being best-sellers. So strong was the position of non-Italian authors that the detective stories published in cheap magazines form by Mondadori (called *gialli* from their yellow covers) were always ascribed to American or British sounding names, even if written in characteristic translationese by an Italian. From this more or less commercially successful fiction serious literary culture tended to keep its distance, making what bids it chose to make for a 'popular' readership on the basis of Neo-realist writing. This, whatever its commitment to 'the people', tended to be read mostly by more serious readers, and certainly had a smaller circulation than at least some Neo-realist films.

In some ways so far as books are concerned, the social and economic transformations of the late 1950s and early 1960s took time to take effect. There was no sudden increase in the number of books published for example. Even in 1966 the total was 9,182, that is, not quite four thousand more than the total for 1956. But then in 1967, for reasons that we shall suggest below, there was a sudden leap to 15,119. Between 1967 and 1978 this figure did increase further but then settled at round about 17,000. However in the same eleven year period, the actual number of books printed each year increased by over a third, from just over 100 mill. to 141 mill. (Cadioli 1981, 160).

If the overall expansion of book-production and sales took time, from the late 1950s the phenomenon of the large-scale best-seller had appeared in Italy, and what is more best-sellers included works of contemporary Italian fiction. The first of these was *Il Gattopardo (The Leopard)* of Tomasi di Lampedusa, which sold an unheard-of 100,000 copies in the twelve months following its publication towards the end of 1958. Similar sales were achieved in the early 1960s by various novels by Carlo Cassola and Giorgio Bassani. By the early 1970s it was possible in a few cases for a best-selling paperback to reach sales of half-a-million or more. If one example was the Italian version of *Love Story* (1971), another was *La Storia (History)* by Elsa Morante, which within a few months of its appearance in 1974 sold 600,000 copies.

Neither of these commercial successes would have been possible without large well-orchestrated publicity on the part of the publishers of the two novels. In the case of *La Storia* Einaudi opted for a great deal of advertising and immediate release in paperback at an unusually low price, whereas for *Love Story* Garzanti (admittedly at a late stage in the sales programme) reached an agreement whereby the book was given away with boxes of Baci chocolates. Both manoeuvres were exceptional, but that they could be mounted is a sign of how far Italian publishing had come since the 1950s. Even in the 1970s there were still a very large number of small firms involved in publishing and many of them continued to combine artisanal production with close co-operation with the writers whose work they published, inevitably in small print-runs. Some of the major firms too, such as Mondadori and Einaudi, have a tradition of publishing more or less unprofitable texts for cultural reasons, often, again, in small quantities, but this aspect of their work has diminished in importance as they have developed as large commercial enterprises, sometimes controlling every stage in the manufacture of their products. Most of the modern bookshops, which since the early 1960s have existed in every town of any size, are owned by publishing firms, though this does not mean that the shops will sell only proprietary books. Given this kind of development it is not surprising that by the mid-1970s Mondadori and Rizzoli should have become the fifty-first and ninety-first companies respectively in the whole country.

In this process of expansion and re-organization by the major firms, one vitally important step was the introduction of the modern paperback. Cheap series already existed, most notably the B.U.R. (Biblioteca Universale Rizzoli), which included a wide range of Italian and foreign classics but which was austere, even drab, in format. More attractive paperbacks, similar to those to be found in other countries, did not appear in Italy until 1965, partly because publishers were not so aware of potential markets as they would later become. But when Mondadori launched its Oscar series in that year, there followed a paperback boom, which gradually drew in the other principal firms, including those which initially felt that, with the paperback, literature was being all too blatantly made into a commodity. And that of course was what Mondadori was doing with some force: indeed they were looking for new markets among the mass of habitual non-readers. They registered the Oscars as a periodical, brought out fresh titles every week (drawn initially entirely from fiction, Italian and foreign) and they put the books on sale not only in bookshops, but also, and primarily, in the newspaper-kiosks (*edicole*) scattered through Italian towns, large and small. The period of spectacular sales was, however, fairly short, and when it ended some of the moderately-sized firms were driven into liquidation. But it was largely the discovery of a mass-market that brought about the re-structuring of the larger firms. It was also a result of the paperback revolution that a very great range of books of all kinds became easily and cheaply available throughout the late 1960s and for most of the 1970s. As some English readers of Italian were aware, up to the onset of the recession in 1978, it was often cheaper and easier to buy academic studies in Italian paperback than to buy them in their language and country of origin.

All these developments point to a large increase in the number of people reading books, although how large and how solid the increase was is difficult to estimate with any accuracy. The most important single factor behind this expansion was undoubtedly the educational reform which made secondary schooling compulsory throughout the country from 1964. The knock-on effect of this reform was an increase in the numbers of students in higher education. Already in 1964 there were 360,000 students registered with Italian universities. In 1972–73 there were just over 800,000 (*Aspetti*, 73). Apart from the fact that all surveys indicate that all former students read books, it is clear that the student public itself is vitally important to the publishing industry, and not solely for text-books. Since the early 1970s almost all paperbacks with even modest literary or intellectual pretensions have had introductions and notes that both make them serviceable in schools and universities and indicate that the projected readership is one that is familiar with such aids and will not be put off by them.

Almost certainly it was as a direct result of educational reform and expansion, coupled with a general rise in the standard of living and in social expectation, that there was such a large increase in book-production in the later 1960s and that paperbacks were as successful as they proved to be. Indeed the general rule that the reading of books is closely connected with educational experience seems to work particularly strongly in Italy. This means that, apart from actual teachers and students, those sections of the population which habitually buy and read books are those which have been through the educational system and put a value on education, that is, roughly the middle classes and aspiring middle classes. In employment terms it is the tertiary sector of the economy – public administration of all kinds, media, etc. – and the liberal professions which have the highest concentration of readers. In commerce and industry readers are to be found primarily at managerial and clerical levels.

This concentration of the reading public in particular sections of society has important implications. Although we have been emphasising expansion, it is clear that the expansion has had very definite limits. Even the mid-1970s annual production of 140 mill. books meant producing less than three books per inhabitant per year. In fact as everything we have said suggests, it is not the case that all Italians read very few books, but that large sections of the population read hardly anything. It would seem that these non-readers are concentrated among those with less formal education, that is, amongst industrial workers and manual workers of all kinds, especially those who work on the land.

The evidence that this is in fact so is quite strong. In the first place what might be called 'popular' or 'cheap' literature is not well-established. In 1973 adventure-stories, thrillers and detective novels constituted only 2.8% of all books published, as against 16.5% for novels and stories of other kinds. Although there are some romantic writers who have been very successful (such as Liala), it also seems that within that second category of novels and stories romantic and romantic-historical fiction is not particularly significant. There is no equivalent of Mills and Boon, and there has been little attempt (except in isolated cases such as *Love Story*) to find alternative selling-points to the kiosk and bookshop. The implication is that the readership for 'popular' products is more restricted than in some other countries. In particular it seems that a certain female readership is less extensive in Italy. In 1973 it was found that overall more men read books than women. On the other hand illustrated weeklies – which have been generally very successful amongst all classes of Italians – were read by more women than men overall (*Aspetti*, 17). Then there are still problems of literacy and language. Although by 1973 total illiteracy had been virtually wiped out, it was estimated that still a quarter of the population were semi-literate. Related to this is the fact that even in the 1970s the national language was still far from being the prime spoken medium of the majority of Italians. The movement from the land, mass-education, the omnipresence of the mass-media, especially television, had steadily undermined the dialects and dialect culture, and made Italian a much more widely spoken language than it had ever been. But in 1974 it was calculated that 28.9% of people still used dialect as their normal spoken language, that 35.5% alternated dialect and Italian, and that only 25% used Italian exclusively (De Mauro 1978). Given the large number of people who were still more or less estranged from the Italian language, it is to be expected that a similar large number should be more or less estranged from Italian writing in any form.

This configuration of the Italian reading public as primarily educated and primarily middle-class has been a source of preoccupation both to the publishing industry and to the intellectual left. The publishing industry has tried at times to break into a large market which it knew existed, but which has effectively proved resistant except in one or two instances. The intellectual left has been aware that there has been little possibility of reaching a popular readership through writing. One reason for the decline of literary Neo-realism was the recognition that it made little contact with the working-classes that were its apparent focus. Similarly that Dario Fo and Pier Paolo Pasolini should have resorted to other media than the printed word was partly because of the evident social limits of the latter.

As Fo and Pasolini were also well aware, the problems of reaching out to non-readers were connected with the nature of literary culture itself, and especially with the kind of language in which books tended to be written. Commercially successful writers and their public seem to have favoured a continuity of development, not to say a conservatism, in terms of style and of general cultural reference. Noticeably enough the first best-selling Italian novel, *Il Gattopardo*, centred on the impossibility of any real social or political progress and was written in an extremely literary language. Literariness of various kinds is apparent in many successful novels of the 1960s, though it has since diminished – so that the language of, say, Sciascia or Calvino now seems much closer to what might be considered 'good' spoken Italian. All the same commercially successful narrative prose is commonly a good deal more refined than is the case with its American or even British equivalents. And in one important area of writing that has a bearing on creative literature, although its field is overall much wider, there has been a remarkable survival of a highly literary style. Italian discursive prose, as it is used for historical, sociological, philosophical and critical writing (that is, for what Italian calls *saggistica*), has remained remarkably complex – abstract in vocabulary, Ciceronian in syntax and conceptually sophisticated. Thus in the very medium that it uses Italian intellectual culture in general and to some degree literature itself (even leaving out of account literature which is deliberately 'difficult') has tended to maintain the barrier between insiders and outsiders, even if the insiders have come to constitute a large minority within the population as a whole.

This situation has had very positive aspects. It has meant that the intellectual and stylistic level of Italian writing, including much best-selling fiction, has been high. It has meant that from the early 1960s onwards there has been a readiness in writers and to some degree amongst readers too, to assimilate and develop new ideas and new strategies for writing within the broad limits we have been discussing. Partly from a widespread sense that a new culture was developing which needed to be articulated, partly from a feeling that in many ways Italy needed to catch up with other countries, new foreign writing has been rapidly translated and made readily available. Semiotics, structuralism, modern Marxist thought, new theories of psychoanalysis all penetrated Italian literary culture before they were well known in Britain. With this general intellectual sophistication have come moves away from conventional fiction in the successful novel. Since the late 1960s Calvino and Sciascia have had considerable successes with non-realist writing, to the point where they have become the established novelists of contemporary Italy.

But literary culture is not of course homogeneous, and at this point we shall make a broad division, though not one that implies complete opposition, between 'high' and 'middle' writing. In the former we can include more serious and demanding writing of all kinds, such as experimental or avantgarde fiction, all poetry and, to a large extent, literary criticism, philosophy, and other forms of academic writing. Though in the aftermath of 1968 there was a great increase in the sales of political and sociological texts, on the whole the reading public for this 'high' writing has been small, as might be expected. A successful volume of poetry, for example, might sell 2–3,000 copies at the most. Even in the 1970s there were gloomy estimates that 'strong' readers amounted to no more than 10,000 people in all. Within 'middle' culture we can locate the more commercially successful writing we have already mentioned, adding to it from recent years the journalistic and investigative work of such figures as Oriana Fallaci, Giorgio Bocca and (once again) Alberto Moravia. Some writers have moved from one category to the other, Calvino and Sciascia being cases in point. Others, such as Umberto Eco, with his journalism and his novel, *Il nome della rosa* (*The Name of the Rose*) or, more strikingly, Morante with *La Storia*, have made the transition with particular parts of their production. All the same, in general the distinction holds, and holds between different writers.

Overall 'middle' writing has been more accepting of the social, political and economic order of the country than has been the case with 'high' writing, although the acceptance has often been resigned and pessimistic, with strong elements of nostalgia or escapism. Most best-selling novels have been overtly a-political, which, as some critics have been quick to point out, involves at the very least a lack of opposition to the *status quo*. The more recent investigative writing we have just mentioned has been much more critical, but generally from a point of view that lays claim to rationalism, common sense or basic human values and which would seem to have much to do with the political consensus of the mid-1970s that the republic must be defended both against internal corruption and against violence of the extreme left and the extreme right. Whatever its critical position, 'middle' writing has inevitably been deeply involved in the commercialization and consumerization of literature. For many critics from 'high' culture, this involvement has not stopped at methods of production and sales, but has concerned the actual social function of much 'middle' writing, which has been commonly seen to be to console or to provide escape as much through the mechanisms of 'good' writing as through the actual matter of the books in question.

As will be apparent in several essays on individual writers, 'high' culture has consistently set its face against the established order and against the consumerization of literature. This resistance has been by no means exclusively left-wing, and rarely has it been a resistance which coincided with the policies of the PCI or of any other major party. All the same it is quite clear that the DC and the right have failed to generate a sizeable or convincing intellectual culture. Instead the overwhelming tendency of 'high' writing has been to denounce, from a variety of points of view, the new industrialized and consumerized Italy as a physical and moral wasteland to which alternatives must be found. It has thus voiced, often aggressively, what 'middle' culture has sometimes acknowledged more surreptitiously and circumspectly.

It now seems obvious, although in the 1960s it was not so clear, that writers and intellectuals have regularly risked adopting critical positions which they could not in fact sustain or else have risked creating illusory alternatives to a society into which they had in fact been absorbed. Romano Luperini (1981, 722) perhaps expressed a widely-shared view when he wrote that dissenting writers had become part of the 'mass of technician-intellectuals' whose function it is to oil the machinery of the bourgeois-capitalist system. But certainly, for all its opposition, the literary culture, 'high' and 'middle', with which we are concerned in this book, is effectively the established literary culture of modern Italy. The writers discussed by us are amongst those discussed in any text-book of modern literature or thought and represented in school and university anthologies. In fact, the tension between the writer's position in the 'system' and his or her subjective stance is itself a vitally important strand in much of what has been written since the 1950s.

Certainly as individuals few writers have been willing or perhaps able to withdraw to the social or geographical periphery of the country. There are no grants for creative writing, only literary prizes, which of course have been open to commercial manipulation. There are no posts for creative writers as such in universities, although some writers are also academics. Since in absolute terms sales are usually small even for moderately successful authors, it has been difficult for all but a few to make an income solely from writing literature. Instead, like much of their readership, most writers have worked at middle-class jobs, as teachers, businessmen, administrators and journalists. This does not mean that they tend to be unknown to a wide public. Since at least the mid-1960s poets, novelists and academics have been regularly invited to add their often discordant voice to arguments on topical issues – divorce, terrorism, drugs, etc. It is debatable whether such interventions are to be interpreted as a trivialization of the more complex social and political role that literary culture demanded for itself in the 1950s and earlier or whether they might not also be seen as signalling a partial end to literary élitism.

(c) Writers and Writing

Everything we have said so far in this introduction reinforces the idea that the 1960s were a turning-point in Italian affairs. This was the decade during which the economy took off, consumerism was born, education spread, culture found new markets, and social tensions exploded. Inevitably literature too was deeply affected. Although, as we have suggested, a strong vein of continuity runs through Italian literary culture from the 1950s to the 1970s, the 1960s saw writers exploring new paths largely in response to changes in the society in which and for which they were writing. Put in general terms, this meant that a good deal was written which attempted to interpret the reality of the new Italy and, in some cases, to act upon it. But it also meant that new areas of language and new techniques were investigated, often on the basis of advanced theories of literature. Indeed experimental modernism became one of the strongest trends in both verse and prose of the 1960s, but even poets and novelists who were more cautious in their approach, found themselves modifying and modernizing the way in which they wrote.

Any discussion of post-war writing must, however, start farther back. For Italian poetry of the last thirty years, the major reference point has been hermeticism (*ermetismo*), the movement which dominated poetry of the 1930s though its archetypes lay in the poems written by Giuseppe Ungaretti during the second decade of the century. There were strong reactions against it in the 1940s and 1950s, but it survived in more or less identifiable form well into the 1960s and is still traceable in at least some more recent poetry. The reasons for this long and not easily definable life lie in the inseparability of hermeticism from what has been felt to be the central tradition of twentieth-century Italian poetry, a tradition which could find theoretic sustenance in Mallarmé and Valéry, but which located its own essence and the essence of Italian poetry as a whole in Leopardi and Petrarch. Overall pre-war hermeticism aspired to absolute or pure poetry, and, if it was the loss of both that figured large in many hermetic poems, still the result was mostly private, self-absorbed verse, fragmentary and delicate in form, pastoral but also cosmic in imagery, allusive, even impenetrable, in its intuitively glimpsed meanings.

Already by the late 1930s the original father-figure of the movement, Ungaretti, was beginning to write the more accessible, more 'human' verse that would characterize the remainder of his long, but, so far as Italian poetry is concerned, increasingly marginal career. In the immediate post-war years, though hermeticism was continued in the work of Mario Luzi, Leonardo Sinisgalli and others, the changed climate raised for poetry as for prose questions of political and social commitment and fuelled a demand for less rarefied, more public verse. Non-hermetic poetry of the 1930s (such as that of Pavese) was rediscovered. Some former hermeticists made apparent about-turns; most striking was the case of Salvatore Quasimodo, who by 1950 was asserting the need for a poetry that affirmed in everyday language the basic human and moral values of Western culture as a resistance to the inhumanity of contemporary history. And a good deal of verse was written which deliberately put subject-matter before formal elaboration.

By the mid-1950s many poets felt that other ways of writing poetry had to be found apart from hermeticism, on the one hand, and preoccupation with subject-matter (*contenutismo*), on the other. Both were arguably exhausted and out of phase with what was happening in the country. The poets usually grouped together as belonging to the *Linea lombarda* (Nelo Risi, Luciano Erba and some other Northerners) opted for a disillusioned, self-deprecatory irony, that was one way out of the difficulties. But more assertive programmes were also needed. One such is associated with the founding of the periodical *Officina* in 1955 in Bologna by Pier Paolo Pasolini, Francesco Leonetti and Robert Roversi, who collectively and individually attempted to work out a new role for the poet as well as new rules for poetry. Pasolini explained what was involved in this 'neo-experimentalism' in an article of 1957 entitled 'La libertà stilistica' ('Stylistic freedom'). He demanded that formal and stylistic invention should be radically innovative but regulated by an awareness of political and social realities. At the same time he recognized that this awareness could not be absorbed into the official ideology of any party: instead there would have to be 'a continuous, painful effort to keep abreast of a present that cannot be grasped ideologically' (Pasolini 1960, 487–8). In effect he was calling for 'experimentalism' without the ivory tower associations of hermeticism and 'commitment' without party strings. To a large extent the work of Pasolini in verse after 1957, as also that of Leonetti and Roversi, was an attempt, often very successful, to carry out that programme (see Chapter 6).

There were other younger poets grouped around another review, *Il Verri*, who also in the mid-1950s were thinking along similar lines, though in more cosmopolitan, more flamboyantly modernistic terms, and who were to develop into the poetic wing of the Neo-avantgarde (see Chapter 2). Over the same years of the late 1950s and early 1960s older poets were also cautiously evolving their individual responses to the pressures at work both in the *Officina* group and in the *Novissimi* (as the *Verri* poets proclaimed themselves in their anthology of 1961). For some – such as Andrea Zanzotto (see Chapter 5), Mario Luzi, and Vittorio Sereni – the way forward lay in modifying, perhaps transforming hermeticism in the direction of a poetry that was less obviously elevated but still in some measure transcendentally poetic. Others took difficult paths that were both anti-traditionalist and anti-experimental. Franco Fortini, who is discussed in Chapter 4 principally as an essayist, aimed as a poet at a severe precision that owed a good deal to the more 'classic' and 'Chinese' aspects of Bertolt Brecht (whom he translated into Italian). More striking is the case of Eugenio Montale, the best-known and perhaps the best Italian poet of the century. If Montale was ever a hermetic poet, it was principally in the sense that his work from the 1920s up to and including his third volume *La bufera e altro* (*The Storm et cetera*, 1956) was difficult to understand. His fourth book, *Satura* (*Medley*) published in 1971, but containing work going back to the late 1950s, marked a shift towards foregrounding the discursive, prosy elements that had always figured in his poetry and a discarding of the richer, imaginative features that had previously accompanied them. And this tendency is strengthened in the three further books that Montale published. So what Montale was writing during his years of maximum celebrity, was in fact an anti-poetry, fiercely critical of consumer and technological civilization, pessimistic in a jokey way about the chances for real change and real knowledge, scholastic and simultaneously conversational in its tone and terminology.

This later production of Montale was well received on the whole. What it did not do was to establish him as a leader or model for other poets. From the late 1960s onwards the individualism that we have already implicitly indicated as existing before then, is confirmed as the general rule, with most poets following along the lines they had already drawn for themselves. New interesting voices appear (such as Fernando Bandini, Maurizio Cucchi, Giovanni Ramella Bagneri) and the 1970s also see a new 'popular' poetry, associated in part with *cantautori* (singer-songwriters) such as Lucio Dalla and Fabrizio de André, and partly with highly politicised, anti-literary working-class poets, such as Luigi di Ruscio. If, as was claimed, something of a poetic resurgence occurred during the 1970s, it was in the name of no orthodoxy other than anti-traditionalism, and by the end of the decade even that was in question, as certain poets half-humorously but also half-seriously turned to forms such as the sonnet and to pastiches of the old literary language.

Whilst hermeticism is the starting point for talking about poetry, discussion of the novel has to begin with Neo-realism, which was a dominant aesthetic up until the mid-1950s not only in the cinema, in the work of such directors as Rossellini and De Sica, but also in the novel (and, to a lesser extent, in poetry). In fiction, the Neo-realists looked back to Giovanni Verga, the leading exponent of the late nineteenth-century school of *verismo*, but they also had far more recent models in the writing of Cesare Pavese and Elio Vittorini. Pavese and Vittorini were surprising mentors in some ways, for their writing contained mythopoeic and surrealist elements which were apparently at odds with the more documentary tradition of realism. But behind them lay the example of the American realists which they had done much to promote in the 1930s and early 1940s (Steinbeck, Saroyan, Hemingway, Dos Passos). In the footsteps of these masters, the Neo-realists produced a fiction which set out to represent to the reader a supposedly 'undiscovered' or 'hidden' Italy: the impoverished, hungry, violent, unemployed Italy suppressed by Fascist rhetoric. Neo-realist fiction explored the Italy of the regions and the dialects, but in an anti-provincial spirit: its themes were universal with a local accent. Its connection with social and political reality was immediate: it either took topical events or situations as its subject-matter, or, in more epic vein, drew on working-class history, often the recent history of the Resistance, though one of the very best of Neo-realist novels, Francesco Jovine's *Le terre del Sacramento* (*The Lands of Sacramento*, 1950) describes the rise of agrarian fascism in the South in the early 1920s. Neo-realism was imbued with moral, and increasingly with political purpose. It was, in a broad sense, 'committed' literature, especially in the years immediately after the war when writers were both called upon to participate and willingly did participate in the efforts of culture to do its bit towards the 'renewal', the 're-creation' of Italian society.

The demise of Neo-realism, however, was brought about by both political and literary pressures. Politically, it became increasingly the terrain of Stalinist critics who would sustain the most banal realism as a bulwark against what they saw as literary decadence, irrespective of the fact that a genuine commitment to popular causes was frequently slipping into no more than sentimental populism. From the literary point of view, after the initial post-war flood of enthusiasm and identification with the subject-matter of Neo-realism, it was becoming more problematical to take the realist aesthetic for granted. And by the mid-1950s, the public had had its fill of peasant culture, positive heroes and 'national-popular' values.

The objections did not, however, for the moment at least, diminish the force either of the documentary strain in Italian writing or the particular concern with the South, both of which had been important elements in Neo-realist writing as in Neo-realist cinema. Elio Vittorini, who remained one of the most active figures on the literary scene up until his death in 1966, continued to publish documentary and autobiographical 'testimonies' as well as novels and stories, by unknown and non-professional authors as well as established ones, in the *Gettoni* series he edited for Einaudi between 1951 and 1958. And when a sympathetic critic came to describe the work of 'young Italian writers' in 1962, what he emphasized most was the novel as 'essay' or 'document' or 'inquiry', and the writer as 'investigating', 'debating', 'recording' every aspect of reality: a thoroughly traditional project, albeit freshly presented in the striking new clothes of the *nouveau roman* (Mariani 1962, 5 and *passim*). Indeed, it is remarkable how in the debate over the relations between literature and industry promoted by Vittorini in the pages of *Il menabò* (1961–62), at the very moment when the contributors were denouncing the seemingly limitless capacity of neo-capitalist industry to reify all productive life and to reduce all social relations to a condition of alienation and mystification, they yet seemed entirely confident in the ability of literature to 'know', 'represent' and 'communicate' the new human condition successfully. The robotization of men in industrial work, the standardization of behavioural patterns, the depoliticization of consumer society were some of the themes that now had to be confronted (and were, in a number of 'industrial' novels of the late 1950s and early 1960s, notably Ottiero Ottieri's *Donnarumma all'assalto*, translated as *The Man at the Gates*, 1959, Paolo Volponi's *Memoriale, Memorandum*, 1962, and Goffredo Parise's *Il padrone, The Boss*, 1965).

Although the star of Neo-realism had for a time obscured all other forms of fiction, this is not to say of course that they were not being written. Among the many novelists to emerge after the war, there was a strong 'psychological' line of writing, working particularly in the vein of Proustian memory (two outstanding examples were *Il giardino dei Finzi-Contini, The Garden of the Finzi-Contini*, 1962, by Giorgio Bassani, and Natalia Ginzburg's *Lessico famigliare, Family Words*, 1963). Others worked in different registers altogether, those of fantasy or fable for example, while even the most socially committed or aware of the novels discussed in this volume (for example, Pasolini's Roman novels or Calvino's tales of urban life) bear only an oblique or critical relation to Neo-realism. In this connection it was the discovery or re-discovery of an older non-realist, Carlo Emilio Gadda, that was probably most significant.

Born in 1893, Gadda achieved fame late in life when two earlier novels, republished in their final form in 1957 (*Quer pasticciaccio brutto de Via Merulana*, translated as *That Awful Mess on Via Merulana*) and 1963 (*La cognizione del dolore*, translated as *Acquainted with Grief*) made a powerful impact on a new generation of readers, mainly for three reasons. Firstly, Gadda had no hesitation in using fiction as a vehicle for vituperation and diatribe. Not only was this quite contrary to the earnest objectivity of Neo-realism, it also had the effect of forcing attention back on to the narrating voice, away from the reality supposedly being represented. Secondly, in spite of a professed (but tongue-in-cheek?) desire for rounded characters and completed plots, Gadda was quite incapable of producing them. The labyrinthine tangle of detail which baffles the detective in *Quer pasticciaccio brutto*, the inhibiting weight of pain which shrouds the 'last hidalgo', Gonzalo, the hero of *La cognizione del dolore,* in fact, everywhere in Gadda the density of reality defies structure or completeness. It is, however, a reality which Gadda knows to be mediated, already represented in the minds of men; the novelist represents a representation, and language is a further complication in the mess. Gadda's own narrative language – and this is the third reason for Gadda's impact – is non-representational. It is a bewildering concoction of archaicisms, Latinisms, dialect (real or invented), slang, jargon, neologisms, word-play, unusual syntax, extravagant metaphor. It is entertaining, frustrating, disturbing and incomprehensible by turns. It refuses to take itself seriously at the same time that it underlines its own pre-eminence in the narrative at the expense of the reality represented and of conceptual structures.

Gadda's importance to the avantgarde of the early 1960s lay in his showing – in practice rather than in theory – that the way forward for fiction lay beyond simply renewing its content within a broadly realist consensus. He injected a note of scepticism into the innocent craft of fiction and invited literature to begin to doubt creatively its own procedures. Just as much fiction of the 1940s and 1950s had aspired to 'realism', so in the 1960s and early 1970s the touchstone for many novelists became 'experimentalism'. The avantgarde's concept and practice of fiction is discussed in Chapter 2, but not all writers who regarded themselves as experimental identified with the avantgarde. Inside and outside the avantgarde certain lines of what was often called 'research' at the time were particularly favoured.

One major concern was of course the language and the continuing endeavour to free writing from the conventions of Neo-realist language. This was one area in which Gadda exerted a major influence: the appeal of his *plurilinguismo* ('multi-lingualism') can be clearly seen – to take but one example – in the macaronic prose of Sebastiano Vassalli (especially his early books, *Narcisso, Narcissus,* 1968 and *Tempo di massacro, Time of Massacre,* 1970). The linguistic concern though was also in part a recognition of the new situation of the language as outlined in the previous section. Pressure both from below (new masses of people, brought in by compulsory education and the spread of TV, communicating in Italian rather than dialect) and from above (new scientific and technological sublanguages) led towards a simplification and 'derhetoricization' of the language (Corti 1978, 132).

A second direction of research was strongly influenced by the expansion in Italy in the late 1950s and early 1960s of the 'human sciences' (linguistics, sociology, psychology, semiology, cultural anthropology, etc): this direction was the renewed interest in dream and the unconscious, fruitfully explored by writers such as Francesco Leonetti, who is a novelist as well as a poet, Giuseppe Berto (*Il male oscuro, The Obscure Disease,* 1964) and Luigi

Malerba (*Il serpente, The Snake,* 1966). But the interest in the unconscious (and in the pathological) did not necessarily imply an empirical 'I' that was tangible to the reader on the page; thus it is complementary to a third tendency of the experimental novel, namely the dissolving of 'believable' character into minimal character-substitutes – names on the page, attributes detached from any personality, occasional, sometimes repeated phrases. For example, Giuseppe Pontiggia's 1968 novel *L'arte della fuga* (which translates as 'The art of the fugue', or 'The art of flight'), is a murder story in which not only the murderer but also the victim is unknown. The absence of psychology in turn produces a sort of draining of time, with no perceptible development or action for the story to narrate.

One other trend in a way presupposes and contains the others: the lasting achievement of experimental writers in the 1960s was to have restored wit to Italian fiction. Language itself was exploited as a rich source of the comic, with its almost infinite possibilities of pun, irony and incongruity – almost all the writers of the period make use of these possibilities, but Gianni Celati's particular brand of verbal slapstick, owing not a little to the devices of the early movies, is an outstanding example. The renewed interest in the unconscious brought with it a new sensitivity to the role of jokes seen from a Freudian perspective and to the multiple folds of meaning concealed beneath the surface of apparent meanings. Finally, the experimentation with narrative structures was an open invitation to pastiche and parody, a mixture of the genres with a consequent scrambling of the message.

This refreshing rediscovery of wit in Italian fiction was by no means confined to those writers who identify with the avantgarde. Play with forms of the detective novel, for instance, characterized a whole phase of Sciascia's fiction (see Chapter 10, pp.247 – 250), while Calvino, who has always kept his distance from the more formalized avantgarde, is the writer who, as well as being the best known of his generation outside Italy, has also explored most consistently the rules of fiction as a 'game'. The result of all this experiment, and attention to experiment, has been a highly sophisticated literature, in which the subject very frequently is literature itself, an exploration of the devices and mechanics of narration. Thus, those writers who were less obviously innovative in their work and who, in however refined a way, drew on traditional narrative structures ran the risk of being ignored in the 1960s and early 1970s (Buzzati and Morante, among the writers discussed in this volume, are striking examples). Others were 'discovered' or 'rediscovered': Alberto Savinio, Antonio Pizzuto, Tommaso Landolfi, Guido Morselli.

But there was always the danger that experiment would become mere refinement, that the self-referentiality of the text would become exclusive rather than illuminating. There are indeed signs that experimentation *per se* in the Italian novel is running into the sands and has been doing so for a number of years. The consensus around the experimental novel that existed at the beginning of the 1970s was lost in the middle and later years of what Alberto Arbasino called that 'unloved' decade. There have been single texts of special significance – Stefano D'Arrigo's *Horcynus Orca* (1975) or Vincenzo Consolo's *Il sorriso dell'ignoto marinaio* (*The Smile of the Unknown Sailor*, 1976) or Carmelo Samonà's *Fratelli* (*Brothers*, 1977) are all outstanding achievements – but these have been curiously one-off affairs, their authors failing to repeat or develop the performance. The most encouraging sign has been the emergence of younger writers whose expressionist style is in its directness and rawness a far remove from the oblique manner of the avant-garde. Reading the new fiction of the past five or six years, it seems as though reality has re-imposed itself, almost as in the days of Neo-realism, though it is a very different reality from the agrarian, regional Italy of the years after the Resistance. Italy is in many ways a more fragmented society than it was thirty years ago. New social groups, or new social identities, are emerging and seeing literature as a means of giving voice to their concerns: redefinitions of sexuality, explorations of all kinds of 'emargination', social and psychological, awareness of language as a prisonhouse rather than a plaything. The interesting point is that writers and readers alike appear to have been focussing their attention on these themes for their own sake – the 1970s were a serious and, in their way, committed decade – and much less than their experimental predecessors on the 'literariness' of the finished text.

BIBLIOGRAPHY

WORKS CITED

Acquaviva, S. S. and Santuccio, M. *Social structure in Italy*, transl. Colin Hamer, Martin Robertson, London, 1976

Allum, P. 'Political Terrorism in Italy',*Journal of the Association of Teachers of Italian*, 25 (1978) 5–18

Aspetti. *Aspetti delle letture in Italia (Quaderni di vita italiana,* 9), Istituto poligrafico dello Stato, Rome, 1975

Berlinguer, E. 'Riflessioni sull'Italia dopo i fatti del Cile' (articles originally published in *Rinascita,* 28 Sept, 5 and 9 Oct 1973), in *La "questione comunista",* a cura di A. Tatò, Editori Riuniti, Rome, vol. II, 1975, 609–639

Cadioli, A. *L'industria del romanzo,* Editori Riuniti, Rome, 1981

Censis. Rapporto sulla situazione sociale, cited in *La Repubblica,* 4 Dec. 1982

Corti, M. *Il viaggio testuale,* Einaudi, Turin, 1978

De Mauro, T. *Storia linguistica dell'Italia unita,* Laterza, Bari, (2nd ed.) 1976

—, *Linguaggio e società nell'Italia d'oggi,* RAI, Turin, 1978

Luperini, R. *Il novecento,* Loescher, Turin, 1981

Mammarella, G. *L'Italia dalla caduta del fascismo a oggi,* Il Mulino, Bologna, (2nd ed.) 1978

Mariani, G. *La giovane narrativa italiana tra documento e poesia,* Le Monnier, Florence, 1962

Moss, D. and Rogers, E. 'Poverty and inequality in Italy', in V. George and R. Lawson (eds.), *Poverty and Inequality in Common Market Countries,* RKP, London, 1980, 161–94

Pacifici, S. *A guide to Contemporary Italian Literature. From Futurism to Neorealism,* Preface by Thomas G. Bergin, Meridian Books, Cleveland and New York, 1962

Pasolini, P. P. *Passione e ideologia,* Garzanti, Milan, 1960

Podbielski, G. *Italy: Development and Crisis in the Postwar Economy,* Clarendon Press, Oxford, 1974

Sylos Labini, P. *Saggio sulle classi sociali,*Laterza, Bari, 1975

FURTHER READING

Allum, P. *Italy – Republic without Government?,* Weidenfeld and Nicolson, London, 1973

Asor Rosa, A. *Scrittori e popolo,* Samonà e Savelli, Rome, 1965

Castronovo, V. (ed.) *L'Italia contemporanea 1945-1975,* Einaudi, Turin, 1974

Debenedetti, G. *Poesia italiana del Novecento,* Garzanti, Milan, 1974

Ferretti, G. C. *Il mercato delle lettere,* Einaudi, Turin, 1979

Fraser, J. *Italy: Society in Crisis/Society in Transformation,* RKP, London, 1981

Gatt-Rutter, J. *Writers and Politics in Modern Italy,* Hodder and Stoughton, London, 1978

Kogan, N. *A Political History of Postwar Italy: From the Old to the New Center-Left,* Praeger, New York, 1981

Manacorda, G. *Storia della letteratura italiana contemporanea 1940-1975,* Editori Riuniti, Rome, 1977

Spinazzola, V. (ed.) *Pubblico 1978,* Milano Libri, Milan, 1979

Christopher Wagstaff

2 The Neo-avantgarde

After the Second World War, Italian literary movements picked up what they considered to be some of the literary threads broken by the Fascist 'interlude', and so many of them were called 'neo' something or other. The pre-Fascist avant-garde of Futurism and the post-war Neo-avantgarde, as well as having many technical and superficial affinities, had in common the fundamental purpose of making art reflect in its form the social and economic conditions which it inhabited. In the case of Futurism, this was an enthusiastically embraced imperialist capitalism; in the case of the Neo-avantgarde, it was to be a 'demystified' neo-capitalism. A number of Neo-avantgarde writers had been working together, conscious of a developing group identity, for several years when, in 1963, they called a meeting and baptised themselves the *Gruppo 63*, which then became a label interchangeable with *neo-avanguardia* for a literary movement operating in Italy between 1956 and 1969.

The group had first formed around the periodical *Il Verri*, founded by Luciano Anceschi in 1956 in Milan. Anceschi and many of his collaborators were strongly influenced by the phenomenological school, whose method was that of the disinterested observation of actual experience, and for whom poetry should be an expression of the present rather than an attempt to bring about a specific future. Anceschi and Lombard phenomenologists had promoted for several years a 'poetry of objects', in opposition to the idealism and elevated style of the hermetics; not for nothing was the first group motto of the Neo-avantgarde 'la riduzione dell'io' ('the reduction of the "I" '). *Il Verri* did not apologise for its attention to literature; Anceschi's opening *Discorso generale* had this to say: 'poetry and literature come second to no other activity worthy of man, and to dedicate . . . attention to them is an act . . . as necessary as that of solving any other problem, not just philosophical and moral, but social, economic and political as well' (*Il Verri* 1). This is not art for art's sake; this is art seen as having its greatest practical value in its very autonomy, and the Neo-avantgarde will elaborate, along phenomenological lines, but also under the influence of the Frankfurt School, a poetics which gives precedence to the superstructure (of which art is a part) over the base (i.e. economics).

The innovation of *Il Verri* was to work as a team of specialists, rather than as a circle of polymath humanists. This enabled the writers to carry out a systematic de-provincialization of Italian letters, with competent analyses of structuralism, ethnology, Russian formalism, semiology, and veritable campaigns of promotion – for example of the *nouveau roman*, known at the time in Italy as the 'école du regard'. Italian society was seen as having moved into the phase of neo-capitalism, where the managing of consensus took priority over revolutionary confrontation. Intellectuals began to see themselves as ideological technicians, part of the machinery of consensus whether they liked it or not. Self-knowledge (one of the goals of phenomenology), in the sense of understanding the machinery of the 'system' (i.e. how you do function and how you can function in it), was the path towards what little freedom was to be conquered. *Il Verri* therefore set about mapping the ideological superstructure of contemporary Italy.

The next landmark in the story of the Neo-avantgarde was the publication in 1961 of an anthology of poetry, edited by Alfredo Giuliani (*Il Verri's* specialist on poetry), containing the work of Giuliani himself, Elio Pagliarani, Antonio Porta, Edoardo Sanguineti and Nanni Balestrini. The anthology's title borrowed from Anceschi's previous *Lirici nuovi (New Lyric Poets)*, and went further, calling these poets *I novissimi (The Newest)*, in a conscious assertion of an avant-garde ambition. The poetry of the *Novissimi* will be one of the main topics of this essay, and here we need only situate it in its historical context. The works of Giuliani, Sanguineti and Balestrini in the anthology constituted a complete rejection of conventional language, not just of poetic language, and the anthology had an enormous impact not only in presenting this new work to a wider public, but also in confronting, on a practical level, the question of language's hold over our experience. While formally syntax was brutally assaulted, on the level of content rationality was simply exorcised by the oneiric, the erotic and the demented. All this was presented by the poets (who contributed theoretical essays and notes to their poems) as a mimetic exercise: the schizophrenia of the poetry was a mirror to the schizophrenia and alienation of neo-capitalist society.

Two years later, from the 3rd to the 8th of October 1963, just outside Palermo, a number of writers gathered to discuss matters of concern to them: the function of intellectuals in contemporary society, the role of literature, and most of all, what the writer should be doing. Public discussions were held, and there were meetings where texts were read and theatrical pieces performed. The press response was far greater than the participants had expected, and the *Gruppo 63* acquired its name (deliberately echoing the German *Gruppe 47*). Further meetings were held in 1964, and the meeting in 1965 discussed the matter of the experimental novel. Anthologies of critical and theoretical writings, reports of debates at the meetings, and the works of participants were published. By now the firm of Feltrinelli had become the group's official publisher, and from 1964 onwards it produced *Materiali*, an important series of theoretical and critical books by members of the group. The group was now not only established as an avant-garde, but was achieving considerable media exposure, partly by chance, but in large part by design. The team had its periodical, but also a friendly big-league publisher, and numerous collaborators in the press and in the universities. An avant-garde whose products could in no way be considered commercial was succeeding in penetrating the capitalist market-place. It is not surprising that some saw that success as proof that the movement was not genuinely avant-garde.

The next landmark in the movement's history is its demise, a story told in the pages of the periodical which it founded in June 1967, *Quindici (Fifteen)*. The Neo-avantgarde was committed to working within the autonomy which art conferred at the level of ideology; its members believed this to be the only effective area of operation available to them. When, in 1968, Italy seemed to offer significant opportunities for direct political action, the *Gruppo 63*, saw its *raison d'etre* disappear, and members responded in very different ways to the situation. Certainly, the literature which Anceschi had put on a par with social, economic and political activity in 1956, and which the *Gruppo* had seen as a vanguard, was in danger of being left far behind by the students and the metalworkers of 1968. *Quindici* ceased publication in July 1969.

Much of the artistic activity of the Neo-avantgarde becomes more accessible when elements of the theories which lie behind the activities are brought together. Therefore, the first task of this survey will be to expound some of the basic theoretical positions of the group, against which individual positions can be more clearly picked out, and the creative works can be seen in some sort of logical perspective. We shall find Umberto Eco expressing preliminary general theoretical considerations, Sanguineti taking them further and applying them in a very personal way, while Balestrini works almost exclusively through the application of his principles in his creative writing. As the survey widens its embrace, we shall see these elements of theoretical homogeneity give way to a variety of different solutions to the problem of writing in the modern age. But it is with Eco that we shall begin.

In *Opera aperta* (*The Open Work;* cf. Chapter 3 for a fuller treatment) Eco asserts that modern avant-garde artists have not only exploited ambiguity in order to give a novel representation of the world, but they have gone further and, using an 'open' formal structure for their works, have given to the recipient of works of art the task of partly creating the works himself or herself. The more 'open' the work is to the receiver's creative participation, the more it evades the perpetuation of conventional perception and representation.

In his essay 'Del modo di formare come impegno sulla realtà' ('On the Manner of Giving Form as a Committed Way of Acting on Reality'; see Chapter 3, pp. 67–68) Eco continues the debate, stretching back to the end of the war, on Neo-realist fiction, taking up Vittorini's statement that 'the products of the so-called "école du regard" which in their content seem not to know of the existence of factories, technicians, workers, are in fact much closer to the industrial world, through the new relationship with reality that their language establishes, than all that so-called industrial literature which has factories for its subject-matter' (*Il Menabò*, 4, 1961). Eco points out that a writer's 'form', his language, is the true 'content' of his work. A writer who attempts to criticise or delve behind the images promoted by and for a certain social and economic 'system', and uses, to do so, the language of that system, merely reproduces that system, and perpetuates a mystification. Therefore the avant-garde artist innovates at the level of form, by destroying the ordered system of conventional language. The disorder that he creates is an open expression of conflicts in reality which the system wishes to homogenise in a make-believe harmony.

To explain why 'disorder' plays such an important part in the artist's operation, Eco uses information theory, according to which information is carried by a message in a quantity determined by the unpredictability of that message. Where language is concerned, codes impose on information an order (a measure of predictability) which enables messages to be clearly communicated. The more ordered and predictable the elements and the structures of a message, the more clearly it can be comprehended, the more it is 'meaningful'. Information, therefore, is quantitative; meaning is qualitative. A very meaningful communication is so predictable as to be telling you nothing you did not already know. (Christmas cards are very predictable; they are clearly meaningful, but low in information content. However, such a card from your worst enemy is less predictable, and has higher information content.) Information results from a disturbance in the predictability of the message; the more of a certain type of disorder, of unpredictability, the message has, the more information it carries. But you will not be able to understand a message that is too disordered, that is too devoid of meaning; too much information makes the message unclear (what is the *meaning* of my enemy's Christmas card?). Eco places artistic communication on this scale of order and disorder, and locates the avant-garde a great deal further towards disorder than conventional art: 'the contemporary poet . . . introduces forms of organised disorder into a system to increase its capacity for information' (110). To avoid reproducing the 'system' he is opposing, he subverts, to a greater or a lesser extent, its codes. The conclusion is again, and it is a fundamental one for the Neo-avantgarde, that the artist innovates on a formal level, that of language, rather than on the level of content.

At the root of Eco's theory lies the concept of the artist as one 'alienated' from the 'system' of meanings which offers us a world to live in. In his art, the artist wishes to represent something truer than what convention proposes. At bottom, so does Sanguineti: 'The experience of words conditions (precedes) that of things . . . Literature is the experimental space where the dialectic of words and things is decided' (1975, 132-3). Here words precede things and, as with Eco, the artist's true content is his language.

To explain how Sanguineti sees 'words' preceding 'things', and indeed his concern with the relationship, which he sees as fundamental, between ideology and language, it is necessary to summarise those elements of structural linguistics and of French Marxist thought which he is introducing into the poetic theory of the Neo-avantgarde. From structural linguistics he takes the idea of language as a system of signs, consisting of the signifier and the signified. The signified is a concept ('tree' conjures in your mind the concept, not the literally mind-boggling botanical object itself). To relate language to the real world Sanguineti borrows Marxist theories according to which the concepts denoted by the process of signification are the product of a dialectic between on the one hand what is 'out there', reality – whatever that is – and on the other what you want to be out there, what you need to be out there and what you have been taught is out there. This dialectic is ideology. Through language we construct, appropriate, perceive 'reality-as-ideology-would-have-it'. Sanguineti, the avant-garde poet, wishing to change 'reality', believes that he must change ideology; to change ideology, he must change language. Hence it is at the level of its language that he can work on the system of neo-capitalism. He cannot change ideology in a positive way as long as the 'he' that would do it is ideologically conditioned, but he can destroy the ideological constructs in existence by shattering the linguistic norms that operate at a given moment, thereby opposing the concepts of reality that people have, and so opposing what they do at a practical level.

From this it should be clear that Sanguineti would accuse the Neo-realists of merely reproducing the existing ideological representations of 'reality'. But the position of the Neo-avantgarde with reference to the political commitment of the realists is complicated by the influence of the phenomenological tradition. Sanguineti believes that there is a reality beyond the mystification of ideology, and would have literature 'put us in touch' with it. To achieve this, the artist must rid himself of his 'history', he must de-ideologize himself. Phenomenology offers a method: the suspension of the 'I', with its desire and interests, so that the seeker for knowledge watches disinterestedly his mind experience the world. Neo-avantgarde writers attempt to shine a spotlight on the ideological mystifications of neo-capitalism, exploiting the (relative) autonomy of art for the privileged position of disinterested observation it offers, and never pretending that they themselves can more than very partially elude the ideological conditioning that they are trying to highlight. Someone like Sanguineti, therefore, believes himself to be committed to the struggle for a better society in a far more sophisticated and less naïve way than the Neo-realists.

Sanguineti holds that avant-garde art is a product of, and can be completely absorbed by, the neo-capitalist system, in which the products of men's labour have the exchange value of commodities in a market; one commodity competes with another. The avant-garde artist, aspiring to a pure and uncontaminated product, to avoid having his works of art turned into commodities, tries to escape the commodity condition *(mercificazione)* either by disdaining to compete with more marketable and conventional works (Sanguineti calls this the 'heroic' attitude), or by resigning himself to the fact that his work will not be understood or accepted by the market (the 'pathetic' attitude), or by deliberately sprinting out in front and beating the competition with his *virtuosismo*, his startling innovations (the 'cynical' attitude). But any threat the work might pose to prevailing ideology is neutralised by the fact that the market reduces all works to the value of competing commodities, and those works which refuse to compete are soon absorbed into the 'museum', which is an equally effective way of subjecting them to the values of the market-place; it is a place where 'the tumult of money finally dies down, reality hides its head in the clouds, and the work of art embodies what no money can buy' (1975, 66). The fact that works are destined either for the market-place or the museum introduces a divorce into what should be a 'dialectical unity' of culture and politics. In neither case can the work draw attention to the mystifications of ideology, nor can it break through to new knowledge. This divorce, and this neutralization of the work of art (concepts owed to the Frankfurt School, and in particular the different threads leading from Benjamin, Adorno and Marcuse) constitute Sanguineti's version of Eco's 'alienation' (see Chapter 3), and the theory of the avant-garde which Sanguineti develops constitutes a strategy for bringing this state of affairs out into the open.

One way of opposing dominant ideology is to 'ideologize the avant-garde', to present a personal counter-ideology. Once you have washed yourself clean of conventional ideology it is hard to find another one which is not compromised, but Sanguineti seeks it in what he considers to be the universal symbols and myths of Jung's 'collective unconscious'. Influenced by Barthes's *Mythologies* and by Lévi-Strauss, he sees these myths as forming an ideology, a language, in which the mind expresses its own structure. The dream is a disordered communication, but in its latent order lies its hidden meaning; it has an organization, to which Sanguineti attempts to break through. To borrow from Eco's version of information theory, Sanguineti wants both 'meaning' and 'information', order out of disorder. The destruction of the rationality of the 'system' produces a chaos from which Sanguineti strains to achieve a oneness. The polemic with the 'rationality' of dominant ideology was one of the Neo-avantgarde's main platforms, and one of their major objections to Neo-realism. But for the writers of the Neo-avantgarde irrationality was also a strategy and a weapon to be used to break through the armour of the dominant ideology. Disorder could be positive, the bearer of information; it could be negative, the destruction of meaning.

Sanguineti's early poetry (1951-1964) consists of the working out of this struggle between order and disorder. *Laborintus* (1951-1954) is a Dantesque journey through the *complicazione* ('complication') of the mind, a story of an erotic love of Ellie who is this disorder in the Jungian anima, and at the same time the attempt to achieve an integration of all this disorder and diversity into a meaningful whole, a *semplificazione* ('simplification'). The artist is like a watchmaker; he tries to produce 'articolazioni pensose per convincere una materia ribellante' ('articulations of thought to tame a rebellious material'). *Laborintus* is a poetry that is about its own poetics, but which uses the personal events of the mind as a language. The *complicazione* is a condition of the neurotic psyche undergoing a sort of nervous breakdown. But this expresses the alienation of the mind in a world which divorces, for example, the political from the cultural, the rational from the irrational.

From Jung's *Psychology and Alchemy* Sanguineti has borrowed the parallel between the process of psychic individuation, or integration, the bringing to one of the many, and the process that the alchemist is attempting to bring to a conclusion, the refinement of base metals, purification and salvation. Disorder, alienation and splitting are expressed in a mixture of erotic and mythical images: sex and death, descent, the labyrinth, or, as in the opening of the collection, the Palus Putredinis (Stinking Swamp). In his most famous statement of his poetics he calls the procedure: 'hurling oneself straightaway headfirst into the labyrinth of formalism and irrationalism, into the Stinking Swamp, in fact, of anarchy and alienation, in the hope – which I persist in believing is not illusory – of then truly emerging from it all with one's hands dirty, but also with the mire once and for all behind one' (*Novissimi,* 204). Sanguineti is Lukácsian in his negative view of formalism and irrationalism (and in this he contrasts with

Balestrini, for example), and sees the procedures of the avant-garde as a means to an end, an 'ideological realism', in which poetry will reflect what really is the case, and will be the vehicle of liberation. Indeed, his third volume of poetry ends with: 'come ti giustifichi? (. . .) ma vedi il fango che ci sta alle spalle? (. . .) e i bambini che dormono (. . .) (sognando adesso)' ('How do you justify yourself? (. . .) but do you see the mud behind us? (. . .) and the children sleeping (. . .) (dreaming now)'): *Purgatorio de l'Inferno, Purgatory of Hell*. Death leading to rebirth is Sanguineti's recurring topos.

The verse of *Laborintus* (and of the later collections) is described by Giuliani as 'atonal', and Cesare Vivaldi called it 'action poetry', alluding to abstract impressionist painting. There is no rhythmical scheme, no regularly measured line (twenty-five syllable lines are part of the normal scheme, but so is a line with one word); instead there is the fluid movement of recitative. Words, phrases, sentences, quotations and fragments of quotations, a diversity of languages (mainly Italian, French, English, German, Latin, Greek) are mingled together in a dreamlike hubbub from which threads and themes spiral out, so that the whole work is one long poem, broken into lyrical sections. The same goes for his next volume of verse, *Erotopaegnia* (*Love Songs*, 1961), in which the same fearsome plunging into the labyrinth of the unconscious is treated more playfully, with the same dream-perspective, a love-story again, but where chronology is distorted, where word-play becomes a mimesis of the erotic play being expressed. The language has descended further towards the linguistic gesture of the grunted exclamation (*uh*, *oh*, etc.), and the fragmentation of the discourse has been taken further. Inside this disorder there are fragments of a discursive polemic which has appeared already in *Laborintus* against war and the intellectuals' tolerance of it, and the book ends with a satire of America. At the same time, the intensity of the lyricism has sometimes increased – section 11 is justly celebrated.

The third volume, *Purgatorio de l'Inferno* (1964), while increasing the fragmentation of the discourse, actually increases the discursive content of the poetry. It has been referred to as Sanguineti's 'Neo-contenutismo' ('renewed concern with content') where he tries to emerge from the disorder and direct his poetry to some clear statement of commitment.

At this point it is best to turn to an examination of his novels. The first, *Capriccio italiano* (*Italian Caprice*, 1963), is one of the most successful of all the works of the Neo-avantgarde, and it draws upon the poetry of *Laborintus* and *Erotopaegnia*. Its diction is an anti-style: there is an overabundance of adverbs (*ormai, adesso, invece, intanto, già*) used almost like hand gestures; the conjunctions *ma* and *e* regularly turn sentences into exclamations; the conjunction *che* joins propositions that have no syntactical business with each other; anacoluthon is everywhere; sentences are short, paratactic, and repeat themselves with minor variations, relying on accumulation of data rather than concise expression to get across their meaning. The narrative diction is lowered below the colloquial to the very lowest common denominator of speech, a neutral diction whose verbal nature is almost incidental. This antithesis of literary style, this glorification of the stock expression is so stereotyped as not to 'belong' to anyone – in the same way that bureaucratese could not be called a style that 'belonged' to anyone (there are parallels here with the 'found' language of Balestrini's writings). This diction functions as a neutral vehicle for the optical ambiguity of dream perspective, in which a person or object does not remain the same for long, and in which the dreamer has constantly to qualify his references to an experience that is not clear and unequivocal, but which may well have changed between one utterance and the next. Characters in the novels are not (usually) identified by name or sex: they are given a letter, while the 'character' signified by a letter may keep changing radically: the *moglie* (wife), *figli* (children), and the letter-characters are projections of the dreamer's psyche, phonemes in the discourse of the dream. The diction is mimetic, expressing the process of the dream; as language it is indifferent: it denotes, it never connotes, it has no resonances. Behind the words are the perceptions, nothing more. The real language of the novel, therefore, is the dream itself, the gestures, the events, the experiences which the dreamer perceives, all of which do have resonances and conceal a number of levels of meaning. Sanguineti has tried to reduce his diction to a neutral vehicle for something else which *is* a language.

The whole novel is a process, consisting of the working out of a conflict within the psyche of the narrator between the imminent birth of a child and his fear of that birth, which is also a fear of death, disorder, and a fear of his own unconscious mind. This conflict is worked out on three symbolic levels: firstly through the narrator's immersion in his unconscious, the encounter between persona and anima, which is the level of the dream *per se*. Secondly, there is the level of ritual, in which the descent into the unconscious becomes the fairy-tale descent into death, in which memories of school-life become initiation rites, and in which impotence is connected with circumcision and mutilation. The third level is that of alchemy, symbolising what Jung calls the 'process of individuation'. The process of the novel is that of the resolution of the conflict in the oneiric sphere on the three levels we have mentioned, coinciding, in the sphere of waking reality, with the birth of Michele. On the first level, that of the dream *per se*, the conscious becomes acquainted with the unconscious, persona with anima, male with female; the acceptance of the unconscious by the conscious is often expressed in the gesture-language of the dream as copulation between the narrator and an anima figure. On the level of ritual, the narrator undergoes an initiation entailing a rebirth after death (a descent into the tomb with female characters, for example). The initiation leads towards the acceptance of life and death (which is the axiomatic, as it were, interpretation of initiation which Sanguineti is following). On the alchemical level, the dreamer learns to see the light of salvation at the bottom of the alchemist's flask (e.g. the 'fontana calda' ('hot spring') of chapter LXXII) – which eventually becomes the umbilical cord of his son about to be born (CIII), and in the process of individuation, the 'many' become 'one' in a huge painting done by B – and here the sense of the novel as an expression of the author's poetics becomes clear, for the painting bears the message which the myths alone can convey in unmystified form: the myths are the objects which the work of art has somehow reproduced uncontaminated by the dominant ideology, through a process of regression (not unlike a regression proposed by the Surrealists). In writing about dream, myth, ritual, Sanguineti has by-passed the problem of ideology interfering with his representation of reality, for he is representing not reality but a *representation* of reality, the dream, which has a language evolved phylogenetically (not 'historically'), in which the contradictions of social life evade rational or historical deformation and censorship, and in which the mind expresses itself in universal symbols.

The novel's 111 chapters are like cinematic sequences, whose contents are dreams, broken up and scattered among separate chapters, as though the 'film' of each episode had been cut into pieces and interspersed with fragments of other episodes. The reader has to interpret everything: the dreams are 'told', they are not 'told about', they are not given meaning by the narration. It is as though someone were describing the initiation rites of a tribe of people by describing objectively the behaviour of the participants, without in any way revealing why they were behaving the way they behaved. This 'distanced' perspective is a characteristic of much of the Neo-avantgarde's narrative, as we shall see, and owes much to the lesson of the *nouveau roman*.

Il giuoco dell'oca (*The Goose Game*, 1967) takes the procedure of the novel as a representation of a representation even further. It consists, like *Capriccio*, of 111 short chapters. Each describes a square on a huge board ('il gioco dell'oca' is a board game played with the throw of dice similar to snakes and ladders). As in the first novel, what is described is merely 'described'; it is not explained. The squares, or 'boxes', as they are called, contain the 'representations' created by our culture, and include: newspaper clippings, comic strips, cinema posters, nudie calendars, graffiti from lavatory walls, rebuses, bits of an auction catalogue, advertisements, collages, Rorschach tests, descriptions of dreams, all viewed with that oneiric perspective that has become Sanguineti's trademark. The narrator is dead, looking back at the world, seeing reality through ideology's representation of it. Sometimes paintings or sculptures seem to be described, in the style of Delvaux, Ceroli, Festa, Dali, Bosch, Warhol, Lichtenstein. Indeed, the whole novel is often compared to Pop Art, and the narrator sees himself at a desk (seen from his coffin?) on which is a Pop Art ornament and his own skull. This artistic re-presentation of the products of contemporary culture is a feature of much art of the 1960s, and of much Italian visual poetry, and both the novel and the collection of poems which parallels it, *T.A.T.* (1968), have been called descriptions of visual poems. The objects are stripped of meaning, only to be used as a satirical portrayal of the ideology they represent; it is literature about language, and it throws together into conflict all the contradictory forces operating on a man of the 1960s, lying dead in his coffin, trying to tap out morse code messages to his family.

Balestrini takes the process of 'desemanticisation' even further. He does not describe representations, he simply presents them: his novel *Tristano* (1966) consists of ten chapters of ten paragraphs of thirty-four lines each. It is a scissors and paste job: he has taken sentences from novels of romance on the one hand, and technical handbooks on the other, and juxtaposed them. No 'meaning' is really intended. How has he arrived at so radical a procedure?

Balestrini wishes the poet to 'take, as the object of poetry, language, understood as a *verbal fact*' (*Novissimi*, 196). Language is normally used to communicate an ordered system of values, and it is through values and order that power is wielded. Balestrini, therefore, strips language of its communicative function, and offers it as a formal entity, an object like any other. His poetry is a verbal collage. An early poem, *De cultu virginis* (*On the Cult of Virgins*), is a collage of pieces of conversation, quotations and recondite references, not really requiring to be interpreted, but simply experienced. It is not true to say that Balestrini's collages are meaningless, just that they do not require an exegetic activity; one reads them, some fragments make sense, some seem arbitrary, the juxtapositions are plainly there, and the reader makes of them what he or she wants. In the poem *Il sasso appeso* (*The Suspended Stone*, 1961), for instance, the collage allows certain things gradually to come into focus: the 'sasso' as a symbol for time and history, looming menacingly over us; images of flight; the sense of not moving from a static position; the statement that we shall be free if we cut the rope that holds the 'sasso' over us. The poem reflects the state of the intellectual, unable to escape history, but needing to reject it if he is to be free of his frenzied, useless activity; he must accept, for his survival, to move without a goal. *Lo sventramento della storia* (*The Disembowelment of History*, 1963) is laid out visually in such a way as to isolate fragments of the collage, and here the elements used for the collage are more frequently 'found' elements, natural descriptions, scraps of poetry, mingled with Balestrini's own statement of the bankruptcy of communicative language. As a result, the 'personal message' of Balestrini that percolates through the poem sends us back to the form of the poem, which is using language 'objectively'. So far there has been a progression from the collagistic use of conventional poetic material to the use of 'found' material, or sentences and phrases from a pre-existing text. His next text is a series of *Cronogrammi* (*Chronogrammes*, 1963), consisting of collages of words and phrases cut out of newspapers in their original typography, pasted together in a pleasing visual layout, and giving rise to unexpected semantic concoctions.

Art, however, offers an aesthetic ordering of the disorder of communication for Balestrini and so he needs a formal method of producing his texts, his objects. In *Ma noi facciamone un'altra* (*But let's us make another one*, 1964–1968) he uses typography to order the text: a set number of characters per line, and the fragments assembled in incompleted patterns of repetition; or a line of type (containing normal language) which is shorter than the piece of discourse, and which only contains part of the discourse, so that you have a series of repetitions of the same thing, but each repetition slightly different from the others because it cuts off the discourse in different places. Another way he produces his form is to programme a computer to assemble the collage according to principles which he enters into the machine at the outset (*Tape Mark I, Tape Mark II*). *Tape Mark I* is a sort of *sestina* (six stanzas of six lines, with constant repetition of certain elements) mixing fragments from various sources with a description of a nuclear explosion. Balestrini engaged in many different experimental forms, notably visual poetry, but the computer-composed verse is the furthest point to which he took his notion of a neo-capitalist use of language. If culture is now an area where the sphere of reproduction (media industries) conditions production, cultural artefacts have become commodities. The information which culture communicates is no longer organized by the artisan on the basis of use value, but by the capitalist forces of production on the basis of commodity value (what is new). Computer composition, where form is everything (where form is content), offers a system for infinite reproduction of commodities, and makes it impossible to treat language as anything else.

To return to the novel we referred to earlier, *Tristano* is a typographically formed collage, with its 10 x 10 x 34 structure. The collage is made up of phrases and sentences cut from texts of four quite separate kinds: novels of romance, textbooks of photography and geography, descriptions of the female body in terms of lines and shapes, and fragments of a discussion of post-war Italian history. All characters, places and proper nouns are replaced by the letter C. This permits what appears to be one sentence to start talking about a person and end by referring to an object, or for a character to change sex in mid-sentence. In fact, there are no characters, no plot and no continuous discourse. A notable feature is that the fragments from which the collage is built are repeated, frequently more than once. If it were not for the repetition, there would be no form to the book, and it would be unreadable. As it is, the repetitions create a rhythm, and once the reader has learned not to look for any conventional forms in the novel, he or she can experience the purely artificial form of this rhythm. Meanings do percolate through: the alienation of sexual relationships, the problems of seeing clearly ('themes', if you like, emerging from three of the sources), the sense of the Resistance as a failed revolution (from the fourth source). The reader inevitably creates for himself or herself a context for the fragments, both in *Tristano* and in the 'source'. This means that rather than the tragically predestined, 'closed' story of Tristan, Balestrini's novel offers no destiny at all, and is totally 'open'. As for his theoretical position, it is that the novel should be a 'purely verbal mechanism', and the formal structure is the level at which it is to be experienced.

After *Tristano*, and after the upheavals of 1968, Balestrini threw himself into direct political activity, and his art took back on board a strong semantic content. *Vogliamo tutto* (*We Want Everything*, 1971) is a first-person account, almost a diary, of the experiences of a worker at the Fiat plant during the 1968–69 uprisings, containing manifestos, communiqués and documents relating to the events narrated. *La violenza illustrata* (*Violence Illustrated*, 1976) is once again a collage, but of bureaucratese, describing the institutionalized violence of capitalist society (massacres in Vietnam, accidents at work, and the more indirect violence of the amassing of huge wealth).

Balestrini was the most radical experimenter of the *Gruppo 63*, and also the most uncompromising in his attitude to language, in his desire to let poetry and the novel merely reflect reality by destroying the order with which language articulates dominant ideology. His collages are the nearest thing to the *opera aperta* of Eco (whose model was really aleatory music) that the Neo-avantgarde produced. He is also the artist who let the form of the work be determined by the methods of production of the reality whose form he was trying to illuminate. At the same time, he was one of the very few members of the group who did not employ irrationality as content: none of the fragments from which his collages are made are 'deviant'. Unlike Sanguineti or Giuliani, or in another way Manganelli, he does not produce a Rimbaldian 'dérèglement de tous les sens'; rather, as Eco says, 'he does not create disorder by overturning order, but discovers it in the place of order' (1967, 280n.).

Eco, Sanguineti and Balestrini form part of the ideological wing of the Neo-avantgarde, but the anthology *I novissimi* contained the work of three other very different poets, Elio Pagliarani, Alfredo Giuliani and Antonio Porta. Despite the diversity of ideological position and poetic technique, all the *Novissimi* are primarily engaged in a linguistic struggle with conventional lyrical forms, and they all attempt to open their linguistic doors to what the world in which they live 'says', rather than imposing a subjective lyrical perspective on reality.

Pagliarani's reaction against the solipsism of contemporary lyric poetry was to reject the purity of the lyric *genre* and to reflect the reality of a class society in what he calls 'the *genre* of the extended poem, of the narrative, didactic *kind*' (*Novissimi*, 199). Thus his poetry can expand its contents by expanding its vocabulary and adopting a 'plurilinguistic lexical material'. The most obvious influences on his long poem *La ragazza Carla* (*The Girl Carla,* 1960) are Parini and Gadda. Pagliarani's poem describes the life and environment of a young woman who has just left school in Milan. She lives with her family and is in the process of growing out of a terror of her own sexuality, persecuted by the advances of men, following a course at a secretarial college, after which she gets a job in an import-export company office – where the boss molests her, and where she starts a relationship with a young colleague. The narrative of this poem is, however, by no means straightforward; although what the reader is offered is a slice of life, this is presented not in an objective way but as reflected in the minds of the characters and the narrator – or even as a product of the language. This allows the didactic-narrative poem to function as a multi-layered lyric poem, a compendium of the lyrics of the many classes and institutions that make up the society depicted. The narrative uses a multiplicity of voices, and rather than carrying out a suppression of his 'I', Pagliarani uses his own, reflective, commentative voice as just one more of the voices in the choral effect. Much is made of Pagliarani's 'plurilinguistic' technique by critics, partly because this is what ties him most firmly to the Neo-avantgarde. Satirical-didactic-narrative poetry is very content-oriented, while the Neo-avantgarde is thought of as directing its attention to form. Certainly *La ragazza Carla* uses a large number of different registers and vocabularies: familiar colloquial language, quotations from typing manuals and from international law textbooks, business jargon, and refined poetic discourse. The transitions from one to the other are abrupt and fragmentary, and the end result is akin to that of collage. The office where Carla works, for example, is evoked by the multiplicity of the languages and discourses produced by it. Nevertheless, while at the level of form the poem partakes of the fragmenting, dissociated, collage technique of the Neo-avantgarde, at the ideological level it is much closer to the committed reformist ethos of Neo-realism than the radical mimesis of the other *Novissimi* poets.

Pagliarani's main concern in a work like *Carla* is to put the *reader* in a more immediate relationship with reality, whereas Giuliani and Porta are concerned with the *poet's* relationship with reality. Like Pagliarani, Alfredo Giuliani constantly returns in his writings to the problem of 'content': 'what poetry *does* is precisely its content' (*Novissimi*, 17). In his poem *Le radici dei segni* (*The Root of signs*, 1964), an exposition of his poetics, the universe is an organization of signs, where one has to 'get some movement out of words which are so sure of themselves' in order to try and bring about a rapport with reality.

Giuliani wants poetry to have the force of material objects, and to achieve this he must see the world of material objects as signs. Then poetry can work on the world: 'if to live means to "represent", or to write, biologically to inscribe memory traces, then writing poetry is a way of forcing life to rewrite itself, to jumble up and reassemble memory traces in new configurations, forcing life to free itself from the fetishisms of representation' (*Novissimi*, 14). From Dylan Thomas he takes the function of poetry to be that of revitalizing experience, and he takes Thomas's biological paradigm too. The image is to do this job, which is seen very much in phenomenological terms, of bringing the objective world into vigorous contact with the mind through the experience of concepts (which are the images) that have the density and impact of material objects or gestures. If one stands back from this a little, there is much that is familiar from post-symbolist poetry, and indeed, Giuliani's early poetry (*Il cuore zoppo*, *The Lame Heart*, 1955) is very hermetic in its language, its imagery and its seemingly metaphysical aspirations. In *I novissimi* he says he is trying to 'make thoughts as visible as things rather than concepts', but his own notes to his poems in the anthology show how much many of the images depend on logical systems of reference outside the poems. I am not at all sure that Giuliani ever achieves his aim, but he certainly developed a poetic method which brought him further away from the sentimental, autobiographical lyric he abhorred. In *La cara contraddizione* (*The Dear Contradiction*) he affirms life in the existentialist manner against its negation in death, treating it as a dance, an adventure, as something producing a lunatic joy. Indeed, the lunatic or the lycanthropic (believing you are a wolf when the moon is full) quickly become Giuliani's way of creating

his 'novel configurations'; the *Predilezioni* (*Predilections*) affirm
life at its lowest, instinctual level of experience, conveyed with
images of lycanthropic love. But at around this point Giuliani
moves (with the poem *Azzurro pari venerdì*, a title not accurately
translatable) to the use of collage, using scraps of conversation and
elements from different sources in a composition that is
characteristic of the Neo-avantgarde. Giuliani's collages, however,
are not intended merely to reflect, to 'be' contemporary society;
they are to be illuminative, their organization is intended to
produce sudden startling imaginative discoveries.

A statement of Giuliani's nicely highlights a fundamental
difference between him and Antonio Porta: 'poetry is not a form of
knowledge but a form of contact' (Barilli-Guglielmi 1976, 98).
This statement accurately describes Giuliani's aspirations; with
Porta precisely the opposite is true. Poetry is 'contact' for Giuliani;
it is 'knowledge' for Porta. Indeed, with Porta the theoretical
discourse of the Neo-avantgarde has been reduced to so generic a
level as to refer to almost any cognitive and communicative
process. Even the *Gruppo 63* writers find themselves treating
Porta's poetry from the point of view of the psychology of the
writer rather than from the standpoint of his poetic theory. Porta's
version of avant-garde disorder is not ideological but emotional; it
is not an organized subversion of codes, but an incomprehension,
created formally by a process of omission and negation. The poet is
engaged in a cognitive quest, to penetrate reality: 'directly tied to a
poetics of the objective is the problem of truth and reality, in
symbiosis with the search for images and the need for penetration.
. . . Objects and events, highlighted and ordered in a rhythmic
whole, can immerse us deeply in reality' (*Novissimi*, 194).

Porta's is a judgemental vision and, whatever Giuliani may say
about the 'riduzione dell'io' which unites the *Novissimi*, in Porta's
first collection, *La palpebra rovesciata* (*The Peeled Eyelid*, 1960),
the eye that would like to shut and cannot is the poet's. He writes of
the violence and destruction in existence: in nature and in civilized
life. His affinity with the rest of the *novissimi* lies in the extreme
poverty of his poetic diction, in the way his poetry accumulates
data in disconnected fragments of facts, actions, news items and
behaviour, producing a total effect, a collage of the horror of life,
rather than a conventionally coherent discourse:

> Un incidente, dicono, ogni ora,
> una giornata che c'era scuola nell'aria

un odore di detriti, crescono
sulla piazza gli aranci del mercante.
Il pneumatico pesantissimo (tale
un giorno l'insetto sfarinò)
orecchie livella occhi voce,
le scarpe penzolano dal ramo,
orecchie livella occhi voce,
le scarpe penzolano dal ramo,
evapora la gomma della frenata.

(Europa cavalca un toro nero, Europe Rides a Black Bull)

(An accident, they say, every hour,/ a day in which there was
school in the air/ a smell of rubbish, in the square/ grow the
oranges of the fruit-seller. /The heavy tyre (just as/ it once
pulverised the insect)/ levels ears eyes voice,/ the shoes dangle
from the branch,/ the rubber from the skid evaporates.)

Knowledge produces anguish, deservedly so, for that 'need for
penetration' on a cognitive level occurs everywhere in the poetry as
a violent penetration, as, for example, the famous super-
imposition of the sex act on the skinning of the beaver in *La
pelliccia del castoro (The Beaver Pelt)*:

In gola penetra scuotendo
le anche l'animale impellicciato,
dilata la bocca dell'esofago,
lo stomaco si distende, in attesa
d'essere venduto e lavorato
come pelle per guanti.

(He penetrates into the throat the furry/ animal shaking its
haunches,/ he dilates the mouth of the oesophagus,/ the
stomach distends, waiting/ to be sold and worked/ as leather
for gloves.)

Porta's indecision in the face of existence gives a form to *Zero*
(1963), a verbal collage in which he uses many devices typical of
the work of the *Gruppo 63*. The lines of the poem are justified, in
the typographical sense, at either margin, cutting words off
sometimes at either end of the line, and different stanzas have
different widths of margin. The language consists of words and
phrases (which look very much as though they might easily have
come from other poems of his), juxtaposed, rarely with a semantic
connection, but always with a total break from line to line, as

though verbal material were missing between the end of one line and the beginning of the next (though nothing suggests that the missing material would confer greater sense on the whole).

The same issues of the cognitive relationship of man with the world are at the heart of the discussion of the novel by two members of the *Gruppo 63* who are the most important representatives, together with Sanguineti, of the movement's literary criticism, Renato Barilli and Angelo Guglielmi. Their contributions to the debate on the avant-garde novel (some of which took place at the 1965 meeting of the *Gruppo*) are what best highlight their positions. Barilli's background is in phenomenology, which leads him to a rejection of naturalism or any utilitarian aim for literature. The writer, establishing a contact between the subject and an object, tries to 'reach the highest possible level of integration with respect to the world' (in Balestrini (ed.) 1966, 18), rather than trying to change the world, so that man can live the 'ecstasy' of his experience of material reality. The novel is the action that makes possible this ecstasy; it is the construction of an invented mechanism in which the mind watches itself experience the world. For Barilli one of the important steps in the achievement of this 'free' contemplation is the *nouveau roman* and the work of Beckett, both of which he sees as fathers of the Italian experimental novel. He then situates the whole contemporary movement in an historical continuity with the experimental novel of the beginning of the century (Joyce, Proust, Svevo, Pirandello, Kafka), so that the Neo-avantgarde is almost a democratization of the twentieth century avant-garde novel, bringing the devices of the latter into the mainstream of contemporary narrative.

Guglielmi's position is, on the surface, almost diametrically opposed to that of Barilli. In a world of false values you cannot substitute true ones directly, you can only reduce existence to an elemental, physical level, and so free material reality from these false values by a completely neutral description. Both Guglielmi and Barilli were vigorously opposed by the ideological wing of the movement (among whom Sanguineti and Pagliarani), who sustained that contemplation and neutral description evade the problem of ideology, and that the collective role of artists is to oppose dominant ideology with an alternative ideal, using changes in style, form and structure as a means of re-structuring meanings and so operating on reality. At a different extreme from this position was that of Balestrini, for whom the novel was a 'purely verbal mechanism', 'self-sufficient', which has 'cut all its connections with reality' (in Balestrini (ed.) 1966, 132-4). Sanguineti linked this attitude, as one in which the novel is an 'organism of total purity and autonomy', with that of Giorgio Manganelli who, in a famous essay, *Letteratura come menzogna* (*Literature as Lie*, 1967), sees literature as a negation of bourgeois rationality, as a rhetorical, ceremonial ritual of the unconscious celebrated by the artist as priest of the underworld, liberating, through language, life's inexorable leaning towards death. Manganelli's novel, *Hilarotragoedia* (1964), is true to its author's precepts. It is a *romanzo-saggio* (essay-novel), a disquisition on the *balistica discenditiva* (downward ballistic) or the state of being *Adediretto* (Hades-bound). The prose glories in archaism and pedantry, in the circular sequence of appositions which are Manganelli's wallowing in the utterance of the aberrant. No very profound philosphy is expounded either in the novel or in the essay; instead, Manganélli plays with the sound, the resonances and the registers of literary prose, and applies them to the expression of the alternative to rationalist, bourgeois ideals: death rather than life, the base rather than the lofty, decay rather than generation, hell rather than heaven. All follows from an introductory premise: 'CHE L'UOMO HA NATURA DIS-CENDITIVA. Intendo e chioso: l'uomo ̀e agito da forza non umana, da voglia, o amore, o occulta intenzione, che si inlàtebra in muscolo o nerbo, che egli non sceglie, né intende; che egli disama e disvuole, che gli instà, lo adopera, invade e governa; la quale abbia nome potestà o volontà discenditiva' ('THAT MAN HAS A DESCENSIONAL NATURE. I intend and gloss: man is controlled by a non-human force, by will or love or occult intention, which lurks in muscle or nerve, which he does not choose, nor intend; which he disloves and unwills, which indwells him, uses him, invades and governs him; which is called descensional power or will': 7).

Manganelli's stance is one of satire, the negative reflection of prevailing ideology. Alberto Arbasino's novel *Fratelli d'Italia* (*Italy's Brothers*, 1963) is also satirical, and it is also a *romanzo-saggio*, consisting of long conversations between the characters, who are blasé, wealthy young people touring Europe attending festivals, in the presence of a narrator who participates in the events and conversations. Not only long sections of the novel, but also an entire second book (*Certi romanzi, Certain Novels,* 1964) are given over to discussions of the form, style and content of the novel which Arbasino is writing, and the author, in 1976, entirely re-wrote the novel in greatly expanded form (and it was a very long novel to begin with). Thus it must surely be one of the most self-conscious undertakings of its time. The conversational form permits narrative sophistication (the reader is not required to accept a narrator's omniscience) and allows Arbasino to use informal, spoken Italian as his language, which he does with great attention to the fashionable, world-weary colloquialisms of the period. Everything is of the period, deliberately so: names, events, products of the time – for example, a film that one of the characters is making is clearly a reference to Antonioni's *L'avventura* and the circumstances surrounding its filming. Arbasino rejects the practical aspirations of naturalism in favour of a poetics of *divertimento* ('entertainment'); nevertheless, he wants a complete realism of detail and reveres Gadda's 'sete per ogni segno dei tempi' ('thirst for every sign of the times'). This rejection of macroscopic realism and obsession with a microscopic realism is a characteristic of post-war avant-gardes in general.

Arbasino has called his novel 'structural', and in a sense it carries within it many literary narrative structures: the picaresque novel, the journey as quest for initiation, the Grand Tour and the *éducation sentimentale,* all mixed in a cauldron of tragicomedy. Embedded in the 'low' style of the conversations is a dazzling wealth of cultural reference, 'tutti gli aspetti essenziali della società e della vita, non rifiutarsi a niente a priori, molto "il gusto come criterio di giudizio" ' (50: 'all the essential aspects of culture, society and life; don't reject anything a priori; very much a case of "taste as a criterion of judgement" '). This brilliance is not merely superficial. Arbasino is importing into the Italian novel a whole cargo of European and Anglo-Saxon culture which, he says in his essay *La gita a Chiasso* (*A Trip to Chiasso*) (in Barilli-Guglielmi 1976, 180-3), Italians could always have had, even under Fascism, for the price of a railway-ticket over the Swiss border.

Arbasino asks in *Fratelli:* 'how would a novelist of the "école du regard" deal with a blind protagonist, reduced to "movements of the heart"?' (42), and certainly it would have posed a problem for Germano Lombardi, in whom the influence of the *nouveau roman* is very strong. His novel, *Barcelona* (1963), and his collection of stories, *L'occhio di Heinrich* (*Heinrich's Eye,* 1965), use the eyes and ears of their protagonist, Giovanni Zevi, as openings on a world about which the reader is given no further information. Events and behaviour are described, but not explained, not rendered into a logical scheme for the reader's understanding. The novel consists of eighteen chapters, in the first six of which Giovanni prepares to leave Paris for Barcelona by train, the journey occupying the next six chapters. In the final six he settles into Barcelona and prepares inconclusively for his task, which is to be part of a plot to assassinate General Felipe Acerro. Giovanni's view at times takes in events in chronological order, but also dreams, memories, fantasies, the most important of which concern his relationship with his anti-Fascist grandfather, Columbus, whose death is skilfully recounted in a story in *L'occhio* which blends objective narrative of a bomber pilot dropping his bombs and Columbus being killed by them. The chapters from the novel and the stories from *L'occhio* can all be taken as fragments of a biography of Giovanni, an alcoholic, perhaps almost psychotic, depressive, living in Paris, London and Barcelona, after a childhood in Fascist Italy. Because Giovanni is at times drunk, drugged, depressed, paranoid or asleep, the *regard* he offers the reader on reality is confused, incomplete and distorted. The result is to convey intensely the inner world of a man, but with the use of a completely dead-pan factual description, narrated in a very spare but elegant prose, as a completely unaberrant example should show:

> Giovanni si avvicinò al comodino, prese la boccetta, ne svitò il tappo e inclinando ne fece uscire una pillola di colore bianco. La pastiglia era a forma di discoide, egli la inghiottì e bevve un sorso. Si era seduto sulla sponda del letto. La pelle delle gambe si era increspata e i peli ogni tanto si rizzavano mentre i muscoli delle gambe si contraevano. Anche le mani tremavano e la pelle delle braccia guizzava per improvvisi brividi.
>
> (*Barcelona*, 23)

> (Giovanni went over to the cupboard, took the bottle, undid its top and tilting it spilled out a white-coloured pill. The tablet was discoid-shaped, he swallowed it and took a sip of water. He had sat down on the edge of the bed. The skin of his legs had wrinkled and hairs now and then stood up, while the muscles of the legs contracted. His hands trembled too and the skin of his arms twitched from sudden shivers).

Nothing, anywhere, explains this or prepares the reader for it. The 'author' could have said: 'Giovanni felt feverish and took an aspirin', leaving the reader to supply the white, discoid tablet. Instead, he narrates the behaviour, and leaves the reader to supply the interpretation. Lombardi's work seems to reconcile the apparently conflicting requirements of Barilli and Guglielmi: disinterested contemplation, and the reduction of narrative to a neutral description of material reality; and yet it shows how much intensity and refined craftsmanship can be put at the service of that task.

An enormous number of criticisms have been levelled at the theory of the Neo-avantgarde and at what its application implies. Some of the most important criticisms can be summarised by saying that the issues of language and ideology and of the relationship of the subject to the object are dealt with by amputating one or other of the sign's poles: either the signified is arbitrarily deemed 'neutral' and free from the history of the signifier, or else the signified is dumped altogether in order to reduce the sign to a mere signifier. Moreover, how is it possible for the subject, who is constructed by ideology, to innovate freely? Is not the destruction of meaning (notwithstanding all the claims that it truly reflects the contradictions of neo-capitalist society) an admission that the writer cannot do anything but confess his incoherence? To what extent can the art of an élite act, through the superstructure, on the base? As far as aesthetics is concerned, it is noteworthy that, for an avant-garde that was vindicating the autonomy of art, its members justified it, used it, and explained it almost exclusively in terms of its ideological usefulness.

Extravagant claims on behalf of the Neo-avantgarde are not made by anybody, inside or outside the *Gruppo 63*. By Sanguineti's own criteria, a lot of their work was *mercificato* and *museificato* almost before the ink had dried on the paper (or the glue dried on the collages). The Neo-avantgarde went simultaneously into the market through Feltrinelli, the large publishers, and into the museum of academic respectability. The artists were already members of the Italian cultural establishment when they formed the group, they remained so, and are so today. Even while they were writing, other artists in Italy distanced themselves from the Neo-avantgarde for precisely that reason: it was the establishment dabbling in a little daring experimentation. Nevertheless, their ideas and theories were new to Italy, and were a breath of fresh air in a culture divided between traditionalist provincialism and social realism. It will be a long time before the Italian Communist Party will try to stigmatise avant-garde art as reactionary, and impose a tepid, populist realism again. But the ideas were borrowed ones, from Paris and Frankfurt. The artistic experimentation was also in large part derivative: an immense debt was owed to Italian Futurism, to Dada, to Russian Formalism, to Surrealism, to Brecht, to the *nouveau roman*, and to the *Tel Quel* movement. Nevertheless, just to make this list of influences (and let Paris, Frankfurt and Russian Formalism expand into the immensely rich veins which those few words encapsulate) and to imagine them being injected efficiently and under high pressure into the Italian scene over the brief period between 1956 and 1966 gives one some idea of the powerful impact that the Neo-avantgarde had on Italian culture. It was difficult to write prose or verse any more in the way it had been written before the founding of *Il Verri*.

The *Gruppo* writers were as acutely aware of the flaws in their theories as any critic is likely to be. Their strongest point was that their primary aim was to produce an art that would reflect its time, to penetrate behind the smooth, mystificatory façade of consensus and harmony that characterizes liberal-bourgeois society, and to represent some of the conflicts and uncertainties that neo-capitalist ideology chooses to hide. They attempted this as a group of writers united by this and other aims. With the demise of the *Gruppo 63*, Italian avant-garde literature has become once more a world in which isolated individuals pursue their separate investigations in the face of a largely indifferent public.

BIOGRAPHICAL NOTES AND BIBLIOGRAPHIES

UMBERTO ECO: for biography and bibliography see Chapter 3. *Opera aperta*, ed. cited Bompiani, Milan, 1967 (2nd ed; includes 'Del modo di formare come impegno sulla realta').

EDOARDO SANGUINETI (born 1930, Genoa; professor of Italian literature; he has written poetry, novels, plays, opera libretti, and is an important

academic literary critic; he is a journalist and since 1979 has been a Member of Parliament)
Poetry: *Laborintus*, Magenta, Varese, 1956; ed. cited *Catamerone*, 1974. *Erotopaegnia*, Rusconi e Paolazzi, Milan, 1961; ed. cited *Catamerone*, 1974. *Purgatorio de l'Inferno*, in *Triperuno*, Feltrinelli, 1964; ed. cited *Catamerone*, 1974. *Catamerone 1951-1971* (containing the above, plus *T.A.T. and Wirwarr*), Feltrinelli, Milan, 1974
Novels: *Capriccio italiano*, Feltrinelli, Milan, 1963; ed. cited 1967. *Il giuoco dell'oca*, Feltrinelli, Milan, 1967
Essays: *Ideologia e linguaggio*, Feltrinelli, Milan, 1965; ed. cited 1975
Further reading: *Gabriella Sica, *Sanguineti*, La Nuova Italia (Il Castoro), Florence, 1974

NANNI BALESTRINI (has used the pseudonym L. Giordani; born 1935, Milan; works in publishing; poet, novelist, critic and political activist: editor of *Il Verri* and *Quindici*)
Poetry: *Come si agisce*, Feltrinelli, Milan, 1963. *Ma noi facciamone un'altra*. Feltrinelli, Milan, 1968. *Poesie pratiche 1954-1969*, including a selection from the above, Einaudi, Turin, 1976
Novels: *Tristano*, Feltrinelli, Milan, 1966. *Vogliamo tutto*, Feltrinelli, Milan, 1971. *La violenza illustrata*, Einaudi, Turin, 1976
Anthologies: joint editor with Alfredo Giuliani: *Gruppo 63. La nuova letteratura*, Feltrinelli, Milan, 1964. (Editor) *Gruppo 63. Il romanzo sperimentale*, Feltrinelli, Milan, 1966

ELIO PAGLIARANI (born 1927, Viserba; variously government employee, secondary school teacher, joint editor or contributor for various periodicals and newspapers, including *Paese sera*, *Il Verri* and *Quindici*, poet and theatre critic)
Poetry: *La ragazza Carla e altre poesie*, Mondadori, Milan, 1962; ed. cited *La ragazza Carla e nuove poesie*, Mondadori, Milan, 1978, which includes a selection from his other major collection: *Lezione di fisica e Fecaloro*, Feltrinelli, Milan, 1968
Anthology: (editor) *Manuale della poesia sperimentale*, Mondadori, Milan, 1968

ALFREDO GIULIANI (born 1924, Pesaro; teaches Italian literature at the University of Bologna; contributor to *Il Verri* and editor of *Quindici*; poet and literary critic)
Poetry: *Il cuore zoppo*, Magenta, Varese, 1955. *Povera Juliet e altre poesie*, Feltrinelli, Milan, 1965. *Il tautofono*, Feltrinelli, Milan, 1969. *Chi l'avrebbe detto?* including selections from the first two collections above, Einaudi, Turin, 1973
Essays: *Immagini e maniere*, Feltrinelli, Milan, 1965
Anthologies: (editor) *I novissimi. Poesie per gli anni '60*, Rusconi e Paolazzi, Milan, 1961; ed. cited Einaudi, Turin, 1965. (Ed. with J. Risset) *Poeti di 'Tel Quel'*. Einaudi, Turin, 1968

ANTONIO PORTA (pseudonym of Leo Paolazzi; born 1935, Milan; works in publishing; poet and literary critic; co-editor of *Il Verri* and contributor

to *Quindici*)
Poetry: *Quanto ho da dirvi* (collected poetry, 1958-1975), Feltrinelli, Milan, 1977
Novel: *Partita*, Feltrinelli, Milan, 1967

GIORGIO MANGANELLI (born 1922, Milan; journalist, novelist and critic)
Novels: *Hilarotragoedia*, Feltrinelli, Milan, 1964. *Nuovo commento*, Einaudi, Turin, 1969. *Agli dèi ulteriori*, Einaudi, Turin, 1972
Essays: *Letteratura come menzogna*, Feltrinelli, Milan, 1967. *Lunario dell'orfano sannita*, Einaudi, Turin, 1973

ALBERTO ARBASINO (born 1930, Voghera; novelist, literary critic and journalist)
Works: *Piccole vacanze*, Einaudi, Turin, 1957. *L'anonimo lombardo*, Feltrinelli, Milan; 1959; *Parigi o cara*, Feltrinelli, Milan, 1960. *Fratelli d'Italia*, ed. cited Feltrinelli, Milan, 1963; revised ed. Einaudi, Turin, 1976. *Certi romanzi*, Feltrinelli, Milan, 1964. *La narcisata. La controra*, Feltrinelli, Milan, 1964. *Super-Eliogabalo*, Feltrinelli, Milan, 1969; revised ed. Einaudi, Turin, 1978

GERMANO LOMBARDI (born 1925, Oneglia; has been sailor, manual labourer, advertising executive; novelist and dramatist)
Novels: *Barcelona*, Feltrinelli, Milan, 1963. *L'occhio di Heinrich*, Feltrinelli, Milan, 1963. *La linea si può vedere*, Feltrinelli, Milan, 1967. *Il confine*, Feltrinelli, Milan, 1971

RENATO BARILLI (born 1935, Bologna, where he teaches History of Art; he is an art historian, literary critic and journalist)

ANGELO GUGLIELMI (born 1929, Arona; works for Italian state broadcasting; literary critic)

*BARILLI and GUGLIELMI (joint editors), *Gruppo 63. Critica e teoria*, Feltrinelli, Milan, 1976

FURTHER READING

Barilli and Guglielmi. *See immediately above*
Esposito, R., *Le ideologie della neo-avanguardia*, Liguori, Naples, 1976
Smith, L.R. (ed. and transl.), *The new Italian poetry, 1945 to the present: a bilingual anthology*, University of California Press, Berkeley, Los Angeles, 1981

David Robey

3 Umberto Eco

Umberto Eco's first published book was the thesis with which he graduated from the University of Turin, and deals with problems of aesthetics in the works of St. Thomas Aquinas (*Il problema estetico in San Tommaso*, 1954). Twenty-four years later, in 1980, he published his first novel, set in the fourteenth century; *Il nome della rosa* (*The Name of the Rose*) is a lengthy detective story filled with discussions and descriptions of a great many aspects of medieval culture and medieval politics. But between this medieval starting-point and this temporary return to the Middle Ages Eco's remarkable energy has been directed almost entirely at problems and issues of the present: modern art and modern culture, modern mass-communications and the modern discipline of semiotics. It is Eco's involvement, or rather the particular mode of his involvement, in the present that will be the main subject of discussion here. For he is very consciously an intellectual, and like many Italian intellectuals he has assumed the obligation of marrying theory with practice, of combining a high degree of political and social engagement with a coherent set of abstract principles. The combination that Eco has achieved in this respect is a particularly instructive one, whether or not one agrees with his views. He provides a clear and powerful model of the relationship between the intellectual and society, a model that illustrates strikingly the advantages and difficulties of the marriage of theoretical speculation with social practice. This is the aspect of his writings that I shall have particularly in mind in the following pages.

Opera aperta (*The Open Work*), published in 1962, was the first

---

Part of this chapter was previously published in the *Times Literary Supplement* and is reprinted by kind permission of the Editor.

of Eco's books on a modern topic, and it was with it that he made his name in Italy. It is a polemical book, in marked conflict with the Crocean aesthetics that dominated the Italian academic world in the 1950s and early 1960s. It arose partially out of Eco's work on general questions of aesthetics, which was strongly influenced by the anti-Crocean, though still idealist, philosophy of his mentor at the University of Turin, Luigi Pareyson. But the immediate stimulus for writing it came from his contacts with avant-garde artists, together with the study of the work of James Joyce, in whom, as we shall see, he had a particular personal interest. In fact the book has at least to some extent the air of a theoretical manifesto for certain kinds of avant-garde art; for the *Gruppo 63* (the subject of Chapter 2), which was formed in the year after its publication and of which Eco himself became a member, it effectively served as such.

In *Opera aperta* the idea of the 'open' work serves to explain and justify a development relevant to a number of essays in the present volume, the apparently radical difference in character between modern and traditional art. The idea is illustrated in its most extreme form by what Eco calls 'opere in movimento' ('works in motion'); he cites the aleatory music of Stockhausen, Berio and Pousseur, Calder's mobiles and Mallarmé's *Livre*. What such works have in common is the artist's decision to leave the arrangement of some of their constituents either to the public, or to chance, thus giving them not a single definitive order but a multiplicity of possible orders; if Mallarmé had ever finished his *Livre*, for instance, the reader would have been left, at least up to a point, to arrange its pages for himself in a variety of different sequences. Works of this kind, evidently, are for the most part of recent origin, and even today are very much the exception rather than the rule. Eco's point, however, is that the intention behind them is fundamentally similar to the intention behind a great deal of modern art since the Symbolist movement at the end of the nineteenth century.

Traditional or 'classical' art, Eco argues, was in an essential sense unambiguous. It could give rise to varying responses, but its nature was such as to channel these responses in a particular direction; for readers, viewers and listeners there was in general only one way of understanding what a text was about, what a painting or sculpture stood for, what the tune was of a piece of music. Much modern art, on the other hand, is deliberately and systematically ambiguous. A text like *Finnegans Wake*, for Eco the exemplary modern 'open' work, cannot be said to be about a particular subject; a great variety of potential meanings coexist in it, and none can be said to be the main or dominant one. The text presents the reader with a 'field' of possibilities, and leaves it in large part to him to decide what approach to take. The same can be said, Eco argues, of many other modern texts that are less radically avant-garde than the *Wake*: for instance Symbolist poems, Brecht's plays, Kafka's novels.

This is where the analogy with works like Mallarmé's *Livre* obtains: just as Mallarmé's reader would have arranged the pages of the book in a number of different sequences, so the reader of the *Wake* perceives a number of different patterns of meaning in Joyce's language. In the *Livre* it is the material form that is 'open', in the *Wake* the semantic content, but in each case, according to Eco, the reader is in substantially the same position, because in each case he moves freely between a multiplicity of different interpretations. The same analogy obtains, he argues, between abstract visual art and mobiles; and between the aleatory music of Stockhausen, Berio or Pousseur, and the serial music of a composer like Webern. All these characteristically modern forms of art are said by Eco to mark a radical shift in the relationship between artist and public, by requiring of the public a much greater degree of collaboration and personal involvement than was ever required by the traditional art of the past.

The deliberate and systematic ambiguity of the 'open' work is associated by Eco with a well-known feature of modern art, its high degree of formal innovation. Ambiguity, for Eco, is the product of the contravention of established conventions of expression: the less conventional forms of expression are, the more scope they allow for interpretation and therefore the more ambiguous they can be said to be. In traditional art contraventions occurred only within very definite limits, and forms of expression remained substantially conventional; its ambiguity, therefore, was of a clearly circumscribed kind. In the modern 'open' work, on the other hand, the contravention of conventions is far more radical, and it is this that gives it its very high degree of ambiguity; since ordinary rules of expression no longer apply, the scope for interpretation becomes enormous. Moreover conventional forms of expression convey conventional meanings, and conventional meanings are parts of a conventional view of the world. Thus, according to Eco, traditional art confirms conventional views of the world, whereas the modern 'open' work implicitly denies them.

This function of modern art plays an important role in Eco's thesis, and I shall be returning to it shortly.

In *Opera aperta*, then, there is an equation between the degree of 'openness', the degree of ambiguity, and the degree of contravention of conventions in a work. (Eco adds a further term to this equation, that of 'information', which there is unfortunately no space to consider here; but see Chapter 2, p. 39 for further discussion.) But the equation does not tell us anything about the distinction between art and non-art or good art and bad, since the contravention of conventions and the consequent proliferation of possibilities of interpretation, etc., is not in itself a guarantee of artistic value. To distinguish good art from bad Eco takes over from Pareyson's aesthetics of 'formativity' the concept of organic form, which for him as for Pareyson is closely allied to that of artistic intention. Thus he argues, first, that the contravention of conventions in modern art must, if it is to be aesthetically successful, produce 'controlled disorder' (110), the 'organic fusion of multiple elements' (137). Second, the interpretation of the modern 'open' work is far from entirely free; a 'formative' intention is manifest in every work, and this intention must be a determining factor in the interpretative process. For all its 'openness', the work nonetheless directs the public's response; there are right ways and wrong ways, for instance, of reading *Finnegans Wake*.

The concepts of organic form and artistic intention are important qualifications of Eco's notion of 'openness', but it must be said that they are qualifications of a very problematic and elusive kind, as modern literary theory in particular has shown. How does one distinguish between organic and non-organic or 'failed' form, especially in a work characterized by a multiplicity of different meanings? How does one identify, especially in a work of this kind, the 'intentions implicitly manifested' by the author (153), and why in any case should one's interpretation be bound by them? Eco gives no real answer to the last questions, and only a partial and unsatisfactory answer to the first; we shall return to this answer, and to these questions, in connection with his later work. Such difficulties are not, perhaps, major grounds for objecting to the thesis of Eco's book; as he emphasized in the preface to the second edition (*Opera aperta* 1972, 8), it is more concerned with the aims of certain kinds of art than with their success or failure, with questions of poetics (*poetica*: a work's artistic purpose) rather than aesthetics. Yet much of the impetus of *Opera aperta* derives from its

conception of the special function or effect of the modern
'open' work in relation to the world in which we live, a conception
which depends to a large extent on Eco's general aesthetic theory.
This conception is most fully developed in an essay published
shortly after the book appeared and reprinted in subsequent
editions (e.g. *Opera aperta* 1972, 229–84), 'Del modo di formare
come impegno sulla realtà' ('On the manner of giving form as a
committed way of acting on reality'). The essay was written for
Vittorini's journal *Il Menabò*, apparently at his suggestion, in the
second of two issues on the relationship between literature and
industry, and it represents a viewpoint quite closely allied to
Vittorini's own. Even more than *Opera aperta* it has the character
of a manifesto for certain kinds of avant-garde art, by virtue of the
conviction it expresses, characteristic of the *Gruppo 63* and of
Vittorini, about avant-garde art's special political function.

In the essay, as in *Opera aperta*, Eco argues that the modern
'open' work represents through its formal properties a
characteristically modern experience of the world. Like all art, it is
an 'epistemological metaphor': not only does it reflect aspects of
modern philosophy (phenomenology, Pareyson's aesthetics) and
modern science (the theory of relativity, mathematical information
theory), but equally importantly, through its lack of conventional
sense and order, it represents by analogy the feeling of
senselessness, disorder, 'discontinuity' that the modern world
generates in all of us. Thus while 'open' works are not the only
kind of art to be produced in our time, they are the only kind that is
appropriate to it; the conventional sense and order of traditional
art reflect an experience of the world wholly different from ours,
and we deceive ourselves if we try to make this sense and order our
own.

What, then, do we gain from art-forms that reflect what can only
seem a negative aspect of the world in which we live? Eco's essay
answers this question through a discussion of the concept of
alienation, in which he outlines a position that has remained
characteristic of all his activity as an intellectual. In one sense
alienation is both necessary and desirable, in that we can say that
we are alienated *to* something other than ourselves, and therefore
lose full possession of ourselves, whenever we become involved in
it. Losing possession of ourselves is not something to be lamented;
it is simply part of the back-and-forth movement between self and
the world that is the condition of a truly human existence. What we
must do is accept our involvement in things other than ourselves,

and at the same time assert our selfhood in the face of the world by actively seeking to understand it and transform it. Art, Eco argues, can contribute significantly to this process of understanding and transforming the world, because its function is essentially cognitive. 'Art knows the world through its own formative structures', he proposes (264), referring to the aesthetics of Pareyson once again. Art represents the world – or more exactly our experience of the world – through the way it organizes its constituents (the *modo di formare*) rather than through what the constituents themselves represent. This representation is a form of knowledge by virtue of the element of organic form: 'Where a form is realized there is a conscious operation on an amorphous material that has been brought under human control' (281). Thus the modern 'open' work is a form of knowledge of the world in which we live, insofar as it constitutes a bringing to consciousness of the nature of the contemporary 'crisis'. As Eco said in the first preface to *Opera aperta* (9), contemporary art seeks a solution to this crisis by offering us a 'new way of seeing, feeling, understanding and accepting a universe in which traditional relationships have been shattered and new possibilities of relationship are being laboriously sketched out'. Art is therefore political in its own special way; it produces new knowledge that can serve as a basis for changing the world, but it does not necessarily have an explicitly political content.

Together with the essay, *Opera aperta* contains, if sometimes only in germ, most of the main features of Eco's later theoretical work: the notion of the special function of art, the sense of living in an age of crisis, the emphasis on awareness and on the need for change. The book's style of thought has also remained characteristic: a taste for broad, synthesizing generalizations, and a consequent tendency to stress the similarities between concepts and phenomena at the expense of the differences, and to neglect local problems in the interests of the overall view. The great change that occurs in Eco's later work is his discovery of semiotics. As he has repeatedly said, *Opera aperta* was written before he came to know the semiotic and structuralist theories of which he has since made so much use – though it is notable that, with its insistence on the element of multiplicity in art, it anticipates a major theme of the structuralist criticism (that of Barthes in particular) of the mid-60s. As we shall see, the semiotic framework will not only clarify and develop Eco's earlier notions, especially his Pareysonian aesthetics, but will also bring about a redistribution of focus and emphasis.

Yet in a curiously personal and paradoxical way *Opera aperta* looks forward to this shift of interest to semiotics. A large section of the first edition consists of a discussion of the poetics (*poetica*) of James Joyce, which was removed from subsequent editions and published separately. As well as providing further illustration of the main theme of *Opera aperta*, this discussion points to a clear analogy between Joyce's artistic development, as Eco sees it, and Eco's own personal history. What interests him in Joyce is the novelist's move from a Catholic, Thomist position to the disordered, decentred, anarchic vision of life that seems to characterize *Ulysses* and *Finnegans Wake*. Yet Eco also finds in Joyce's mature work a degree of persistence of his youthful faith, a nostalgia for the ordered world of medieval thought that is most notably expressed in the system of symbolic correspondences that underlies the surface chaos of *Ulysses; Ulysses*, he suggests, is a 'Thomist *summa* turned upside down' (288). Similarly, as he himself tells us, when Eco began working on his university thesis, he did so in a 'spirit of adhesion to the religious universe of Thomas Aquinas', a spirit which he then lost as he worked on it (*Il problema estetico*, 6). Yet a nostalgia for the ordered world of medieval thought seems to have remained with him as well, expressing itself not only in occasional excursions to the Middle Ages, culminating with *Il nome della rosa*, but also, much more indirectly, in his interest in semiotics. For Eco's semiotic theory has an ordered, comprehensive, rationalist, architectural character that also bears comparison with that of the Thomist *summae*, though with at least one radical qualification: while St. Thomas's system is metaphysical, Eco's very definitely is not; the urge to system and order is displaced by him from the sphere of being to that of method alone. Eco's later work contains a vigorous criticism of French structuralism – which he himself compares (*Il problema estetico*, 258–64) to Thomist thought – for what he calls its ontological rather than methodological character: its conviction that the ordered systems it describes are the systems of the world itself rather than the provisional constructions of a science. For Eco the world is a disordered, chaotic place onto which order can only be projected by a process of thought. One of the most interesting features of his semiotic theory is this association of order and disorder, of a rationalist explanatory structure with the conviction that nothing, finally, can ever be explained.

But between *Opera aperta* and Eco's first major semiotic text there came another book which pursued a line of interest that has since constituted an important part of Eco's activities, the study of mass culture and the mass media. Published in 1964, the book had as its title *Apocalittici e integrati* (*Apocalyptic and integrated* [*intellectuals*]), the two terms of the title standing for two opposite attitudes to the mass media and their effect on contemporary culture: the apocalyptic view that culture has been irredeemably debased by the mass media, and that the only proper way to treat these is to disregard them; and the wholly positive view of those so well integrated in the modern world that they see the nature and effect of the mass media as necessary and even desirable. Eco's own view lies between these two extremes. The mass media, he argues, are such an important feature of modern society as to require the serious attention of intellectuals, and, far from being a necessarily negative influence, they are to be welcomed for providing universal access to cultural experiences previously restricted to an élite. They are not to be accepted as they are, however; the intellectual's task is to analyze their nature and effect and to seek actively to transform them, by criticizing their deleterious features and pointing the way to the improvement of their cultural content.

What this means in practice is shown by the discussion in *Apocalittici e integrati* of such things as comic strips, pop songs and television programmes, a discussion which is supplemented by two essays that were published in the following year (now in *Il superuomo di massa*, 27-67, 145-84), on Eugène Sue's *Mystères de Paris* and on the James Bond novels of Ian Fleming. The main purpose both of these essays and of the discussion of specific mass media in the book is to lay bare the ideological implications of different forms of popular entertainment, particularly, in the case of the comic strips and the novels, the relationship between ideology and narrative structures. From the analysis a distinct set of common themes emerges. The kind of entertainment that Eco criticizes, as did Vittorini, is that which is consolatory, in the sense of reaffirming the public's sense of the essential rightness and permanence of the world in which they live. One means by which this effect is produced is by systematically excluding political issues. For instance both the Superman comics and Sue's *Mystères* are not political, Eco argues, but purely civic; that is, they only deal with the righting of private wrongs, and never suggest that the social system as a whole is in any way at fault. The wholly predictable plot structure of popular narrative texts such as the James Bond novels, the fact that such stories tend to end happily, the fact that they tend to reproduce the most stereotyped ideals and prejudices of our society, all these features also contribute to the same conservative effect. The great fault of the mass media, for Eco, is to convey a standardized, oversimplified, static and complacent vision that masks the real complexity of things and implicitly denies the possibility of change.

There is nothing intrinsically wrong, Eco suggests, with pure popular entertainment; all of us feel the need to read a James Bond novel or listen to pop music from time to time. The problem is that for most people *bad* popular entertainment has come to be a major part of their cultural experience, and its effect has been to exercise a strongly reactionary influence. The solution, therefore, is not to raise popular entertainment to the level of art – Eco is not saying that the public should be fed on a diet of modern 'open' works – but to work for forms of entertainment that are 'honest'. This means on the one hand entertainment that does not have false artistic pretensions; the concept of kitsch is discussed at some length in *Apocalittici e integrati*, and is defined as non-art that aspires to artistic status by borrowing devices from true art-works, devices that automatically cease to be artistic when they are used outside their original 'organic' context. On the other hand, and more importantly, 'honest' entertainment is that which is ideologically sound, not in the sense of propagating the dogma of a political party, but by virtue of more widely acceptable qualities: because it acknowledges the complexity, the problematic character of the historical circumstances in which we live, because it allows for the possibility of change and serves as a stimulus to reflection and criticism, because it generates a sense of independence and choice instead of conformism and passivity.

This should help to make clear what kind of political commitment Eco expresses in his writings. The emphasis on change, the hostility to conformism and conservatism must mark him as a man of the left. Yet however he may personally vote, there is no recognizably party-political element in his books. This is partly because his intellectual task, as he conceives it, is cultural rather than narrowly political, but more importantly because his values are broadly democratic rather than specifically socialist or communist. In particular, as a writer, he has always kept his distance from the Italian Communist Party. *Opera aperta*, with its insistence on the special function of the modern 'open' work, was in conflict with the view of art at that time favoured by the Party. In *Apocalittici e integrati* the emphasis on criticism, debate and the complexity of things also seems implicitly opposed to the Party line, at least at that period. Eco particularly favours the television discussion programme 'Tribuna politica' as a form of 'education for democracy' that helped viewers become aware of the 'relative' character of politicians' opinions (351); and in his analysis of the Bond novels (170) he argues that the 'democratic' attitude is that which recognizes the nuances in things and rejects schematic views. Finally the arguments about the limitations of systematic world-views in his later semiotic works, to which we shall turn shortly, again tend to set him apart from mainstream Marxist ideas. Marxism has been an important influence on Eco's thinking, but this relativism, individualism, even liberalism are major qualifications of his left-wing position.

Eco's shift of interest to semiotics began as he was supervising the translation of *Opera aperta* into French. He was introduced to the structuralism of Jakobson and Lévi-Strauss (*Opera aperta* 1976; V ff.), and as a result revised sections of the book along structuralist lines. This contact with structuralist thought was the main source of Eco's semiotics, and in particular of his first major semiotic work, *La struttura assente* (*The Absent Structure*), an 'introduction to semiological research' (according to the sub-title), published in 1968. This was followed by a collection of essays entitled *Le forme del contenuto* (*The Forms of Content*, 1971), which developed some of the ideas of the earlier book, and by *Segno* (*The Sign*, 1973), a monograph aimed at a wide readership on the central concept of semiotics. Finally, in 1976, there appeared Eco's most advanced and systematic semiotic text so far, which incorporates and elaborates most of the main ideas of *La struttura assente* and *Le forme del contenuto: A Theory of Semiotics*, written originally in English, and then translated into Italian as *Trattato di semiotica generale*. In discussing Eco's semiotic theory I shall concentrate on this last text, though I shall also have to refer to *La struttura assente* in connection with certain arguments that play a less prominent part in Eco's subsequent writing. There is, however, a difference of emphasis between the two works that seems to reflect something of a shift in Eco's interests and concerns after *La struttura assente* was written. While the earlier book shows much the same polemical and socially committed character that we saw in *Opera aperta* and *Apocalittici e integrati*, such a character is much less apparent in *A Theory of Semiotics*. This is not to say that Eco has abandoned his earlier view of the intellectual's task, but simply that a clearer separation of functions has come to govern his writing: in his journalism, to which we shall return later, he pursues the line of attack mapped out in *Apocalittici e integrati*, but his theoretical work becomes much more specialist and academic. Eco says something to this effect himself in his preface to *Il nome della rosa*, though it is not certain how far he is really speaking in his own person; in 1968, he suggests (15), it was widely held that one should write 'involving oneself in the present, in order to change the world', whereas now, in 1980, 'the man of letters . . . can console himself with the thought that one can write purely for the sake of writing'.

This element of specialization and academicism in Eco's writing in the 1970s must to some extent be a consequence of his increasing institutional commitment to semiotics as a discipline – founding and editing the semiotic journal *VS*, acting as secretary-general of the International Association for Semiotic Studies, and occupying the first chair of semiotics at the University of Bologna. But it is also interesting to relate it to the political events of 1968 and the consequent dissolution of the *Gruppo 63*. Eco himself has told, in an article of 1971 on 'The Death of the *Gruppo 63*', how the 1968 workers' and students' movements had an outflanking effect on the group's and Eco's own, position concerning the artist's duty to attack the social system indirectly, through the aesthetic medium, rather than by direct political action. In 1968, according to Eco, artists and intellectuals were confronted, for the first time in years, with the opportunity and challenge to involve themselves directly in politics, an opportunity and challenge which the *Gruppo 63* failed to take up, thereby bringing about its own demise. One effect of this crisis on Eco, it would seem, was to reduce his polemical insistence on the special political function of art, though his new interest in semiotics no doubt contributed to the same effect. It is noteworthy, however, that Eco's response does not seem to have taken the form of a more direct involvement in political affairs, at least in his main writings, and that he seems to have moved, if anything, in quite the opposite direction. There may be in the new specialization and academicism of his theoretical work signs of a degree of post-1968 disillusionment.

To turn now to *A Theory of Semiotics*, what view of the subject does the book contain, and what can a theory of it do? Semiotics deals with processes of communication; and since, according to Eco (22), the whole of culture should be studied as a 'communicative phenomenon', a theory of semiotics can claim to be a theory of culture as well. Semiotics thus embraces in its grasp all subjects concerned with culture in the broadest possible sense, from logic, information theory and linguistics, to ethnology, social psychology and the study of literature and other forms of art. It embraces them in the sense that its ultimate objective is to provide them with a unified set of categories with which to conduct their research, on the grounds that all involve, in one way or another, the study of modes of communication. With some, such as linguistics, its role will apparently be that of a collaborator; others, notably logic and social anthropology, it hopes to unite one day within the boundaries of a single semiotic discipline founded on a general semiotic theory. These dreams of empire are, however, for the long term, as Eco himself admits. For the present the most a theory of semiotics can do is propose a tentative general model of the process of communication and of the systems of signification, or codes, on which the process depends; the model can then be adjusted and improved through contact with the various existing disciplines in which semiotics has an interest. In proposing his model in *A Theory of Semiotics* Eco hopes merely to indicate the possibility of a unified approach to cultural phenomena, and to trace the limits of future semiotic research.

Because linguistics is the field in which the study of communication is most advanced, linguistics is inevitably the principal source of semiotic theory. However the relationship between the two disciplines has been the cause of considerable disagreement. Saussure, to whom semioticians always refer, called in his *Cours de linguistique générale* for a general science of signs (*sémiologie*) of which linguistics would eventually be no more than a part. In the early 1960s structuralists such as Barthes altered Saussure's emphasis and modelled their semiology or semiotics almost exclusively on linguistics, assuming a strongly language-centred view of culture, but Eco follows Saussure in insisting that linguistics should be seen as a subordinate part of a general semiotics. *A Theory of Semiotics* is divided into a theory of codes (systems of signification) and a theory of sign production (the process of communication). Codes are sets of conventions which connect systems of 'expression' to systems of 'content'; that is, they enable us to recognize a word, a gesture, an image, etc. ('units of expression'), as standing for a particular meaning (a 'unit of content'). Both kinds of system are, according to Eco, structural, in the sense in which the term is used in linguistic theory: the identity of every unit depends entirely on its relations with other units in the same system. These relations, Eco argues, are in the last analysis binary; they can be explained as deriving from two-term oppositions similar to those which structural linguistics uses to explain the sound-system of verbal language. We shall come to the implications of this position shortly.

Eco's arguments on the subject of codes are largely a restatement of structural linguistic theory in such a form as to make it applicable to all forms of signification, though he does add elements of his own. His theory of sign production, on the other hand, is much more original. Semioticians have usually accepted C.S. Peirce's distinction between symbols, indices and icons. In all three cases something is seen as standing for something else. But for Peirce in the case of a symbol the 'standing for' relationship is arbitrary and therefore coded, in the case of an index it is causal, and in that of an icon it is one of resemblance; the content or meaning of indices and icons thus depends on their relationship with the real world, whereas that of symbols does not. Eco rejects this trichotomy, and substitutes for Peirce's (and Saussure's) notion of the sign that of sign function; whenever something is perceived as standing for something else, whether Peirce would have called it a symbol, an index or an icon, a sign function occurs, and whenever a sign function occurs, it depends on a coded relationship between a unit of expression and a unit of content. Such differences of kind as seem to exist between sign functions are to be accounted for, not by employing Peirce's three discrete categories, but by distinguishing between different modes of sign production: different ways, that is, in which the unit of expression may be structured, different ways in which it may be connected with the unit of content, and different ways in which it may be related to the real world. In no case, however, does the meaning or content of the unit of expression *depend* on its relationship with the real world. The second half of Eco's book consists mainly in the development of a taxonomy of sign functions based on these considerations.

Let us take an example to clarify the implications of this very technical argument. When we recognize a picture of a horse as a picture of a horse, we establish a relationship, according to Eco, not between an image (a unit of 'expression') and a real animal, but between an image and a unit of an internalized cultural system (a unit of 'content') - the (culture-bound) idea of a horse. What is more, as far as his semiotics is concerned, the internalized cultural unit 'horse' can only be defined structurally: its significance derives entirely from its relationship with other internalized cultural units, never from its relationship with the real animal kingdom. For Eco the world of meaning or signification is a closed system, a sort of parallel universe related in various ways to the world of sense experience, but in no way directly dependent on it. This conception, for which he uses the phrase 'unlimited semiosis', is, Eco insists, vital to the constitution of semiotics as a subject. If one can argue that all forms of meaning or signification are the product of structure, then all these forms must be analysable in a way in which they would not be if their identity depended on reference to the real world; they can be studied by semiotics in their own terms, without interference, at least in the first instance, from other branches of knowledge. The notion of 'unlimited semiosis' is the condition for the existence of an independent discipline of semiotics with its own specific subject-matter – the nature of sign functions, what they communicate, and how they communicate – and its own set of methods and concepts.

It is worth emphasizing, however, that Eco is not denying that we use sign functions to refer to the real world, and still less is he denying that the real world exists; he is simply maintaining, as Saussure had maintained, that the structure of sign functions is a grid which we impose upon reality and in this sense pre-exists any use to which it may be put. Moreover to view it in this way does not, for Eco, entail cutting it off from history. His 'methodological' rather than 'ontological' conception of structuralism and semiotics, to which I referred earlier, was developed as a criticism of the view prevalent in the late 1960s, and due above all to the influence of Lévi-Strauss's anthropology, that structural analysis served ultimately to reveal the perennial laws that govern the working of the human mind. *La struttura assente*, which deals with this issue at much greater length and in a much more polemical way than *A Theory of Semiotics*, is called by this title in order to emphasize Eco's belief that the ultimate structure of semiotic systems necessarily eludes our intellectual grasp. We can attempt to describe the individual structures of individual systems, and we can be reasonably confident that our description corresponds to reality to some extent. But the description can only be hypothetical and provisional because its object is constantly developing and because our approach is inevitably selective; it is a product of the historical process, and subject to negation or modification by that process. Thus while we may legitimately try to extrapolate an ultimate structure from all the individual structures that we describe, what we extrapolate must be extremely tentative in character, nor can we know how much it really tells us about the perennial laws of the mind. By means of this argument Eco seeks to avoid the objection of a-historicity with which Marxists have often attacked structuralist thought, and to construct a semiotic theory at least partially reconcilable with Marxist historicism. He also displays a notable element of continuity with the ideas of *Opera aperta*, combining the notions of structure and system with the sense of a world in crisis, without conventional order or conventional meaning, that is such a prominent feature of the earlier work.

Since Eco has told us (*Lector in fabula*, 8) that his interest in semiotics arose out of his work on art in *Opera aperta*, and since this interest is also closely connected to his work on mass communications in *Apocalittici e integrati*, what changes did his new theoretical framework bring to the ideas of the earlier books? Although his new interests broadened Eco's horizons considerably, it is notable that the subjects of art and mass communications occupy almost half the pages of *La struttura assente*, and could still be said to be a central, if less prominent, object of attention in *A Theory of Semiotics* as well. To begin with the theory of art, it is perhaps surprising how many of the aesthetic principles of *Opera aperta* remain in the later works. In *A Theory of Semiotics*, as in *Opera aperta*, Eco maintains that art produces an essential effect of ambiguity through the contravention of conventions of expression, but that such contraventions are only properly artistic if they are part of a specifically aesthetic form. What the later work does, first, is express these ideas in more wide-ranging theoretical terms; like all other forms of cultural activity, the production and consumption of art is seen as governed by codes, and it is the violation of these codes that is said to be the source of the effect of ambiguity. This new formulation opens the way to a different conception of the function of art; whereas in *Opera aperta* the function was said to be essentially cognitive, in the later books it is explained according to the structuralist principle that the effect of the violation of codes in a work of art is to focus attention first on the structure of the work itself, then on the codes which the work employs, and finally on the relationship between the codes and reality, thus generating in the reader, etc., a renovated perception of himself and the world. In *A Theory of Semiotics*, also, Eco argues that in art the violation of codes occurs according to a specific structural pattern, a pattern which is said to be the distinguishing feature of artistic form, and replaces the much vaguer notion of 'organic' properties in *Opera aperta*. There Eco had argued that the language of poetry is distinguished by its 'iconic' properties, a special relationship between sound and sense. Extending and developing this notion, he now suggests that all kinds of art are characterized by what he calls a 'super-system of homologous structural relationships' (271); that is, a code is violated not just at one level of a work, but at all of its levels, and between these different violations there is a fundamental similarity of structure. This structural pattern constitutes what he calls the 'aesthetic idiolect': just as the term 'idiolect' is employed in linguistics to mean the language habits peculiar to an individual, so here it stands for the overall pattern of deviation, the 'general deviational matrix' (271) peculiar to and characteristic of each work of art.

The trouble is, of course, that it is very difficult to see how such a pattern might be realized in practice. It is true that there are numerous cases in literature in which the sound seems to be an echo to the sense (though not as many cases as sometimes is supposed), and stylistic analyses such as Leo Spitzer's have shown parallels between the meaning of texts and other levels of expression, for instance syntax. But to suggest, as Eco does, that there is a multiple set of correspondences in all works of art, beginning from their physical substance – to which Eco attaches special importance: in art matter is 'rendered semiotically interesting' (266) – and proceeding down to the various aspects of their content, seems to require a good deal of clarification and empirical verification, neither of which has been adequately provided in any of Eco's works. Nevertheless the aesthetic theory of Eco's more recent books is interesting for one reason at the very least, because of the extent to which the ideas of his mentor Pareyson have continued to dominate his view of art even after his conversion to semiotics. For the notion of 'aesthetic idiolect' is not only a revision of Pareyson's notion of organic form, but is also strikingly reminiscent of his insistence that it is the 'modo di formare' or style that constitutes the aesthetic essence of any work of art. In another respect as well Eco has remained faithful to Pareyson's principles: in his view that the intention implicit in a work must be the determining factor in its interpretation, a view which in *A Theory of Semiotics* is asserted but not seriously discussed, as in *Opera aperta,* except for the apparent suggestion (the point is far from clear) that it is the 'aesthetic idiolect' by which the intention is manifested. Thus on these two scores, as on others,

A Theory of Semiotics shows not only a striking continuity with Eco's earlier work but also the same tendency which we noted in *Opera aperta* to develop broad generalizations at the expense of more specific problems; and in this case, as modern literary theory has shown, the problems are very much a matter of contemporary debate. While the systematic character of Eco's theory has a great deal of attraction, it is clear that a significant price has been paid for it.

Between them *La struttura assente* and *A Theory of Semiotics* offer general models of the process of aesthetic communication and the structure of works of art. These models are supplemented by a more recent work, *Lector in fabula* (the title, literally 'The Reader in the Tale', is a pun on the Latin expression 'lupus in fabula', meaning 'talk of the devil'), which is exclusively concerned with the process of reading narrative literature, and was published in 1979. Here Eco stays within the framework of ideas developed in the previous semiotic works, but follows the move in much modern literary theory to a more detailed study of reader-response; he also comes full circle back to the main theme of *Opera aperta*, in that the book concludes with an analysis of a modern 'open' work, *Un drame bien parisien* by Alphonse Allais, focussing on the kind of reaction that such a work evokes in its readers. *Lector in fabula* begins with an attack on the structuralism of the 1960s for its insistence on the intrinsic, 'objective' properties of works of literary art. What is offered instead is the idea of interpretative cooperation between reader and text, a cooperation that brings into play not unchanging universal structures of the mind, but sets of presuppositions that vary with the passing of time. The main object of Eco's book is to develop general sets of categories that describe the process of interpretative cooperation, while at the same time making due allowance for its provisional, historical character.

As one might expect, for Eco the process of interpretative cooperation does not involve reference to the real world; instead the reader draws on the various cultural codes that he has assimilated, what Eco calls his 'encyclopaedia'. According to *Lector in fabula*, it is these codes that enable the reader to fill the numerous gaps left by the narrative on the printed page, since so much in fiction depends on what is left unsaid, and to resolve the ambiguities which the narrative presents. The two central concepts used to represent this process are 'frames' and 'possible worlds'. Frames are stock situations or sequences of action which the reader is obliged to insert into the text, following suggestions that the text itself contains, in order to complete its meaning. The concept of possible worlds is borrowed by Eco from modal logic to represent images of the world which the process of interpretation forces the reader to project onto the text, and which the text may either confirm or repudiate. These images may or may not correspond to the world in which we believe ourselves to live; whichever is the case, they are, for Eco, the product of cultural codes. Possible worlds are the main consideration of the analysis of Allais's *Un drame bien parisien*. The distinctive openness of this story, Eco argues, is a consequence of the way in which the text causes the reader to construct one kind of possible world, then to replace it with another quite different one and again with yet another, without ever resolving the question which of these worlds is to be taken as the true one.

The concepts of frames and possible worlds are interesting and possibly fruitful ones for the purpose of literary criticism, though one may not accept Eco's view of reading as a wholly coded process. But it is less easy to see what purpose is served by the degree of elaboration to which he takes his argument in this book, and particularly by the lengthy algebraic formulae with which he represents the structure of possible worlds and their relationship with one another. Eco shows here a passion for a kind of scientific exactness which does not seem especially functional in the study of narrative texts, and which carries to a further extreme the tendency to academic specialization which we saw in *A Theory of Semiotics*. Nor is it clear how relevant his analysis of the story by Allais would be to other more complex 'open' works, of the kind described in *Opera aperta*. Moreover *Lector in fabula* leaves largely unchanged two of the most problematic elements in Eco's earlier discussions of art. His notion of artistic intention is extended, but not significantly altered, by the proposition that every text posits a 'model reader', in the sense that it demands a certain type and range of interpretation and response. The notion of aesthetic idiolect, on the other hand, does not really feature in Eco's argument here, even though one might have expected it to be integrated into his theory of reading. Like *A Theory of Semiotics*, *Lector in fabula* explores new issues, notably by appropriating ideas from other fields of thought, without reconsidering some of the author's more difficult postulates.

What advances did semiotics bring to Eco's views on mass-communications? The semiotic study of this subject takes the form, in *La struttura assente* and *A Theory of Semiotics*, of a discussion of rhetoric (we shall see shortly what Eco understands by this term) and its relationship to ideology; and a consideration of the issues and categories involved in approaching the cinema and architecture from a semiotic point of view. The consideration of the cinema and architecture (which is confined to *La struttura assente*) does little more than show how it is possible to view these in semiotic terms, as sign-systems. The discussion of rhetoric, on the other hand, is a central element in Eco's interests, and he makes a powerful case both for its importance to semiotics and for the advantages of placing it in a semiotic framework.

La struttura assente proposes a conception of rhetoric that is fundamentally classical; it is seen, that is, not as a repertoire of false, stereotyped, emotive turns of expression – as it is commonly seen today – but as a discipline embracing all means of verbal persuasion. Thus rhetoric is also the art of constructing arguments based not on rational proof, which in Aristotelian terms is the domain of strict scientific knowledge, but on people's sense of what is reasonable, acceptable or appropriate. Eco's approach to rhetoric therefore has two principal objects of attention: the various figures of speech or thought classified in considerable detail by classical rhetorical manuals, under such names as metaphor, metonymy, hyperbole, and so forth, all of which are still widely used at all levels of communication; and the connection between techniques of argumentation and ideology, the process of persuasion by reference, tacit or open, to common opinions and responses. In *La struttura assente* Eco shows by a brilliant analysis of examples of advertising how it is possible, through attention to these two types of factor, to expose the manipulations of meaning to which the mass media so frequently subject the public.

One might well wonder, however, what is specifically semiotic about this kind of analysis. *A Theory of Semiotics* answers this question by offering a general justification of the need to insert rhetoric into a semiotic framework. At the most abstract level, since rhetoric is concerned with techniques of communication, it must in principle fall under the heading of semiotics as Eco defines the subject; and on the whole his discussion of rhetoric does show how the use of semiotic terminology can clarify its general nature and purpose. More specifically, semiotic theories of meaning (derived mainly from linguistics) can provide a useful basis for describing the general nature and the particular forms of rhetorical figures of speech such as metaphor, metonymy, etc. What is more, semiotic theories of meaning serve to expose the ideological, in the sense of false, nature of forms of persuasion, when these suppress parts of the meaning of signs and privilege others in order to further the purpose of specific interest-groups, a process Eco terms 'code switching'. This process is one to which he attaches particular weight, and his discussion of it is one of the culminating points of *A Theory of Semiotics*. The 'heuristic and practical power' of a semiotic theory lies in its ability to show how acts of communication can 'respect or betray' the real complexity of the various sign-systems that constitute culture (297). By describing the structure of these sign-systems in their totality and the structure of the messages generated from them, semiotics can enable us to see how messages can manipulate and distort our knowledge of the world, and it is in this sense that it is a form of 'social criticism' and 'social practice' (298). As Eco says in a note (312), 'Semiotics helps us to analyze different ideological choices; it does not help us to choose'. It serves the cause of social and cultural awareness and provides a basis for political action, but it does not itself provide instructions as to the kind of political action one should take. Once again one can see the important element of liberalism in Eco's thinking.

It should be clear, therefore, that as well as a personal urge towards system there were powerful intellectual reasons of a much more specific kind for Eco's interest in semiotic theory. Semiotics provided him with concepts and principles that refined and expanded the ideas of his earlier works, united them within a single theoretical framework which must give an enviable sense of clarity, confidence and purpose to the sort of cultural criticism which he regards as the intellectual's task. Yet it must be said that a theory as elaborate and systematic as Eco's is not strictly necessary to this cultural criticism; to those of a more empirical turn of mind a less systematic approach would seem to perform the same task just as effectively, if not more so, simply through a general awareness of semiotic issues and a selective use of individual semiotic concepts. Moreover the claims that Eco makes about semiotic theory's future academic role do seem rather inflated. Semiotics in general – and Eco's work in particular – has served an extremely valuable purpose by bringing to the different disciplines a greater awareness of the nature and scope of processes of communication, and by encouraging the interdisciplinary movement of ideas and methods. But Eco's imperialistic hope that most of the arts and social sciences will eventually be united within a comprehensive semiotic theory seems to ignore both the practical realities of the academic world, and the necessarily open-ended and approximate nature of theoretical work in many of these subjects. This last criticism, however, is directed more at Eco's conception of semiotic theory as a subject than at his conception of his own contribution to it. He believes far too strongly in the value of dissent and discussion, he has been far too actively engaged in the revision of his own past work, and he is far too aware of the limits of human knowledge, to regard the ideas he proposes as anything other than tentative and provisional, as work-in-progress and as part of a continuing public debate.

I have dwelt in this chapter predominantly on Eco's theoretical work because it is this I believe, which gives his writing its exemplary interest, as well as its remarkable sense of direction and coherence. However much of his writing has been, in itself, far from theoretical in character, although it has been to a significant extent inspired by his theoretical concerns. Three of his books, *Diario minimo* (*Minimum Diary*, 1963), *Il costume di casa* (*Domestic Customs*, 1973) and *Dalla periferia dell'impero* (*From the Borders of the Empire*, 1977), are collections of articles of a more or less journalistic kind, originally published in dailies or weeklies such as the *Corriere della Sera*, *Il Manifesto* and *L'Espresso*, as well as more intellectual or artistic periodicals like *Quindici* and *Il Verri*. Unlike the greater part of his theoretical writings, Eco's journalism is often extremely funny; indeed humour is a property to which he attaches considerable importance. As well as a number of parodies, *Diario minimo* contains the well-known 'Elogio di Franti' ('In Praise of Franti'), written in 1962, a celebration of the villain of De Amicis's sentimental and moralistic schoolboy novel *Cuore*. The infamous Franti, who respects nothing and laughs at everything including his dying mother, is a model of evil for De Amicis and his school-boy narrator, but for Eco his smile is better seen as a healthy assault on the dominant social and cultural order; laughter, Eco suggests, is the 'instrument with which the secret innovator places in doubt that which a society holds to be good' (94), and such an instrument is clearly, for Eco, a very important one. This view of laughter underlies much of Eco's journalism, insofar as its humour or wit is usually directed at objects of a wholly serious kind, objects which for the most part belong to the areas of interest explored in his more academic studies, art, mass-communications, and the world of culture in general.

Of the three journalistic collections *Diario minimo* contains the largest element of humour, and also pre-dates Eco's semiotic studies; on the other hand the articles in *Il costume di casa* and *Dalla periferia dell'impero* date from the mid-60s to the mid-70s, and can in a sense be described as practical extensions of his semiotic theory. This is not to say that Eco's arguments are conducted at a high level of theoretical sophistication, or that he draws to a conspicuous extent on scientific notions that he has elaborated himself; the theoretical work merely prescribes the area in which, in most cases, he has worked as a journalist, and provides his journalism with certain simple general principles and simple conceptual tools. Between them the two later collections cover a wide variety of topics, almost all of which are semiotic in the very broad sense that they concern modes of communication or signification. A number of articles deal with aspects of modern art or kitsch; others look at forms of popular entertainment, political debates and criminal cases, comics, films, advertising, the press, television and radio, and various public events. All of them are highly topical, or were when they were written, and all of them participate to a greater or lesser extent in a common undertaking: what Eco calls (in *Il costume di casa*) the 'clarification of the contemporary world' (251). This means analyzing the ideological implications of political, social and cultural products and events through a 'critical, rational and conscious reading' of their meaning (*Dalla periferia dell'impero*, 235); laying bare the confusion, mystification and manipulation to which the contemporary public is subjected by the mass media and the sources of power; inculcating in readers a constant attitude of healthy suspicion (*diffidenza*) towards the modern world.

Eco's novel, *Il nome della rosa*, is to date his most recent book, and provides an interesting commentary on his earlier writings. It is a work of entertainment and escapism (and has been an immense publishing success), but in at least two important ways it expresses themes or preoccupations that run throughout Eco's works: the conflict between intellectual freedom and repression, and the urge towards intellectual system and order. The story takes place in the year 1327 and concerns a series of murders that are eventually solved by an English Franciscan monk, William of Baskerville. It is set in a monastery in Northern Italy, a vast, ancient and beautiful complex of buildings dominated by a citadel, which contains on its first floor a scriptorium and above it a mysterious, labyrinthine library. At the heart of this library, as William eventually discovers, there is preserved a manuscript of the lost second book of Aristotle's *Poetics*, which dealt with the subject of comedy. The monks who died did so because they read the book, which an elderly blind monk, Jorge of Burgos, had smeared with poison in order to prevent the release of the corrupting influence which he believed the text would produce. Jorge is cornered by William and his assistant in the library, and in the struggle which follows the library and the entire monastery around it catch fire and burn down.

The conflict between intellectual freedom and repression is thus an important part of the novel's plot, and the way in which Eco treats it is highly characteristic. Jorge is the representative of a savagely obscurantist type of Christian dogmatism, to which, Eco suggests, the power of human laughter presents the most serious of threats. The danger of the lost book of Aristotle's *Poetics* for him and his like is that it makes laughter intellectually respectable, not scurrilous. Moreover the theme of repression is also a major feature of the novel's setting, which is dominated by the negotiations between the Avignon Papacy and the Franciscan order, represented by William, on the question of the Franciscan doctrine of apostolic poverty, negotiations which take place against the background of the savage repression of the Franciscan *fraticelli* by the Papal forces. This association of intellectual and physical repression, together with the notion of laughter as a countervailing force, clearly reflect concerns that lie at the heart of Eco's activity as a writer, and particularly his journalistic activity.

The urge towards system and order can be seen in the novel, I would suggest, in a less direct way. The measured succession of activities prescribed by the monastic rule, the geometrical layout of the complex of buildings, the striking image of the library, with its maze-like structure and the initially incomprehensible but actually intricate and highly organized classification of its books, are all an embodiment, in the first place, of the ordered system of medieval scholastic thought, to which, as we have seen, Eco initially adhered, and which he then abandoned early on in his career. It is significant not only that the monastery is burnt down at the end of the novel, but also that the events take place during a period which Italians term the 'low' middle ages, when medieval culture was declining and the world of the Renaissance, at least in Italy, was beginning to be formed. However the setting of the novel seems to convey as well the qualities of system and order that characterize Eco's own mature intellectual work, especially *A*

Theory of Semiotics. The burning of the monastery thus may be more than a symptom of medievalist nostalgia; can we not see it also as a metaphorical recognition by Eco of the precariousness of his whole theoretical enterprise, a precariousness due above all to the irresoluble tension between order and disorder, between reason and chaos, that is such a striking feature of his work?

BIOGRAPHICAL NOTE

Umberto Eco was born in 1932 in the Piedmontese town of Alessandria. He studied philosophy at the University of Turin, where he graduated in 1954, then worked on cultural programmes for the state television network in Milan, the city where he still lives today. From the early 1960s onwards he taught aesthetics, then visual communications, then semiotics at the universities of Turin, Milan, Florence and Bologna, and since 1975 he has held the chair of semiotics at Bologna, the first of its kind to be estalished in any university; he has also lectured at universities in North and South America. Throughout his career he has collaborated actively with a number of academic and literary journals, particularly *Quindici*, as well as the semiotic review *I'S* which he founded and still edits; in addition he has written regular series of articles for the daily and weekly press, in particular *L'Espresso, Il Corriere della Sera* and *Il Manifesto.* He has been a leading member of the International Association for Semiotic Studies, and as secretary-general organized its first international congress in 1974 in Milan. Since 1959 he has also worked with the Milanese publishing-house Bompiani. He is the author of over a dozen full-length books, and has contributed to or edited several others.

BIBLIOGRAPHY

PRINCIPAL WORKS

Il problema estetico in San Tommaso, Edizioni di 'Filosofia', Turin, 1954; ed. cited Bompiani, Milan, 1970

Opera aperta, Bompiani, Milan, 1962; eds. also cited Bompiani, Milan, 1972 and 1976

Diario minimo, Mondadori, Milan, 1963; ed. cited Mondadori, Milan 1978

Apocalittici e integrati, Bompiani, Milan, 1964

La struttura assente, Bompiani, Milan, 1968

La definizione dell'arte, Mursia, Milan, 1968

Le forme del contenuto, Bompiani, Milan, 1971

'The death of the *Gruppo 63*', in *20th Century Studies* 5 (Sept. 1971), 60–71

Il costume di casa, Bompiani, Milan, 1973

Segno, ISEDI, Milan, 1973

A Theory of Semiotics, Indiana University Press, Bloomington, Ind. and London, 1976; transl. into Italian as *Trattato di semiotica generale*, Bompiani, Milan, 1975

Il superuomo di massa, Cooperativa Scrittori, Milan, 1976; ed. cited Bompiani, Milan, 1978

Dalla periferia dell'impero, Bompiani, Milan, 1977

Come si fa una tesi di laurea, Bompiani, Milan, 1977

The Role of the Reader. Explorations in the Semiotics of Texts, Indiana University Press, Bloomington, Ind., 1979; Hutchinson, London, 1981

Lector in fabula, Bompiani, Milan, 1979

Il nome della rosa, Bompiani, Milan, 1980; (transl. W. Weaver) *The Name of the Rose*, Harcourt Brace Jovanovich, New York, and Secker & Warburg, London, 1983

FURTHER READING

De Lauretis, T. *Eco*, La-Nuova Italia (Il Castoro), Florence, 1981

David Forgàcs

4 Franco Fortini

Fortini is known in Italy as a poet and an essayist. It is the latter
Fortini I am going to deal with mostly here, and since this means I
am relegating to the background the conventionally more durable
(creative) part of a writer's work and bringing into the foreground
the conventionally more ephemeral (critical, theoretical) part, I
had better make explicit at the outset the reasons for my choice.
Fortini is, I believe, important for anyone who wants to know
about recent Italian culture because he has been an exceptional
witness of that culture in its development over the last generation.
The value of his testimony lies essentially in the categories and
framework it gives us for looking at a culture. Fortini depicts it as a
contested terrain on which various competitors (political parties,
'capitalism', the state, 'science', the traditional humanistic
intelligentsia) strive for control and come to dominate at different
times. Fortini himself has been no impartial observer of this
struggle in Italian culture. But the fact that his testimony comes
from the inside rather than from a supposedly neutral outside,
from a specifically defined political position on the left and from a
moralistic perspective, enhances rather than diminishes its interest.
It gives his work a self-reflexive quality, because much of what he
writes explores the conditions of writing itself, the ways in which
writing is located in and by a culture, where it is able to exert some
influence and where, by contrast, it is marginal, ignored or
silenced. This exploration is carried on in his poems as well as his
essays and other writings, so the relation between these texts is not
really that of primary and secondary, creative and critical-
theoretical, but a relation simply of different kinds of discourse.
Yet only in the essays is the discussion of culture an explicit theme.

This chapter is arranged by theme rather than chronologically
by text, so although I start in 1956 and trace my main threads from

that year, I move back and forwards in time somewhat. There are five sections, which correspond to the themes of (1) politics (2) culture (3) intellectuals (4) writing (all seen largely through Fortini's eyes and with his categories) and, lastly, (5) a postcript on Fortini seen from the outside. I shall concentrate on his three main essay collections, *Dieci inverni* (*Ten Winters*, 1957), *Verifica dei poteri* (*Verification of Powers*, 1965) and *Questioni di frontiera* (*Questions of Demarcation*, 1977), but I shall also refer to a little of his poetry, to a book of short aphoristic texts and verses called *L'ospite ingrato* (*The Ungrateful Guest*, 1966), a pamphlet-style essay prompted by the Six Day War in the Middle East called *I cani del Sinai* (*The Sinai Dogs*, 1967), a text of 1968, *Ventiquattro voci per un dizionario di lettere* (*Twenty-Four Entries for a Literary Dictionary*), and a collection of critical essays, *Saggi italiani* (*Italian Essays*, 1974). Other titles will be mentioned as they arise.

Politics

The essays in *Dieci inverni* were written in 1947–57, the period on the Italian left of Stalinism and de-Stalinization. Fortini was a member of the Socialist Party throughout this period, and by 1956 had gravitated to a left position within it. Much of his book is a critique of the leadership of the Italian Communist Party for its complicity with Stalinist policies and practices that he disagreed with. In the later 1940s he advocated, like the PSI leadership, socialist neutrality in opposition to the militarist power blocs of the cold war and rejected the 'monolithic' Soviet line in foreign affairs. As he wrote in 1949, 'if we believed that Soviet armoured cars bring the revolution we want, we would already be in the Communist Party' (*Dieci inverni*, 187). At that time, he saw the PSI as representing an alternative to the 'bureaucratic centralism' of the PCI:

> The members of the proletariat and petty bourgeoisie who, consciously or otherwise, criticize the organizational-bureaucratic structures of the left parties *should* . . . be in the Italian Socialist Party rather than in any other political formation.
>
> (*ibid*, 191)

In the early 1950s, he criticized the 'hard line' on art taken by the

PCI, influenced in the cold war years by the theories of A.A. Zhdanov in the Soviet Union. In 1956, he denounced what he called

> the torturing police dementia of the NKVD or the Stalinist police forces in Poland, Hungary, Czechoslovakia etc., the world of trials, the aberrant myths of intellectual discipline, the systematic falsification of the truth.
>
> (*ibid*, 279)

These attitudes build up an identikit picture of Fortini in the 1940s and 1950s. He projects himself as living under a harsh regime of 'ten winters' and, as he puts it in a political poem of 1956 called 'Foglio volante' ('Leaflet'), 'sillabando la nostra verità / che non bastava mai' ('mouthing our truth / which was never sufficient'). The 'winters' in his title allude among other things to the then current imagery of cold war and thaw. An allegorical use of winter is also frequent in his verse collection covering the same period, *Poesia e errore* (*Poetry and Error*, 1959). An example from 1951 is *Agro inverno* (*Bitter Winter*):

> Agro inverno crepiti il tuo fuoco
> incenerisci inverno i boschi i tetti
> recídi e brucia inverno.
>
> Pianga chi piange chi ha male abbia piú male
> chi odia odii piú forte chi tradisce trionfi:
> questo è l'ultimo testo è il decreto del nostro inverno.
>
> Non abbiamo saputo che cosa fare per noi
> della verde vita e dei fiori amorosi.
> Per questo la scure è alla radice dei cuori
>
> e come stecchi che si divincolano saremo arsi.

(Bitter winter let your fire crackle / turn to ashes winter the woods the roofs / cut off and burn winter.

Let him who weeps weep, him who suffers suffer more, / him who hates hate more him who betrays triumph: / this is the last text it is the decree of our winter.

We have not known what to do for ourselves / with the green life and the amorous flowers. / Because of this the axe is at the root of our hearts and like twigs struggling free we will be burnt.)

The period in which *Dieci inverni* was completed and published, 1956-57, was one which Fortini would always regard as a watershed, both for Italy as a whole and for the Italian intellectual left. Two things coincided to make this so. One was the rise of new forms of capitalism, determining new rhythms and patterns of social life and replacing the old Italy by an Italy 'wrapped in the cynicism of weekly magazines, burnt by speculation' (*Dieci inverni*, 30). The other was the breakdown of the culturally hegemonic role of the left parties, primarily the PCI, by what Fortini described as a 'collapse of consensus' (*ibid*, 52). Taken together, these changes signalled the end of a decade on the left dominated by the ideology of post-Resistance democratic unity, of commitment to social progress in the form of collective struggles against the remnants of Fascism and against the right.

This ideology corresponded to a strategy of the left which Fortini and others have called 'frontism'. The strategy had its roots in the 1930s Popular Front against Fascism, the tactical alliance of Communist Parties both with Socialist and with bourgeois anti-Fascist parties. In Italy, frontism had survived the fall of Fascism because of the PCI leadership's decision, in the critical years 1944-45, against attempting a Communist seizure of power and in favour of collaborating in a coalition government with other anti-Fascist parties, including the Christian Democrats. The polarization into left and right groupings during the cold war (1946-53) had then held the left alliance more or less successfully together as the opponent switched from Fascism to American imperialism and the Christian Democrat leadership swung to the right. At a cultural level, frontism meant that the PCI presented itself as a 'third force' party, a broad catchment for middle-class intellectuals who were opposed both to Fascism and to right-wing liberalism and Catholicism. Frontism cannot be reduced to 'Stalinism', but it originated as a Comintern tactic to help protect the Soviet Union against Nazi aggression in 1934-35 and was continued in Italy in accordance with Stalin's desire to establish Communist pawns on the international chessboard in legal ways acceptable to the major Western powers. Thus, when the errors of thirty years of Stalinism were denounced at the Twentieth Congress of the Soviet Communist Party in 1956, one of the reverberations in Italy was to make a number of people start calling into question the correctness of the strategy followed by the PCI since the end of the war. 1956 was a year of symbolic undermining of a whole way of making politics on the left.

1956 was a critical point in Fortini's own political trajectory too. A major group in his party, the PSI, used the occasion of the Soviet repression in Hungary to force a break with the PCI and begin a drift to the right that would culminate in the centre-left governments of the 1960s. At the same time, a number of left intellectuals, like the Socialist political philosopher Norberto Bobbio, began to collapse Stalinism and Marxism together and see in the breakdown of the one the bankruptcy of the other. Fortini, by contrast, reiterated his belief in the possibility of a socialism and communism different both from Stalinism and from social-democracy (see *Dieci inverni*, 269–81). He thus cut himself off from the Socialist Party (he was to resign in early 1958) and he wrote in 1957 of the anti-communist 'neo-socialists':

> They will not be able to understand our obstinate refusal of any formula which deceives itself that it can consider the account with communism settled, precisely because the socialism they talk about is not ours, at least as much as the communism we talk about is no longer, and has never been, that of Stalin and Togliatti.
>
> (*L'ospite*, 33)

The alternative Fortini had in mind to the communism of Stalin and Togliatti provides a key to understanding much of his subsequent writing on politics and culture as well as his poetry. It could be described as a form of socialist humanism, committed to the idea of a liberation of the collectivity as a condition of the liberation of the individual, influenced by a tradition of utopian and messianic Marxism in T.W. Adorno and Walter Benjamin and by a critique of alienation and reification in the young Georg Lukács, but determined also by a Christian-spiritualist component in Fortini's thinking that can probably be traced back to his conversion to Christianity in the late 1930s (see the biographical note and his own account in *Cani*, 52–54). On a visit to China in 1955, Fortini had seen Maoism in practice as a 'welding together of anarchism and communism', the realization of something which had run through nineteenth-century socialist movements as a repressed undercurrent of 'utopian demand' (*Asia Maggiore, Asia Major*, 1955, 27). It was precisely this which he saw forcing its way through to the surface again in 1956 in the workers' risings in

Poznan and Budapest:

> the whole deep libertarian, egalitarian, decentralizing, anti-
> authoritarian current which runs, parallel to Marxism,
> through the nineteenth-century revolutions . . . *has re-*
> *emerged within the system*, as a new formation . . . These
> formations are destroying the model of the Party which has
> lived as an efficiently functioning reality for over thirty years.
> (*Dieci inverni*, 294-95)

This socialist humanism with its utopian streak became overlaid
in Fortini around 1956 by a more orthodox left-wing critique of the
PCI. The small left groups he was associated with in this period,
based round the reviews *Ragionamenti* (1955-57) and *Opinione*
(1956-57), saw in the PCI's adherence to the broad lines of Stalinism
a theoretical backwardness which had had deleterious practical
effects. The revolutionary ideas of Marxism and Leninism had
become diluted by a series of ad hoc adjustments to historical
circumstances and had lost their radical core: the critique of
capitalist relations of production, the notion of revolutionary
rupture and the concepts of socialist democracy and the withering
away of the state. As Fortini saw it, the reformism of the PCI was
characterized by both centralism and frontism, by a disciplinarian
control of the working class and the labour movement by the party
leadership and by a strategy of alliances with other social classes
including the middle class. The point, therefore, was to retrieve the
radical message of a more revolutionary Marxism, oppose these
manifestations of reformism and try to give back to the working
class its autonomy of action, returning, as Fortini put it in 1956, to
'the idea of a party structured democratically from below' (*Dieci
inverni*, 266). In reality, however, there was something too abstract
about these arguments in Fortini's hands. He talked as if there
were a potential counter-movement to the party hierarchy already
ripe within the rank and file, yet in the context of 1956-57 this
seems unlikely. However, these views document accurately
Fortini's dissent as an intellectual from the theory and strategy of
the traditional left, and it is to this that I shall now turn.

Culture

Fortini's critique of the PCI's line on culture makes up the other main thread of *Dieci inverni*. Again, his analysis focuses on the twin articulations of Communist reformism: centralism and frontism. On the one hand, he criticized the party's authoritarian attempt in the cold war years to exert control over culture and the intellectuals. A number of essays identify as characteristic of Stalinism at a cultural level an 'instrumental conception of culture and art' (*Dieci inverni*, 283) and the practice of 'direct authoritarian management of cultural research by the political leadership' (*ibid*, 250). On the other hand, in the periods of coalition and coexistence, the party's desire to build alliances with non-Marxist intellectual sympathisers and thereby establish a power base within cultural institutions such as schools, the press and publishing meant that it took a laissez-faire line with certain intellectuals and certain cultural manifestations so long as they did not openly conflict with the party. Similarly, in the artistic styles and subject-matter favoured by the PCI, there should on the one hand be what Carlo Salinari (responsible for cultural policy in the PCI from 1951 to 1955) described as a correct 'ideological axis' (Salinari 1960, 37) which should avoid 'decadent' treatments of sexuality or psychic experience; on the other hand, literary and artistic works should inherit the tradition of democratic progressivism and realistic depiction of Italian popular life represented by nineteenth-century writers such as Verga. Fortini felt – and he was one of very few writers to express such a dissenting opinion amid the frontist consensus of the early 1950s – that there was little that was either revolutionary or socialist about all this.

Fortini's disagreement with the PCI at a cultural level had already been established at the time of his collaboration on Elio Vittorini's journal *Il Politecnico* in 1945–47. Among the articles he had contributed were several on modernist writers such as Ungaretti, Montale, Kafka and the French surrealists, in harmony with a general line of writing about European and American modern art followed by Vittorini and other contributors. Vittorini was at that time a member of the PCI, and his journal depended on the party's goodwill and support for its distribution and economic survival. Yet *Il Politecnico* came almost from the start into conflict with the cultural section of the PCI, which at that period (and increasingly as the cold war set in) advocated and defended social realist art and the national realist tradition, conducting a campaign against both modernism and the hegemony of American cultural products like the Hollywood film. In a private letter of

1948 to Vittorini, Fortini wrote scathingly of 'the cultural politics of the PCI and . . . its propagandist simplifications about the USA, the USSR, Sartre, Catholicism, Jesus and the Marshall Plan.' (*Dieci inverni*, 75n). In 1947, shortly after the American-backed expulsion of the Socialists and Communists from De Gasperi's Christian Democrat government, *Il Politecnico* folded. It had refused to change its line at the PCI's behest and had thereby lost the party's support. The episode was symptomatic of a toughening of the ideological climate on the left as the cold war started to bite. Viewed retrospectively, it represented a 'hard' phase in the PCI's cultural line, sandwiched between the idyll of the first postwar coalition government (1945–46) (see *Dieci inverni*, 69) and the resumption of a more 'liberal' form of frontism in the period of East-West coexistence and thaw from 1954 onwards (*ibid*, 22). Nevertheless, it became emblematic for Fortini of the kind of coercive, centralist line a political party could take with the intellectuals.

The *Politecnico* episode shows that Fortini's disagreement with Communist culture involved dissent not just from a form of cultural control but also from an artistic style. This style was what he called the 'illustrative' or 'celebratory' manner of socialist realism and Neo-realism. In an article of 1952 called 'Quale arte? Quale comunismo?' ('Which Art? Which Communism?') he equated socialist realist art with the imagery of mass culture in the capitalist West – the hoarding, the illustration, the poster – and contrasted it with more authentic forms of art which cannot be reduced to such an 'instrumental' function.

> I reject the *content* of celebratory Soviet painting (and also of much of our home-grown socialist realism) in the name of the same principles that led the artists to those works: *because I feel the human idea they depict to be on the whole unacceptable, anti-human, inflated, servile.* Almost as odious to me as the image of man degraded by the instruments of capitalist mass iconography (cinema, magazines, advertisements) is Soviet and Neo-realist iconography; the former with its youths smiling at the future and its heroic or sugary public functionaries, the latter with its workers and cyclists and rice-pickers and strikers framed in compositions as Arcadian and inauthentic as those which contain the peasants of Ettore Tito or Millet. This is not, therefore, an aesthetic judgement. It is a political judgement.
>
> (*Dieci inverni*, 141)

The equation Fortini makes here is straightforward. Given that authentic art, as he sees it, is by definition 'something weighty, serious; and rare' (*ibid*, 145), it cannot be made instrumental to any end so narrowly utilitarian as either the illustration of a party line or the promotion of a commercial product. Any art which is instrumentalized in this way will become inauthentic.

Linked to this critique of instrumental and illustrative art is a generic mistrust of the realist or mimetic conception of art, on the grounds that 'it already knows what it has to discover, all it takes is the will' (*ibid*, 144). Consequently, art produced according to this conception is 'limited to being an illustration of already existing truths' (*ibid*, 144). Thus the illustration and the realist work of art are connected. Insofar as a work puts itself forward as imitating reality, it accepts a role as an illustration of something else and thus accepts a merely mechanical or instrumental cultural function of the same order as a piece of propaganda or advertising. It is only by adopting a different *form* – not transparently realistic, not illustrative – that art can escape such instrumentalization.

Fortini developed these ideas in an essay of 1955 called 'Il Metellismo'. He gives the label 'Metellism' to the sum of attitudes he found Communist critics putting forward in their discussion of Vasco Pratolini's novel, *Metello* (the name of the protagonist), a literary *cause célèbre* of 1955–56. Fortini sees 'Metellism' as a mid-50s extension of the notion of a ' "progressivist" and "popular" function' of literature which he identifies with frontism, as the projection of a nostalgic and mythical image of working-class life and morality which, he argues, is out of touch with a structurally new reality of Italian workers with radio and TV sets and a petty bourgeois life style. 'Metellism' exemplifies

> a 'social-democratic' conception of the function of literature and the novel: an edifying, emotive, enthusiastic or confirming function, which is the opposite of the educative-critical function of revolutionary literature.
>
> (*ibid*, 124)

It followed that what Fortini meant by this alternative 'revolutionary literature' was not an alternative realism but 'a *different* technique, not . . . that of one's opponent [the bourgeoisie] turned on its head' (*ibid*, 125).

In a long retrospective essay of 1964–65 called 'Mandato degli scrittori e fine dell'antifascismo' ('Writers' Mandate and End of Anti-Fascism'), Fortini analyzed the historical connections between the ideology of the Popular Front, the postwar strategy of the PCI, and the theories of a progressive social realism, and attempted to expose the political and theoretical bankruptcy of the whole package. This essay, included in *Verifica dei poteri*, was one of the reasons for that book's clamorous impact on the new left in Italy, and together with Alberto Asor Rosa's *Scrittori e popolo* (*Writers and People*), also published in 1965, it came to constitute the classic 'liquidation' of the PCI's postwar cultural policy from a radical position. Fortini argued that just as, at a political level, frontism meant exchanging the struggle of class against class for the struggle of all the 'democratic forces' against Fascism, so at a cultural level it meant exchanging the demand for a truly revolutionary art and literature for the attempt to resurrect and prolong a radical bourgeois realist tradition. This frontist cultural line was exemplified in the 1930s by Lukács, and it had won out both over the 'Trotskyist "avant-gardes" ' (André Breton and Diego Rivera) and over the line followed by Bertolt Brecht, who wanted a more militant communism, rejected the bourgeois humanist tradition and looked instead for experimental and non-European cultural forms. A major reason for frontism's success, Fortini argued, was that it gave back to the intellectuals what the Russian poet Mayakovsky had termed their 'social mandate', their Enlightenment status as the critical consciousness of society as a whole. Around the beginning of this century, the rise of monopoly capitalism, the rationalization and specialization in social organization and the end of liberal-democratic progressivism had put this mandate in jeopardy. The writers therefore sought a new mandate from the mass political parties, and frontism was precisely the broad ideological net which allowed them to be attracted into the Communist Party. But this consensual alliance under Communist hegemony, in force since the 1930s, in turn began to break up in Italy

> above all when – in a process that can be situated between 1957 and 1962 – almost all Italian writers seemed to accept, along with the perspective of parliamentary democracy and existing institutions, the private forms of organization of the culture industry.
>
> (*Verifica*, 143)

The strategy of frontism had been sustained by the belief that Italian capitalism was moribund. It was based precisely on the 'common struggle against a power equilibrium *incapable of securing a development of society'* (Magri 1966, my emphasis). But the cycle of economic expansion based on the mass-production for export of mechanical consumer goods and on petrochemicals made it clear by the late 1950s that capitalism was more vigorous, not weaker, than before, and was establishing powerful new forms of consent around itself.

Intellectuals

The 'migration' *en masse* of the intellectuals from under the wing of the left parties to the 'culture industry' was to dominate Fortini's writing throughout the 1960s and 1970s. In 1956, in line with his left critique of the PCI, he had launched in collaboration with the other editors of *Ragionamenti* a group proposal to devolve the control of culture from the party hierarchy to the intellectuals themselves (see Guiducci et al. 1956). The object was to create the nuclei of a breakaway socialist culture within bourgeois society, as an alternative to the PCI's reformist strategy of trying to 'inherit' bourgeois culture by adopting the latter's artistic styles and by taking over its cultural institutions (education, publishing, etc.). In polemic against what he saw as the PCI's strategy of assimilating specialist intellectuals and converting them into 'politicians' in the sense of party functionaries, Fortini wrote that the development of these new cultural nuclei 'must be *the work of the intellectual-politicians themselves* and indeed their *specific* political manifestation as producers of specialist culture.' (*Dieci inverni*, 252). As a revolutionary proposal this sounded impeccable. The only problem was that it was too theoretical and was out of touch with the new realities of Italian culture. For as Fortini himself began to argue within the space of less than a year, the sort of specialist intellectual on whom this hypothesis was based was being replaced by a new type, no longer the functionary of the party but the functionary of the culture industry.

The emergence of this new category of intellectuals, and of a new relationship between the old intellectuals and industry (graphically described in the introduction to *Ventiquattro voci* as well as in *Verifica dei poteri*) rendered obsolete, in Fortini's view, the PCI's postwar strategy of attempting to break down the élitist mentality of the literary intellectuals by getting them to put their work at the service of the party. This strategy dated back to the Resistance and had derived legitimation from the prison writings of Antonio Gramsci, extracts of which had begun to be published in 1945. 'One of the most important characteristics', Gramsci had written, 'of any group that is developing towards dominance is its struggle to assimilate and conquer "ideologically" the traditional intellectuals.' (Gramsci 1971, 10). Behind this argument lay the belief that certain categories of intellectuals had a strong sense of their corporate identity and functioned, directly or indirectly, to reproduce the ideological structures of capitalist society. Literary intellectuals (writers, critics, teachers of literature) were among those in Italy whom Gramsci had singled out as traditionally possessing this corporate mentality. Like the European intellectuals in general, they had either become 'immediate agents of the dominant class' or had 'completely broken loose from it by making up a caste in themselves, without roots in national-popular life.' (1975, 634). Hence assimilating these intellectuals into the party would help break down the ideological defences of the dominant classes and lay the basis of a socialist culture.

These arguments, which had been developed in the 1930s, presupposed a reality in which the intellectuals were ideologically powerful people. But it was precisely this reality which Fortini and others (see, for instance, Cases 1969) now saw as being overtaken by another, where the intellectuals were the victims of a downwards social mobility that reduced them to the status of salaried employees in education and the rapidly expanding communications industries. The 'proletarianization' that Marx had predicted as the fate of the petty bourgeoisie had befallen the intellectuals in late capitalism and they no longer possessed, as individuals, any real ideological and social power to put at the service of the party. Their power had passed, rather, into the hands of the ideological apparatuses themselves (publishing, education, the media), which were becoming increasingly enmeshed with the capitalist economy. As Fortini wrote in 1961:

> The whole new generation of intellectuals is finding or will find job opportunities within public or private cultural institutions (from the engineer to the writer, from the biologist to the film director) but always as *technicians:* the perspectives will not be determined by them. They will have non-power disguised as power. The ruling class will remain unchanged or will be changed by co-opting new members . . .

The power of private employers (banks, the main industries, publishing etc.) will be absolute.

(*L'ospite*, 89)

Fortini's recognition of this 'non-power' coincides with a 'totalist' outlook in his cultural writing of the 1960s. He becomes convinced of the ubiquity and omnipotence of a culture industry which, by absorbing the intellectuals while generating a mass ideological consensus, could absorb and negate any overt criticism against itself and any alternative cultural styles. It was the classic argument of 'recuperation', which Adorno and Horkheimer had put forward in their essay of 1944, 'The Culture Industry':

Anyone who resists can only survive by fitting in. Once his particular brand of deviation from the norm has been noted by the industry, he belongs to it as the land reformer does to capitalism.

(Adorno and Horkheimer 1979, 132)

Fortini's version of the recuperation thesis was influenced by contemporary analyses of new forms of domination being developed in advanced capitalism. The state was no longer seen in the classic Leninist terms of direct agent of class rule by the bourgeoisie but as what Lelio Basso in 1963 called a 'compensation chamber' which mediates between all the competing social groups, including the working class, 'in order to contain their opposition and frictions within the system' (Basso 1969, 165–66). At the same time, the positivist social sciences, unable to comprehend the significance of structural changes in society such as the huge expansion of a white-collar technical and managerial class, misread them as evidence of a transcendence of capitalist social relations rather than of a change within capitalism itself. 'Science' had become so assimilated into the workings of the capitalist system that it was unable any longer to see the fundamental divisions that sustained it. An astute Marxist analyst of neo-capitalism, Mario Tronti, explained this succinctly in 1962: 'When the whole of society is reduced to a factory, the factory – as such – seems to *disappear*.' (Tronti, 1977, 52).

A new broad ideology thus emerged which proclaimed the 'end of ideology' and a democratic-managerial consensus under the beneficent wing of science (a counterpart of this ideology in 1960s Britain was Wilsonian Labourism). But its ends were no less effectively those of class domination. Fortini explains the equivalent ideological operation in literary culture thus:

> *the present phase of neo-capitalist development requires that a whole broad sector of socialist ideas become part of the language or the tasks of the upper levels of industrial management;* and in the sphere of the cultural and literary superstructure this is clearly seen in the liquidation of the old 'right wing', neo-idealist and irrationalist criticism, in the acceptance of sociologism as a substitute for political discourse and in the recuperation within the reformist order of authors who a few years ago still represented not only an opposition but an alternative.
>
> (*Verifica*, 79)

Many of the essays in both *Verifica dei poteri* and *Questioni di frontiera* aim at reinforcing these and related points: that all proposals of a radical literature with a socialist message have been rendered illusory; that a literary criticism which aims to place itself on a more 'scientific' footing is merely accepting its insertion as a 'specialization' into the neo-capitalist ideological consensus; that the poetry of the new avant-garde, while claiming to contest the depreciation of all discourse in a consumer society, is itself just another consumer durable for an educated bourgeois readership. In each case, the intellectuals who succumb to these positions either cling to an outmoded conception of themselves as free producers writing in some abstract space outside capitalist social relations, outside 'the factory' (Fortini describes Vittorini thus in his contribution to the *Menabò* industry and literature forum of 1961–62, 'Astuti come colombe' ('Cunning as doves') in *Verifica*), or else they gleefully accept their integration into the culture industry as a necessary 'modernization' of their old-fashioned humanistic culture (the structuralists and semioticians described in 'Due note sulla condizione della critica' ('Two notes on the condition of criticism') in *Questioni*), or, finally, they misread the real operations of the culture industry and delude themselves that by 'sabotaging' the channels of bourgeois language they are performing a political sabotage, whereas they are merely confirming the culture industry's democratist ideology of 'anything goes' (Fortini's judgement on Sanguineti and the Neo-avantgarde poets in the essay 'Due avanguardie' ('Two avant-gardes') in *Verifica*).

Although Fortini in the 1960s never quite becomes a cultural pessimist of the order of Adorno and Horkheimer, he does share the bleak and negative view of mass culture associated with the 'culture industry' thesis: that the masses are in the grip of a brutalizing capitalist cultural machinery of enormous ideological flexibility. This thesis not only implies that large numbers of people are victims of 'false consciousness'; it also erects an implicit polarity between on the one hand the intellectuals, who are clear-sighted enough to resist such cultural dope, and on the other the people, who are not. It has been argued, convincingly I think, against this thesis in another context (see Hall, 1981) that it over-simplifies the complex and varied ways in which ordinary people live their relation to the mass media, as well as the nature of ideological control in a highly developed and technologized culture. And yet, it is important to see that Fortini does not draw from his negative analyses the conclusion that nothing can be done. Central to his work is the equation between authentic high culture, human integrity and political resistance: if only these things can be effectively meshed together, then the grip of inauthenticity and of oppression will be broken. Moreover, his work constantly poses the problem of the relation between the kind of culture he considers to be authentic and a mass audience. When in 1956 he put forward his proposal of a new socialist culture produced outside the framework of the party, one of his stated aims was to overcome the great divide between high culture and mass culture. Later, in 1968, when the current of student protest had brought back *'in mass terms'* the prospect of a 'secession' by the intellectuals from the social body, a prospect which Fortini had abandoned after the demise of *Il Politecnico* (see *Ventiquattro voci*, 20–22), he began to think of cultural change as taking place from within the educational system. He discussed the possibility of new educational practices, a new 'popularizing' approach to education which could break down the traditional collusion between knowledge and the formation of power élites. The optimism behind this project collapsed under the counter-offensives by the State against the workers' and students' agitations of 1968–69. Yet what Fortini seemed to develop after this see-saw of cultural pessimism and optimistic interventionism was a sharper pragmatic sense about the areas of flexibility or vulnerability in and around the bourgeois cultural shell. A statement in an essay of 1972 was symptomatic of this new approach:

It was always thought that there was very little one could do in such surroundings [journalism and RAI-TV – the State radio and television networks] because the pressure of capitalist interests was too strong there. The events of the last few months have shown, however, a considerable ability by the journalists (or rather a considerable minority of them) to react against the provocations and threats of the right. . . It only needed one courageous attempt on TV (an inquest into the survival of Fascist laws) to provoke a series of violent reactions which have hit even the government. The hardest struggle, in these surroundings, is always with one's neighbour, not with those who are distant.

(*Questioni*, 138)

Writing

Fortini's views on the intellectuals and on the recuperative nature of the culture industry converge with his opposition to the illustrative and confirmative idea of realism. Their point of convergence is the question of how to write. For if mimetic writing is a mere illustration of what exists, if programmatic socialist writing is absorbed into the social-democratic consensus along with experimental 'alternative' writing, and if technical jargons merely underwrite the new intellectual ideologies of specialization and scientific rigour, then the question arises: what kind of writing, whether 'creative' or 'critical', can possess any real political force in the culture? Fortini's answer is to put forward a certain idea of poetry and criticism, and to adopt certain practices in his own writing.

His views on poetry and criticism intertwine, because the kind of criticism he believes in depends on the way he sees the literary work. Right from his early *Politecnico* articles on poetry, Fortini adopted the anti-populist premiss that poems use particular forms of verbal organization which have to be learned. As poems themselves are not linguistically simple or transparent, so they cannot be falsely simplified by the critic for the reader. 'Easy poetry does not exist', he said in a lecture of 1955:

The most terse and transparent lines of verse ever written in this world are a deception, a cunning deception of poetry. Poetry is not for rapid consumption. People are not for rapid consumption.

(*La poesia di Scotellaro, The Poetry of Scotellaro*, 1974, 3–4)

In 'Quale arte? Quale comunismo?' Fortini, as we saw, defined authentic poetry as 'something weighty, serious; and rare'. He has on various occasions since then described this authenticity as consisting in *ambiguity, irony, duplicity* (*Verifica*, 179) and *hypocrisy* (*L'ospite*, 128). These terms constitute a set because each of them designates a form of 'doubleness' which distinguishes poems from messages with 'singleness' of meaning, be they practical statements such as commands and promises or scientific arguments and propositions. As Fortini puts it axiomatically in the entry on 'ambiguity' in *Ventiquattro voci*, 'The literary composition is by its nature ambiguous. Indeed, the more successful it is, the more ambiguous it is' (54). He uses 'ambiguity' in a wide sense, so that it includes not only conventional devices of multiple meaning such as the pun, and not only William Empson's 'seven types', but also what he considers to be the 'tension' between the form and the content of any literary work (for instance between a poem's metrical form and what it says) as well as the plurality of meanings and possible readings all literary texts possess (*ibid*, 54, 56). It is in these senses that the term 'ambiguity' starts to shade into those other terms like 'irony' and 'duplicity' which have a particular semantic resonance in Fortini's usage. For, as he says in a number of places, particularly in the 1960s, the doubleness of poetry is not just something found within the text but is also a doubleness of 'status' possessed by the text in relation to other activities and messages around it. On the one hand, poems are important because they construct possible worlds, they make 'proposals of being' which contain certain values and ideals. On the other hand, they are, as mere proposals, ineffectual alongside the 'real hammers' of political activity (*L'ospite*, 128 – the image is André Breton's). Moreover, the presence of more strident and utilitarian mass communications around the poem tends to drown it, make its form appear archaic and crudely simplify its content. Hence the poem in contemporary culture is at one and the same time a source of 'inexhaustible riches' and 'an ode to dust' (*Verifica*, 185).

These views have a number of implications. Firstly, they mean that poetry cannot be reduced to the status of an illustration or confirmation of what exists. In 'Quale arte?', Fortini gave an example of basic double meaning from visual art, a 'found' sculpture by Picasso that was both a piece of wood and a bird. He said that 'the perpetual irony of the work of art is in that oscillation' between its two meanings, so that 'one always finds in one's hands something other than one had expected. Whereas the illustration always keeps its easy promises.' (*Dieci inverni*, 143). This irony, in the case of poetry, gives it a 'power of formal disenchantment' which makes it work as 'a questioning of reality and not just a confirmation of it in disguise.' (*Verifica*, 180). Secondly, they mean that poetry cannot be used as a form of functional discourse, and thus cannot be made to serve the instrumental ends of political propaganda or political exhortation. Thus there will always be, for Fortini, an irreconcilable difference between the specific sphere of competence of the writer-intellectual and that of the political intellectual and the party. In 'Mandato degli scrittori' he describes the 'dialogue of the deaf' that takes place in the 1920s and 1930s between writers and the Communist Party:

> the formal character of artistic and literary expression renders every content ambiguous; and thus, thinking it was meeting the naive requirements of the artists and writers, the Party . . . helps them with contents, with suggested themes. And these, even when they are accepted, are turned upside down into unexpected formal results.
>
> (*Verifica*, 148)

Thirdly, Fortini's views transfer a massive weight onto poetry by making it a privileged site of resistance in an alienated and reified society. With its inner formal tensions, its ambiguity/irony/duplicity/hypocrisy, poetry holds out on a battlefield of cheap throwaway communications and specialized technocratic discourses. In a 'strong' version of this defence of poetry, namely the last section of 'Mandato degli scrittori', Fortini suggests that there is a metaphorical equivalence between the formative nature of poetry, the fact that it shapes 'life' in accordance with a predetermined vision, and the return to an integral relation between individuals and their environment which, in his humanistic Marxism, will be the end of alienation and class-divided society and the beginning of the individual's 'formative' control over his or her own life. Hence 'the poetic work is a prophetic metaphor of the formalization of life'. (*Verifica*, 184).

Fortini tends to talk in these instances about poetry in an unqualified way, as if all poems by definition possessed these inner tensions. And indeed, although he is quite plainly critical of poetry which he sees as effectively compromised with the ideological operations of industrialized culture, from the Neo-realist 'illustration' to the Neo-avantgarde collage of 'micro-quotations' (*Verifica*, 99), there is an overt tendency in his critical and theoretical writing to generalize about poetry, to speak (as Pier Vincenzo Mengaldo has observed) about 'form' in the abstract but not about 'forms' in the concrete (Mengaldo 1974, 13). This tendency stems from Fortini's initial definition of the literary work as ambiguous by nature. Part of this ambiguity depends on the fact that all literary works are 'combinations' of elements about reality with elements from literary tradition. Hence, even the most realist work, insofar as it possesses the artifice of a literary form, embodies a 'dialectical relation' between form and content (*Dieci inverni*, 143) and even the most modernist work must speak about or in some way disclose its own time. As Fortini wrote in 1969, opposing Adorno's stark contrast between 'committed' and 'autonomous' (or realist and modernist) literature:

> All art is an art of combination, and, as in a conglomerate, on analysis we find within it in definite proportions the components of society/reality.
>
> (*Questioni*, 81–82)

The same point holds, in Fortini's criticism, for the political and ideological 'components' of a literary text. They always enter into combination and tension with other components in a medium which 'renders every content ambiguous'. If one effect of this, as we have seen, is to hamstring the possibility of a directly political-practical poetry, another is that Fortini is able to assign a positive value in his criticism to poetry with reactionary political contents. This approach can be illustrated from a long essay of 1959 called 'Le poesie italiane di questi anni' ('Recent Italian Poetry'), included in *Saggi italiani*, where he writes about the language of a poet being in contradiction with his populist ideology (his example is the Catholic poet Mario Luzi), so that his poems cannot simply be written off as ideologically retrogressive from a leftist point of view (*Saggi*, 113–14). Indeed, at the end of the essay Fortini talks about a 'dialectical reversal' by which backward and conservative ideologies can 'form images of human integrity rich with future', whereas more advanced 'democratic' ideologies may be effectively locked into acceptance of the present (*ibid*, 134).

Fortini's criticism is sensitive to the socio-economic context of the text, to the way the meaning and value of literary works are constructed and manipulated by the mechanisms of the culture (the 'agencies' of criticism in publishing, education and the review press which he discusses in the title essay of *Verifica dei poteri*). Yet the intrinsic formal nature of these works (their ambiguity/irony) means that it is always possible to construct their meaning in other ways. The left had ignored Luzi, so Fortini retrieves Luzi's 'integrity' for the left. Conversely, the bourgeois press had feted Lampedusa's novel *Il Gattopardo* (*The Leopard*) and made it a bestseller, so Fortini criticizes Lampedusa's conservative historical pessimism (*Saggi*, 242–51).

As forms of writing, poetry and criticism in Fortini share what might be called a strategy of mediation. Fortini sees his poems and criticism of poems as resisting a false simplification, a single ideological collocation. But at the same time he wants them to steer clear of false complication—calculated obscurity or professional jargon. Just as the 'ambiguity' of poetry is situated midway between the easy univocality of practical discourse and the specialized univocality of scientific discourse, so Fortini's criticism situates itself between that reductive 'contentism' and 'ideologism' which passed for Marxist criticism on the left during the 1950s and the specialized and scientific kind of writing which starts to emerge in literary criticism after 1960. The latter's difficulty, as professional jargon, cuts it off from public access. This in turn is an effect of a widespread cultural operation in which the new literary intellectuals, anxious about the apparent uselessness of their traditional humanistic culture, adopt the intellectual paradigms of positivism in a search for scientific credibility and verifiable results.

> Today [1960] we are in fact witnessing in critical language both *the formalization of sociological analysis* . . . and, inversely, *the sociologization and the pedantic pseudo-scientific classification of unverifiable vitalism* or persistent intuitionism, which, ashamed of its cultural nakedness, now decks itself in . . . clothes deriving from positivism, borrowed from the terminology of the human sciences.
>
> (*Verifica*, 42–43)

Fortini himself rejects the positivist notion of scientific verification as the checking of a hypothesis against the facts because this process all takes place within the confines of 'science' itself. He gives the term his own different meaning of an ability to 'test' literary works and criticism against a real world of human relations, against history. This meaning also underlies his use of the metaphor of the 'verification of powers' (a term from constitutional law which refers to the checking, in elections, of a candidate's right to hold office) in an essay which proposes that literary criticism should situate itself at the level of *'common discourse'*. Against a science of the literary text which recuperates history and sociology into textual analysis, Fortini defends a kind of critical essay where the text is the starting point for talking about the world.

> The literary critic has as his object a work which, precisely because it is non-discursive, non-analytic, but synthetic, has or purports to have the complexity of 'the world', of 'life', of 'man'. Performing criticism, conducting critical discourse, therefore means being able to speak about *everything* in relation to a concrete and determinate occasion. The critic is thus precisely someone who is *different* from the specialist, the textual critic and the scholar of 'literary science'; he is the voice of common sense, a common reader who places himself as a mediator not between literary works and the reading public but between specializations and particular activities, particular 'sciences', on the one hand, and the author and the public on the other.
>
> (*Verifica*, 50)

Other instances of Fortini's writing use this strategy of mediation between ideological simplifications and complications. The form of *I cani del Sinai* is a good case. The text opens with a discussion of media simplifications of the issues at stake in the 1967 Arab-Israeli war. The 'total weapon' of the television news bulletins consists in their conveying a message of objectivity which masks the ideological decisions taken 'behind the scenes' (*Cani*, 11). Radio and TV broadcasts, the informational and party press and the consensual bunchings of public opinion reductively position or 'pigeon-hole' one in relation to themselves by forcing one to take sides within a structure of opinion they themselves have determined (*ibid*, 22–23). At the other extreme, there is the ideology of complication, of the impossibility of making any pragmatic and clarificatory simplification of the issues, which is the characteristic approach of positivist sociology. In order to explore the truth about a complex set of asymmetrically related problems (anti-semitism, anti-communism, the nationalities question, class struggle, the world balance of power) which tend to be either falsely collapsed into each other or falsely prised apart, Fortini makes *I cani del Sinai* a sort of counter-text—fragmentary, analytic, open—to the closed discourses of both the media and social science. It is a continually digressive text, cutting back and forward in time from the present to Fortini's adolescence and weaving snatches of quotation and commentary, social analysis and historical reflection into its surface.

This technique can, I believe, be linked up with a number of theoretical principles Fortini enunciated about writing in 1962 in a short text called 'Poetica in nuce' ('ABC of Writing') which stressed the anti-expressive, anti-emotional and anti-mimetic functions of the language he was aiming at (see *L'ospite*, 106-7). These principles, in turn, appear to be connected to Brecht's notion of the alienation effect as a means of suppressing empathy in the theatre in order for the public to arrive at the truth by adopting a critical judging stance. In the early 1960s, Fortini wrote three political-historical texts to accompany montages of documentary archive film where he brought this Brechtian principle into play. The spectator tended to make an immediate emotional identification with the visual images, to which a rather primitive level of political response corresponds:

> The task of the commentary is therefore to pull in the other direction, that of a more reasoned attempt at an explanation, in tension with the emotional effects of the visual. But this can only be done if the spectator and listener is rhythmically allowed an identifying or distracting relaxation, and thus the text must proceed by continual changes of speed.
>
> (*Tre testi per film, Three Film Texts*, 1963, 7)

Behind these various practices of writing there lies what is ultimately a very simple point, around which all of Fortini's work revolves: these strategies of writing are necessary if one is both to arrive at the truth and reach a desired audience, since the only authentic discourse is a discourse which resists closure; and closure threatens from all sides.

Postscript

I have painted a picture of Fortini as a 'cultural critic': a critic of the culture of the traditional left, the mass communications industries and the new literary culture of writers and theorists. Like all pictures which take the side of the critic, this has made Fortini appear in a strong position, cutting a swathe through the ranks of his enemies. It is time, therefore, to destroy this optical illusion, operate a reversal of gaze and come to the truth of the matter. For Fortini is not in a strong but a weak position—that of a 'displaced person' in relation to what he criticizes. His proposal of an alternative socialist culture in the 1950s collapsed because it was marginal and by then anachronistic. His critique of the culture industry was a traditional humanist's and a poet's cry for help. He himself has been criticized variously by members of the Socialist Party (see *Dieci inverni*, 39), the Communist Party (see for instance Leone De Castris 1972) and the extreme left (see for instance Asor Rosa 1973, 231-71) for his alleged conservatism, ' defence of poetry, 'intellectualism' and 'culturalism'.

I would argue that Fortini has been displaced by history, by the very structural changes in society and the agencies of culture which he began with remarkable prescience to recognize in 'advanced' Milan from the end of the 1940s, but which did not affect Italy as a whole on any real scale before the end of the 1950s. His reasons for resisting these changes have been outlined in the foregoing sections. In a first phase, his criticisms of the Stalinism and frontism of the PCI meant that he refused to take part in the party's strategy of mobilizing and assimilating the intellectuals. He therefore 'stayed put' as an intellectual and defended the right to produce a radical form of culture. In a second phase, the establishment of the culture industry and its assimilation of the intellectuals as salaried functionaries meant that he again stayed put, this time in resistance to trading in his humanistic culture for the culture of positivism and a new specialism, while himself being driven into schoolteaching and then a university job. In both cases these positions were accompanied by a critique of certain forms of writing and a defence of others. Throughout, the theme of intellectual resistance is dominant, and the metaphors of subjection, subservience, assimilation, instrumentalization occur again and again in Fortini's writing to describe it.

It is important to point out that the displacement of Fortini is not just the displacement of an individual but represents the displacement of a whole way of making culture in Italy. Fortini began his literary career in 1930s Florence, the cradle since the beginning of the century of a refined bourgeois culture with a radical reputation whose characteristic form of organization was the close-knit café circle of intellectuals. Literary criticism was conducted by these groups and reviews or by academic critics in a restricted and selective education system. The little reviews continued after the war, and Fortini was associated with a number of politico-cultural ones, notably *Il Politecnico, Discussioni* (1949–53), *Ragionamenti, Opinione, Officina* (1955–58), *Quaderni Piacentini* (first issue 1962). The difference was, however, that these semi-artisanal reviews, however 'professional' they became, were no longer determinant in forming cultural opinion; this role had shifted first to the mass political parties and then to the mass media and the major publishing houses. At the same time, the advent of mass education at all levels from the early 1960s brought a huge 'overproduction' on intellectuals. In the early 1970s, 60 per cent of graduates were employed in teaching, thereby 'contributing to the self-reproduction of the education system' (Canestri and Ricuperati 1976, 271). One effect of this was to take literary criticism away from freelancers and professionalize it in the university, a process which affected Fortini too. Another was to force it, by sheer pressure of numbers competing for research, towards increased specialization and the acquisition of new critical tools. The expansion of the communications industries and the changes in education were of course related. Mass education meant the rise of the cheap paperback to supply school and university courses, so a two-way determination of taste between the big publishers and the education system began (Cf. Chapter 1, pp. 15–25). The mechanisms for producing both literature and criticism thus moved out of the hands of the old literary intellectuals and merged with those of the tertiary economy as a whole. Fortini for instance noted how Calvino's *Il castello dei destini incrociati* (*The Castle of Crossed Destinies,*) was written on commission from the publishers Ricci for a piece on the Visconti tarot pack, after Calvino was inspired by Paolo Fabbri's semiotic analysis of the card-pack as a sign system. On publication, readings of it were made by Maria Corti and Gérard Genot, semioticians writing for other specialist semioticians in education. The text therefore was written, published and reviewed in the space of a few months within a highly closed circuit. What Fortini protested against in this process was the elimination of 'verifiability' in his sense of the term, which requires precisely that this circuit be broken. What frequently appears as retrenchment in Fortini, outmoded 'humanism', overstated pessimism, recourse to a defence of poetry, needs to be understood in relation to these processes as a whole. As Adorno wrote in *Minima Moralia* (translated into Italian by Fortini's colleague Renato Solmi in 1954):

> While the individual, like all individualistic processes of production, has fallen behind the state of technology and become historically obsolete, he becomes the custodian of truth, as the condemned against the victor.
>
> (Adorno 1974, 129)

The 'truth' of Fortini's work lies in its being an accurate barometer of changes that have at once integrated him like everyone else but have also left him emotionally estranged. In a sequence of poems dated 1970–72, entitled 'Il falso vecchio' ('The falsely old man') he metaphorically describes this condition:

> Il verbo al presente porta tutto il mondo.
> Mi chiedo dove sono i popoli scomparsi.
> Il fattorino vestito di grigio in cortile mi dice
> che alcuni stanno nascosti sotto il primo sottoscala.
>
> Ho portato con me sotto il primo sottoscala
> le ceneri di Alessandro, il pianto di Rachele.
> Il verbo al presente mi permette di scomparire.
> Il fattorino non vede piú dove sono scomparso.

(The verb in the present carries all the world./I ask myself where the disappeared peoples are./The delivery boy dressed in grey in the courtyard tells me/that some are hidden beneath the first understairs.

I have brought with me beneath the first understairs/the ashes of Alexander, the weeping of Rachel./The verb in the present allows me to disappear./The delivery boy no longer sees where I have disappeared to.)

BIOGRAPHICAL NOTE

Franco Fortini was born Franco Lattes in Florence in 1917. While studying philosophy at university there he wrote his first verse and criticism. After graduating, he qualified as a schoolteacher. In 1939 he received baptism as a Waldensian Protestant, backdated a year to protect him under the Fascist anti-semitic laws. In 1940 he exchanged his Jewish surname for his mother's maiden name. Conscripted in 1941, he escaped after the 1943 armistice to Switzerland, where he made contact with anti-Fascist emigrés and joined the Italian Socialist Party. In October 1944 he returned to fight in a partisan brigade in the Resistance. After the 1945 liberation he settled in Milan with his wife Ruth Leiser, worked for the Socialist paper *Avanti!* and for the periodical *Il Politecnico* (1945-47). He subsequently took jobs as an advertising copywriter for Olivetti (1947-53), a consultant to various publishers (from 1959) and as a teacher, first in technical schools (1964-71) then at the University of Siena (since 1971) where he is professor of the History of Literary Criticism. Throughout this period he has written many articles on politics, culture and literature and a substantial body of poetry. He has also translated extensively from writers including Goethe, Brecht, Eluard and Proust. Since leaving the PSI in 1958 he has remained on the independent left.

BIBLIOGRAPHY

PRINCIPAL WORKS

Foglio di via e altri versi, Einaudi, Turin, 1946.
Agonia di Natale, Einaudi, Turin, 1948; (republished 1972 with revised title *Giovanni e le mani*)
Asia Maggiore. Viaggio nella Cina, Einaudi, Turin, 1956
Dieci inverni, 1947-1957, Feltrinelli, Milan, 1957; ed. cited De Donato, Bari, 1973
Poesia e errore 1937-1957, Feltrinelli, Milan, 1959
Il movimento surrealista, Garzanti, Milan, 1959
Una volta per sempre, 1958-1962, Mondadori, Milan, 1963
Tre testi per film (All'armi siam fascisti!, Sciopero a Torino, La statua di Stalin), Edizioni Avanti!, Milan, 1963
Sere in Valdossola, Mondadori, Milan, 1963
Verifica dei poteri, Il Saggiatore, Milan, 1965; revised and expanded 1969; ed. cited 1974
L'ospite ingrato, De Donato, Bari, 1966
I cani del Sinai, De Donato, Bari, 1967
Ventiquattro voci per un dizionario di lettere, Il Saggiatore, Milan, 1968
Faust I e II (translated from Goethe), Mondadori, Milan, 1970
Questo muro, 1962-1972, Mondadori, Milan, 1973
La poesia di Scotellaro [1955], Basilicata editrice, Rome-Matera, 1974
Saggi italiani, De Donato, Bari, 1974
I poeti del Novecento, Laterza, Bari, 1977
Questioni di frontiera, Einaudi, Turin, 1977
Una volta per sempre. Poesie 1938-1973, Einaudi, Turin, 1978 (collected poems including the four previous volumes: *Foglio di via, Poesia e errore, Una volta per sempre, Questo muro*)

Il ladro di ciliege, (verse translations), Einaudi, Turin, 1982

'Communism' (translation by Angelo Quattrocchi and Lucien Rey of
'Il comunismo' [1958] in *Una volta per sempre*), *New Left Review* 38,
July-August 1966, 81

'The Writer's Mandate and the End of Anti-Fascism' (translation by
Geoffrey Nowell Smith of 'Mandato degli scrittori e fine dell'antifascismo' in *Verifica dei poteri*), *Screen* 15, 1 (Spring 1974) 33–70

'*Fortini-Cani* – Script' (translation by Geoffrey Nowell Smith of the script
of the film by Jean-Marie Straub and Danièle Huillet in which Fortini
reads aloud from *I cani del Sinai*), *Screen* 19, 2 (Summer 1978) 9–40

Poems (a selection translated by Michael Hamburger), Arc Publications,
Todmorden, 1978

WORKS CITED

Adorno, T.W. *Minima Moralia* (first published 1951) translated by
Edmund Jephcott, NLB, London, 1974

— and Horkheimer, M., *Dialectic of Enlightenment* (first published
1944) translated by John Cumming, NLB, London, 1979

Asor Rosa, A. *Intellettuali e classe operaia*, La Novua Italia, Florence,
1973

Basso, L., *Neocapitalismo e nuova sinistra*, Laterza, Bari, 1969

Canestri, G. and Ricuperati, G., *La scuola in Italia dalla legge Casati a
oggi*, Loescher, Turin, 1976

Cases, C. 'Intervention' in *Gramsci e la cultura contemporanea*, ed. P. Rossi,
Editori Riuniti, Rome, vol. I., 1969

Gramsci, A. *Selections from the Prison Notebooks*, translated by
Quintin Hoare and Geoffrey Nowell Smith, Lawrence and Wishart,
London, 1971

— *Quaderni del carcere*, ed. V. Gerratana, Einaudi, Turin, 1975

Guiducci, R. et al. 'Proposte per una organizzazione della cultura
marxista in Italia', *Ragionamenti* 5-6 (supplement), September 1956

Hall, S. 'Notes on deconstructing "the popular",' in R. Samuel (ed.)
People's History and Socialist Theory, RKP, London, 1981

Leone De Castris, A. *L'anima e la classe*, De Donato, Bari, 1972, Chapter 2

Magri, L. 'Il valore e il limite delle esperienze frontiste', *Critica marxista* 3
(1966) 4

Mengaldo, P.V. Introduction to F. Fortini, *Poesie scelte*, Mondadori,
Milan, 1974

Salinari, C. *La questione del realismo*, Parenti, Florence, 1960

Tronti, M. *Operai e capitale*, 2nd edition, Einaudi, Turin, 1977

FURTHER READING

Asor Rosa, A. 'Lo stato democratico e i partiti politici' in *Letteratura
italiana* Vol. I, *Il letterato e le istituzioni*, Einaudi, Turin, 1982

Barberi Squarotti, G. Fortini, in *Grande Dizionario Enciclopedico*,
UTET, Turin, 1968, Vol. VIII

*Berardinelli, A. *Fortini*, La Nuova Italia (Il Castoro), Florence, 1974
Ferretti, G.C. *L'autocritica dell'intellettuale*, Marsilio, Padua, 1970
Scalia, G. 'Due 'diari' dell'engagement', in *Crittica, letteratura, ideologia*, Marsilio, Padua, 1968

Peter Hainsworth

5 Andrea Zanzotto

If any one Italian poet has been felt to stand out amongst his contemporaries, it has been Andrea Zanzotto. Not that this has been the case throughout Zanzotto's career. His first four books were well received and respected, but it has really been since the publication of *La Beltà (Beauty)* in 1968 that his importance has been fully recognized. For with *La Beltà* Zanzotto showed himself to be capable of remarkably adventurous and yet coherent poetry. If he took risks, and sometimes revolutionary risks, he clearly did so for good reason. If he was difficult, he clearly had important things to say which could not be said easily. If he wrote in an apparently disorderly, unpoetic way on unpoetic matters, the aim was still something that had to be called poetry and it was pursued in full consciousness of the Italian and the European traditions. At the same time, though there was a breakthrough in *La Beltà* – which has been extended and deepened in subsequent books – there is also a continuity running through his work. Indeed in retrospect all his books seem to have the same core of principles and preoccupations at their centre whatever their innovations, as if there is basically one set of problems which he is trying to articulate and resolve. Thus there is in Zanzotto's work a rich and complex combination of openness and cohesion, of development and consistency, of traditionalism and novelty, for which it is hard to find parallels in Italy. The pity is that he is not better known abroad: but the one bilingual anthology of his poetry that has appeared (Feldman and Swann 1975) concentrates on his earlier, less unconventional work and understandably so, since his later poems are even less likely to survive translation than most. Perhaps it is an even greater pity that he is not read more in Italy itself. But except for a 1973 paperback anthology *Poesie (1938-1972)* his work is not widely available. As has been the rule throughout the century, critical recognition has not meant for an Italian poet even the readership that a Larkin or a Hughes could expect, let alone a Lowell or an Ashbery.

If those who do read poetry can reasonably think of Zanzotto as a European poet, his first collections were much more what might be expected from a poet who lives in the Venetian provinces and who, as he said himself in a poem entitled *Miracolo a Milano (Miracle in Milan)*, only 'becomes Milanese three times a year'. He had begun writing before the war, although his first collection of poems was not published until 1951. What is noticeable about this book, *Dietro il paesaggio (Behind the landscape)*, is that it belongs very much to the idiom of hermeticism. As was explained in Chapter 1 (pp. 25–27), hermeticism, with its tenuous imagery, its refined modernism, its aspiration to absolute poetic values, had been the orthodoxy of the 1930s. In the immediate post-war years it was partly superseded. The pressure was towards committed poetry, or at least towards a poetry which was more public and less literary.

It is a pressure which *Dietro il paesaggio* chooses to ignore, not even raising the question of the political and social conscience of the thirty-year-old poet, although the return to what are basically hermetic issues and to a hermetic mode is anything but unthinking. 'In my first books' Zanzotto has recently written (1981, 97) 'I had actually cancelled human presence, out of a form of 'distaste' *(fastidio)* caused by historical events. I wanted only to speak of landscapes, to return to a nature in which man had not been active. It was a psychological reflex-re-action to the devastations of war.'

As these words suggest, there are differences from the old hermeticism. The poems are longer and more discursive than most hermetic poems and seem to hint more at a personal trauma than at a flaw which exists in the nature of things. They also centre on a real place, the village of Pieve di Soligo in the hills above the Piave river to the north of Venice where Zanzotto lives, rather than suggesting bucolic images that may not even possess a spatial dimension. In spite of focussing on the landscaping of a small part of the Veneto they are remarkably unprovincial poems in one sense: they draw on, indeed, as Nuvoli (1979) points out, they cite from, the tradition of Italian poetry but also do the same with contemporary European poetry, Rimbaud, Lorca, Hölderlin and Eluard being particularly in evidence. But this openness to other poetry, which seems more a result of choice than of what is commonly called influence, is just one sign of how literary these poems are, of how much Zanzotto rejects the appeals of Quasimodo and others (see Chapter 1, p. 26). Rather than aiming at any illusion of immediacy he prefers to hold the world of raw experience at a distance. Instead poetry turns in on itself. Broadly speaking, as the title suggests (and like all Zanzotto's titles it is emblematic), there is a reaching for what lies 'behind the landscape', that is, for some hidden, special world that the actual physical countryside seems to point towards and which is re-created, or also created, in the language of landscape in poetry. In that world, there is felt to be a reality (in some sense) and, what is more, a warmth and a security, that the rest of life appears to deny. In rough psychological terms the hermetic absolute has become a realm of narcissistic pleasure, of childlike and childish joy, of a welcoming, protective mother. This realm will be the (much-loved) object of almost all Zanzotto's poetry. But at this stage, though the poems speak of pleasurable union or of the pain of loss, they impress as strangely cold creations. Stylistically they are literary pastorals and what guides them is a disturbingly calm consciousness, or perhaps a disturbingly tense one, which repeatedly re-affirms in a delicately unemphatic monotone its own rather distanced position.

> Sul libro aperto della primavera
> figura mezzodì per sempre,
> è dipinto ch'io viva nell'isola,
> nell'oceano, ch'io viva nell'amore
>
> d'una luna che s'oppone al mondo.

(On the open book of spring / midday figures for ever, / it is depicted that I should live in the island, / in the ocean, that I should live in the love / of a moon opposed to the world.)

So ends *A foglia e a gemma* (*In leaf and bud*), laying claim in the way that is typical of the book to lunar isolation and love.

In the next three books – *Elegia e altri versi* (*Elegy and other verses*, 1954), *Vocativo* (*Vocative*, 1957) and *IX Ecloghe* (*IX Eclogues*, 1962) – the lines drawn in *Dietro il paesaggio* become more firm and also more complex. The tone and language become generally richer and more account is taken of historical reality. Rather than being excluded or repressed, the inauthentic, the unpoetic, the whole false world which had been held at a distance gradually begins to make its way into the poems. What lies 'behind' the landscape is still there but increasingly threatened. The late 1950s and early 1960s were the years of transformation for Italy as a whole. The peasant cultures and dialects of rural Italy, the very landscape itself, all were deeply affected by the movement to the towns and the development of the new technological civilization. As a result, what is 'behind' the landscape comes to have less and less support in lived experience and increasingly has to be posited as existing only in, or through, poetry. Simultaneously there is an internal crisis: what 'it' is becomes more problematic, as do its value, its reality or even the possibility of talking about it or making poetry which can (as the title *Vocativo* suggests) call it out, address it. At times it seems impossible to say anything positive or true about whatever it is that poetry alludes to. And yet it is still in that realm, remote, secretive, apparently useless, that a positive is to be found which is not to be found in the rest of experience of the rest of language. *Così siamo (So let us be)* from *IX Ecloghe* is one of the poems which most catches this movement between a fouled contemporary world and something which has been lost to the self and to language – if it was ever there.

> Dicevano, a Padova, "anch'io"
> gli amici "l'ho conosciuto".
> E c'era il romorio d'un'acqua sporca
> prossima, e d'una sporca fabbrica:
> stupende nel silenzio.
> Perché era notte. "Anch'io
> l'ho conosciuto."
> Vitalmente ho pensato
> a te che ora
> non sei né soggetto né oggetto
> né lingua usuale né gergo
> né quiete né movimento
> neppure il né che negava
> e che per quanto s'affondino
> gli occhi dentro la sua cruna
> mai ti nega abbastanza
>
> E così sia: ma io
> credo con altrettanta
> forza in tutto il mio nulla,
> perciò non ti ho perduto

o, più ti perdo e più ti perdi,
più mi sei simile, più m'avvicini.

('I too' said in Padua / my friends 'I knew him'. / And there
was the sloshing of dirty water / nearby, and the noise of a
dirty factory: / amazing in the silence. / But it was night. 'I
too / knew him.' / Vitally I thought / of you who now / are
neither subject nor object / nor normal language nor private
code / nor rest nor movement / nor even the nor that negated
/ and that though my eyes sink / into its needle's eye / never
negated you enough / And so be it: but I / believe with equal
/ force in all my nothing, / and so I have not lost you / or the
more I lose you or you lose yourself, / the more you are like
me, the more you come close to me.)

Not all the poems of *IX Ecloghe* have this paradoxical positive:
others are ironically gloomy about the value of lyric poetry as it has
been and might be in a world which seems to falsify it or ignore it
or which alternatively poetry itself falsifies or ignores. The last of
the nine eclogues from which the book takes its title focusses the
question in terms of schoolteaching, that is, in terms of Zanzotto's
own working life but also in terms of a primary organization and
transmission of knowledge. Following a familiar mythology, the
basics of which he has never doubted, Zanzotto posits that children
come from some richly significant realm, which is the same or
almost the same as that of poetry, into a classroom which at best
mixes a little truth with much falsehood. The danger is not so
much schematization and indoctrination as a chaotic, endless
proliferation of words, ideas, things which is confusible with, but
really at the opposite pole to, the fertile, harmonised complexities
of poetry, at least as it might ideally exist. At most the so-called
master can perform a minimal affirmation of his own presence,
'and, in this, be a pointer, a gift, your gift, given to others' ('e, in
questo, essere indizio, dono, / dono tuo, agli altri donato'). In this
giving may be the seed of something else, the discovery of remains
of an old self and an old wound, and some necessary awareness,
'even if he still does not know either love or teaching' ('anche se
ancora non sa / né amore né insegnamento').

Teaching merges with poetry here, and both, though they still
have a good deal of their literal senses left, are also metaphorical.
Poetry in particular tends to become a metaphor for the authentic
or the real in a very wide sense, but especially for a mode of
language and a mode of being that have their analogues in

children and in memories of childhood but which the normal, adult world rejects. But, following on from *Dietro il paesaggio*, the poems that actually make up *IX Ecloghe* and, to some extent, *Vocativo*, are poems *about* this cluster of metaphors, 'meta-poems' about poetry which recount the loss of everything that the metaphor alludes to, but include elements from the false world which authentic poetry would in some sense transcend. At the same time these poems seem to veer disconcertingly from being *about* 'poetry' towards themselves becoming 'poetry', and that means towards re-enacting for the umpteenth time traditional or hermetic formulae. As they do, they become more and more remote, and less and less able to evoke or include whatever it is that 'poetry' is about. Instead, as Zanzotto recognises in some of the poems, it is in the contrast between the 'poetic' and the 'non-poetic' or in attending simply to the latter, that these 'meta-poems' are themselves most interesting, most poetic. The question is partly psychiatric. In terms of the 'I' an attempt must be made to uncover what has been repressed, whilst recognising that a total inclusion or verbalisation of the self is impossible, if for no other reason, because there must always be a gap between the knowing self and the self that is known: the 'I' is 'a pronoun which has been waiting for ever to become a noun' ('pronome che da sempre a farsi nome attende') as Zanzotto puts it in *Un libro di Ecloghe* (*A Book of Eclogues*), the prefactory poem to the volume. But the issue is also linguistic and stylistic, indeed in a book of poems primarily so. In terms of language these poems come most to life when they admit words and concepts which the closed world of Italian lyric poetry had traditionally disallowed. Yet the title of the book is indicative of a severe, even sublime resistance. The literary, even the antiquatedly literary, is still dominant. It absorbs into itself privileged items from the various sciences and technologies, but, though there are bulges and one or two tears, the barrier keeping out the non-poetic is still standing. The controlling 'I' still will not open itself to all the linguistic dirt or admit that its own cleansing power is an illusion.

Probably because it remained within the traditional limits of poetry, *IX Ecloghe* was not the stuff to win more than serious admiration. Disturbed and aware though it might be, it could also appear academic, isolationist or neo-hermetic in a bad sense. Compared to the *Novissimi* (for whom see Chapter 2), Zanzotto was (apparently) unadventurous and unexciting, although now at twenty years distance there is much in the original anthology-cum-manifesto of the group which seems superficial and much in *IX Ecloghe* which seems barely to have fended off a destructive turmoil. Be that as it may, it was the theory and the polemics surrounding the new anti-poetry which occupied the public centre of the poetic stage in Italy for most of the 1960s.

Zanzotto has never had much time for the new avant-garde. As long ago as 1954, he wrote in a review of Sanguineti's first book of poems that it could only be sincere if it were the record or the consequence of a nervous breakdown. In 1971 he remarked on the obsolescence of literary flag-wavers, 'those young men who were active in the 1960s, sweetly Mithridatified almost as if they had absorbed pus with their artificial maternal milk, so mortally euphoric that they offered us homilies on aphasia through loudspeakers' (1974, 353). But the poems which he wrote between 1961 and 1968 and which were published in that year as *La Beltà* (*Beauty*), if they resembled any poetry that was being written at the time in Italy or in Europe, resembled avant-garde poetry. They practised what the avant-garde called defamiliarization or estrangement: they broke rules as avant-garde poetry did: they showed a similarly appalled hostility to the duplicities of neo-capitalist and consumerist culture. On the other hand there is no trace in *La Beltà* of confidence in revolutionary theory, whether of history or of the self or of language. The past is rather transformed or ambiguously repeated. In many ways *La Beltà* is a metamorphosis of *IX Ecloghe*, returning to almost everything that is in that book but drawing in as much as it can of what it had left out. In that sense it is a move in Zanzotto's own development, dictated more by the breaking of internal tensions than by any encounter with 'new' theories and practices of poetry, except perhaps in their most osmotic permeations.

'Breaking', 'collapse', 'chaos' are the kind of words that are likely to come to mind on a cursory or unsympathetic reading of *La Beltà*. They are also the words which some critics have used in a more or less approving sense of the book. Whether it is to approve or disapprove, this particular chain of association is started off because Zanzotto shatters not only stylistic conventions but also some basic linguistic rules. Up to a point there are few problems. For the contemporary reader of poetry it may even be a relief, after Zanzotto's earlier mode, to find various registers of language confounded in the poems of *La Beltà*, although the confounding is probably more familiar in fiction (say Joyce) than in verse. The highly literary, technical, scientific language of parts of *IX*

Ecloghe re-appears, but mixed with it come the cliché of adverts and everyday conversations, private and regional slang, neologisms, child-language and foreign words in what might well be thought a liberating and liberated farrago. It is probably also not an index of poetic disruption for a contemporary reader that there should be allusions to a whole range of poetic and non-poetic texts and *ad libitum* quotation from them, though the density of reference and the speed of transition may take the breath away – as, say, when Zanzotto juxtaposes an advertising jingle and Hölderlin, or Tasso and Hermann Kahn. But the disorienting rupture is of syntax and semantics. In complete contrast to the complex but formally correct sentences that Zanzotto had previously favoured, words seem to tumble over each other, sometimes with rhyme but frequently without reason. Even more disconcertingly in the course of a poem sentences which are more or less 'normal' will emerge from a sequence of incomplete clauses and phrases only for the 'normal' language to vanish again. Add to this that the various items of vocabulary, the various phrases and more or less incomplete sentences may appear semantically disparate and yet somehow connected, and we may well find ourselves wondering what to make of something that refuses to declare whether or not it is non-sense, or for that matter nonsense. Pasolini voiced some such re-action with his usual force: 'Not only does Zanzotto estrange the reader from any possible semantic fields because in his disgust and disillusionment he rejects them all, but he actually arranges it so that there is not even the semantic field of a lack of semantic field' (Pasolini 1971, 26).

It may be partly the passage of the years, but it is hard now not to feel that Pasolini was exaggerating. Even when the book first came out, more careful assessments argued that, if the poems undermined language in one way, they enriched it in another. The 'normal' significance of words is broken down but other 'abnormal', but interesting, and somehow valid meanings are suggested or released, although they cannot be readily translated or paraphrased in 'normal' – or critical – language. At a primary and material level the poems do not have that deliberate aridity or blankness of those avant-garde texts whose explicit pretext is commonly the destruction of meaning, on the grounds that all meanings, suggested or explicit, are corrupt or inauthentic. Instead they have the dense sound patterns, the complexities of tropes and figures, the formal order and the rhythmic power associated with traditional poetry but attenuated in much modern poetry, including Zanzotto's own before *La Beltà*. The novelty is that this traditional activation of language (which after all is not usually decipherable in terms of meaning in much familiar poetry) is applied to a non-traditional range of language and in non-traditional ways. Rhythmically in particular the old Italian metres have largely disappeared, as has the delicate free verse of hermeticism. In their stead has come what is generally a rapid, irregular insistent movement forwards that seems allied to the rhythms of certain contemporary composers. As Montale put it in his review, Zanzotto is 'a percussive poet but not a loud one: his metronone is perhaps the heartbeat' (Montale 1968).

Such features as rhythm are of course fundamental in the experience of reading the poems and also as ways of suggesting to the reader that these are in some sense still poems (on the whole) rather than 'texts' or something unnameable. Equally obviously it is precisely those features which are unlikely to survive commentary, let alone translation. One entertaining and disturbing poem which poses these difficulties to a slightly lesser degree than some others, at least in its opening lines, is *Sì, ancora la neve* (*Yes, Snow Again*) which follows a poem entitled *La perfezione della neve* (*The Perfection of Snow*). It has the following epigraph: 'Ti piace essere venuto a questo mondo?' Bamb.: 'Sí, perché c'è la STANDA'. ('Are you happy to have come into this world?' Child: 'Yes, because there's STANDA'. – that is, the Italian equivalent of Woolworth's). And then the poem begins:

> Che sarà della neve
> che sarà di noi?
> Una curva sul ghiaccio
> e poi e poi . . . ma i pini, i pini
> tutti uscenti alla neve, e fin l'ultima età
> circondata da pini. Sic et simpliciter?
> E perché si è – il mondo pinoso il mondo nevoso –
> perché si è fatto bambucci-ucci, odore di cristianucci,
> perché si è fatto noi, roba per noi?
> E questo valere in persona ed ex-persona
> un solo possibile ed ex-possibile?
> Hölderlin: 'siamo un segno senza significato':
> ma dove le due serie entrano in contatto?
> Ma è vero? E che sarà di noi?
> E tu perché, perché tu?

(What will become of the snow / what will become of us? / A

curve on the ice / and then and then . . . but the pines, the pines / all coming out to the snow, and even the last age / surrounded by snow. So and simply? / And why has it – the piny world the snowy world – / why has it become baby-abies, smell of Christy-istians, / why has it become us, stuff for us? / And this availing in person and ex-person / a single possible and ex-possible? / Hölderlin: 'we are a sign without meaning': / but where the two series enter into contact? / But is it true? And what will become of us? / And you why, why you?)

And the poem goes on from there for another eighty and more lines. listing and questioning, ranging over pulp-food, drugs, diseases, flowers, freewill, tradition and the avant-garde among other things, but returning eventually to its beginning:

> E il pino. E i pini-ini-ini per profili
> e profili mai scissi mai cuciti
> ini-ini a fianco davanti
> dietro l'eterno l'esterno l'interno (il paesaggio)
> dietro davanti da tutti i lati,
> i pini come stanno, stanno bene?
>
> Detto alla neve: 'Non mi abbandonerai mai, vero?'
>
> E una pinzetta, ora, una graffetta.

(And the pine. And the piny-iny-ines for profiles / and profiles never split never sown up / iny-ines beside before / behind the eternal the external the internal (the landscape) / behind before on all sides, / the pines how are they, are they well? // Said to the snow: 'You'll never leave me, will you?' // And a little clamp now, a little clip.)

It may be that the reader will have only the vaguest sense of what goes on in this poem, of what it is 'about' in the common sense of the expression. And yet the reading of the poem can be pleasurable – so long as no demand is made that it should conform to traditional norms for poetry, even if they are the norms of the modern tradition. The poem does not 'beautify' language: in a blatant overthrow of the dogma of purification, almost any form of language is accepted and then played with, in places in an almost ludicrously childish way (as in the distortions of the words for 'babies' or 'pines'). We might say that it is this game of linguistic manipulation, gratuitous perhaps, narcissistic perhaps, in

Freudian terms close to the happy manipulation of fecal fantasies, that the poem offers, or tries to offer, for our pleasure, as perhaps a great deal of poetry offers us for our pleasure. More simply, one of the things the poem does is to invite the reader to play at being a child, or to play with language as a child plays with it. That, in another sense of the phrase, is (partly) what it is 'about'.

Put this way, the connections with Zanzotto's earlier work should be fairly clear, and also the metamorphosis which has taken place. *Dietro il paesaggio* and subsequent books had posited a poetic realm which was also the realm of childish pleasure and security and also the realm of authenticity, of real being, each of these terms evoking and to some extent standing of each other. But though it had evolved in complexity, this realm had mostly remained severely and remotely objectified. In *Sì, ancora la neve*, as in *La Beltà* generally, the child has been allowed (or forced) into the mode of expression itself. As well as being signified it enters the activity of signifying and drastically deranges it. At the same time, as before, the child is still a metaphor for something else, or a metaphorical representation of something else, something that Zanzotto himself has written of as the creating of meaning or the emergence of the *logos* (Zanzotto 1970). Ideally the poem catches reality as it comes into being.

But there has been a further change, *La Beltà* recognizes that instead of revealing a forgotten joy in the world that the adult might accept sentimentally or gleefully, poetry might produce a joy that is unholy or at least unwelcome. Reality and the poetic idyll as previously formulated might have to part company. If so the former cannot be denied. In an article of 1973 Zanzotto wrote: 'Poetry and childhood come to speak to us of that unspoken something: the risk that it will be terrible, enclosed by a horizon within which revelation and apocalypse coincide, as they do etymologically, cannot justify our not listening.' Reflexes of this position surface repeatedly in *La Beltà*, most astoundingly in the eighteenth and last of a sequence of poems called *Profezie o memorie o giornali murali* (*Prophecies or Memories or Wall-Newspapers*) in which the various stages leading to all-out nuclear war as outlined by Hermann Kahn metonymically provoke images of sexual violence, totalitarian torture, and also poetic violence as practised by, and on, Zanzotto himself. At least in a textual universe the violence is already literally everywhere.

4 E il tentatore riapre la porta
e il torturatore rilegge ciò che che
che aveva fatto rossamente essudare fuori.
Idee tropi nomi e niente.
Un paesaggio-traino di fiori, di grida. Colpisci
trafiggi dunque.
Diecimila frammenti d'acciaio irraggiati intorno.

(4 And the tempter reopens the door / and the torturer rereads
that which which / which he had caused redly to sweat out. /
Ideas tropes names and nothing. / A landscape-sled of
flowers, of cries. Strike / spike through then. / Ten thousand
fragments of steel radiated round.)

Apocalypse now is one possibility. Less dramatic and more
immediately dangerous is the possibility of falsification, of an
intimate corruption of the actual and the metaphorical child. If the
child can believe, or be made to believe, that it is Standa or
Woolworth's that makes the world pleasurable, then the chances
are increased that the language of the child, as we know it, will be a
parody, just as the child of adverts and soap-operas is a parody.
Consequently there is the enormous risk that the real poetry too
will elude the poem. *Sì, ancora la neve* might be not merely collage
or jumble, but a grotesque counterfeit of the childish or the poetic.
From one perspective the childish has definitely entered the poem.
From another it may be as absent as it was from earlier poems.

Zanzotto is serious about child-language. He believes that there
is an archetypal pre-language which is shared by mothers and very
young children. He goes so far as actually to include lines in *petél*
(as baby-talk is apparently called in his own dialect) in his *Elegia
in petél* (*Elegy in petel*) which cannot, he suggests, be translated
because they are private, though they are also on the edge of known
language. The first pair of these run:

Mama e nona te dà ate e cuco e pepi e memela.
Bono ti, ca, co nona. Béi bumba bona. È fet foa e upi.

It is possible to find in these lines a particularly liquid pleasure—
what Fellini, in a letter that became the occasion of *Filò* (and which
is included in the volume as a preface), called 'that sweet broken
burbling of babies in a mixture of milk and dribbled matter' ('quel
cantilenare dolce e rotto dei bambini in un miscuglio di latte e
materia disciolta').

But the juxtaposition of 'elegy' with *petél* points in almost the opposite direction. The reader's more or less regressive pleasure may be primary but it is not sufficient. Childishness does not mean a surrender of awareness or responsibility, and even less so the counterfeiting of childishness. The reader is continually asked to think about what is occurring in the poem, to be conscious of what the language is referring to and of how it is doing so. As well as being invited to return to a pre-rational stage, the reader is being asked to entertain the possibility (or the impossibility) of understanding what is going on. The earlier meta-poems have not been rejected, but now the subject and the object aim to meet in a paradoxical whole – a multiple, open unity. So, to go back to *Sì, ancora la neve*, that poem explicitly and continuously asks pertinent questions: what is going on, what will happen, what do these words mean, what do they conceal, what is the poetry that this appears to be, what do many other things mean etc.? At the same time it seems to nullify the questions by parodying them or by making them pleasurable . . .

Maturity and infancy, true and false, the meaningful and the meaningless, self-consciousness and its absence, what is said and what is not said, the recherché and the trivial, subject and object – the list of opposites which the poems of *La Beltà* bring together or which they recognize they fail to bring together, can be extended endlessly. The constant drive of the book (which takes more manifest forms than my comments on *Sì, ancora la neve* suggests) is to bring together any opposites that can be imagined in one totality which must be, or which must allude to, the whole of life: the urge is to deny nothing and to make failure a failure to include, not to discriminate. If, positively, all that may in the end be offered turns out to be childish pleasure, even counterfeit childish pleasure, Zanzotto gambles that much more is to be won. From the poem which defeats interpretation and categorization but which attempts to include both, something of value, perhaps *the* thing of value, may spring. It is the line which will not go either towards sense or non-sense, or which goes in both directions, what Zanzotto calls in the *Elegia in petél* 'a trembling line' ('una riga tremante') which counts.

Zanzotto's conceptual see-saw is obviously a much riskier and much more ambitious game than that played by most of his contemporaries in Italy and abroad. The poems of *La Beltà* may well not be accepted as poems at all (as of course they admit). If they are accepted as being somehow 'poetry', they may still seem to be attempting the impossible. Again the poems take that into account, but Zanzotto has also said elsewhere that he sees such risks as inevitable in writing what aim to be poems. 'There is no poetry which does not have to do with emargination, and it is precisely when it is completely involved in emargination, that this force from which poetry comes touches the margin, the limit, and perhaps goes beyond everything that one might initially have suspected. Hence poetic activity is still there in its ragged, debatable autonomy, setting up an opposite and necessary pole to all human institutions that are related to the forces of power (*potere storico*)' (Zanzotto 1976).

On the one hand then is established, institutionalised power in all its ramifications, including its ramifications into language and thought. On the other hand, maintaining a stance of opposition already evident in *Dietro il paesaggio*, there is poetry, which may attain to, or point to, the freedom which power subverts. In any event poetry can only exist on the edges of things. Its habitat must be the provinces, not the capitals. Its readership must be eccentric and minoritarian, not the mainstream. And its impulse must be to go beyond everything that has previously been considered possible in poetry or to constitute poetry. In that sense it must risk going over the edge, as well as touching it. The wager is that if a death of poetry occurs, so will a re-birth which can make the past and the world live rather than annihilate them. As Zanzotto says at the end of *Al mondo* (*To the world*):

> Su, bello, su.
> > Su, münchhausen.
> (Up, my beauty, up.
> > /Up, münchhausen.)

The beautiful world and the beautiful poem might come into being or come back into being on the same impossible principles as those applied by the fabled baron. 'La beltà', the antiquated word for beauty which is the title of the book and also the title of one of the poems, might cease to be 'questa scarica, disadattata parola' ('this chargeless, inadequated word'), might once again signify.

Obviously the issue is not only aesthetic. More is involved than beautiful poems or seeing the world in a beautiful light at privileged moments in a more or less hermetic fashion. Because the object is now a totality which admits of no exclusions or categorical divisions, the aesthetic merges with the ethical. The re-birth is as mystical and as all embracing as is re-birth in Christianity.

It is of course hard to say what such a re-birth could be. But Zanzotto gives some indication of what has to die before it can occur. Above all there are the delusions of neo-capitalist civilization, which he sees in a poem entitled *In una storia idiota di vampiri* (*In an idiotic vampire story*) as a banquet of vampires offering spurious satisfactions to the un-dead. But he also makes it plain that for him any theory of history, whether Marxist or not, fails to come to terms with the actual brutality of the historical process, and with the fact that time and life do not move forward in functional, linear progression. It is in this area that Zanzotto can also begin to make affirmations. Words, the self, others, the world are webs of relations which can constitute a form of resistance to the abusive power of history. Instead of progressing, or as well as progressing, perhaps time stands still. *Alla stagione* (*To the season*) rests largely on the paradox that the Italian word for season (*stagione*), that is for something essentially transitory, is etymologically a word for stopping or standing (cf. 'stationary'). In this perspective in *Retorica su: lo sbandamento, il principio 'resistenza'* (*Rhetoric on: Dispersal, the 'Resistance' Principle*) Zanzotto issues an exhortation to quit historical time:

> Va' corri. Spera una zuppa di fagioli
> spera arrivare possedere entrare
> nel templum-tempus.
> Contemplare. Tempo ottimo e massimo.

(Go, run. Hope for a bean-soup / hope to arrive possess enter / into temple-time. / To contemplate. Best and greatest time.)

Of course there is no forgetting historical time. A few lines later the poem makes its adventurous and completely justified end, or lack of end.

> L'azione sbanda si riprende
> sbanda glissa e

(The action dissolves recovers / dissolves slides and . . .)

Contemplation (rather than the dominant look), non-functional time, sacred time are notions which could carry connotations of self-denial. But Zanzotto does not seem, on the whole, to subscribe to those currents of thought which would find pleasure in destroying the ego on the grounds of its deceptiveness or non-being. The ego is obviously a problem and several poems circle round it. But generally there is an extension of the self-affirmation that had been adumbrated in *IX Ecloghe*. Risky though it is, the self is recognized and accepted as present in the world and its desires are recognized and accepted as potentially good, just as the world is potentially good, however disastrous both the world and the self might seem from another perspective. What is impossible is dominance. 'We are all minors, as the grass is minor, as the dew is' ('siamo tutti tra i minori / come l'erba è minore, come la rugiada'). And later in the same poem – which is once again *Retorica* – Zanzotto says that it is time for the hare battalion, the rabbit brigade to attack ('battaglione lepre, brigata coniglio / all'assalto'). Those symbols of fear and flight are the implausible vehicles of resistance, and resistance which is conceptually nonsensical. But in the middle of this complicated multi-layered poem (it is also of course about poetry) there is the unambiguous stating of a banal truth which is as impossible as any such paradox.

> E ho mangiato anche quel giorno
> – dopo il sangue –
> e mangio tutti i giorni
> – dopo l'insegnamento –
> una zuppa gustosa, fagioli.
> Posso farlo e devo.
> Tutti possono e devono.
> Bello. Fagiolo. Fiore.

(And I ate that day too / – after the blood – / and I eat every day / – after teaching – / a tasty soup, beans. / I can do it and I must. / Everyone can and must. / Beautiful. Bean. Flower.)

Everyone in the world, including himself, could and should have the basic meal of beans. It is the vampire world which needs blood.

Such an outlook is more metaphysical than moralistic in *La Beltà*. In any case *Retorica* is probably not the magnet that draws together the various currents at work in the book. If an emblematic summation is to be found, it is probably in the last poem, *E la madre-norma*, (*And the Mother-Norm*) which ends with a kind of *envoi* addressed to the poem, to the reader, to Zanzotto himself and perhaps to that other radical transgressor of paternal norms, Franco Fortini, to whom the poem is dedicated.

> Va' nella chiara libertà,
> libera il sereno la pastura
> dei colli goduta a misura
> d'una figurabile natura
>
> rileva 'i raccordi e le rime
> dell'abbietto con il sublime'
>
> e la madre-norma

(Go in clear liberty, / liberate the serene the pasture / of the hills enjoyed in measure / of a figurable nature // Heighten 'the link and rhyme / of the abject with the sublime' // and the mother-norm)

Zanzotto's next major collection, *Pasque* (1972), is an exasperation of *La Beltà* rather than a change of direction. 'Pasque' are 'Easters', but, says Zanzotto in a note (quoting from a textbook of Italian etymology), *pásque* comes from the Latin *pascha* (itself from the Greek *páskha*, which in turn comes from the Hebrew *pésah*, 'passage') but crossed with *pascua*, 'pasture'. So hidden in itself, the word *Pasque* indicates certain *foci* of Zanzotto's work – re-birth, nourishment, movement forward, rusticity – all of which are once again to be activated. But the threats have never been stronger. The book consists of two groups of eleven poems each, divided by a strange text entitled *Microfilm*, which is a phototypic reproduction, together with manuscript annotations in French, of a hieroglyph (as it might be called) which Zanzotto apparently dreamt. The hieroglyph itself is a triangle containing a patterning of the letters IODIO, from which various crucial nuclei can also be generated – the ego (*io*), God (*dio*), nothing (*O*), hatred (*odio*) and others. The trouble is that the significances that can be released from the hieroglyph and from the word *Pasque*, are unstable, fragmentary, related only obscurely to each other and each in turn ready to release what could prove to be the infinite chains of further signs that had been feared in *IX Ecloghe*. It is this nuclear proliferation of language which the collection largely concerns itself with, the first part centring on teaching (*insegnamento*) but also, given the Italian word, on signs (*segni*), and the second on the actual *Pasque*. Cutting through both is the conviction of the grotesque failure of normal discursive language and, with greater urgency than before, the question of poetry. *La Beltà* had ended with the exhortation to free what it called 'the serene' (*il sereno*). Now the serene of poetry seems once more icily locked in itself and tragically so. 'Lume non è se non vien dal sereno / che non si turba mai' ('There is no light if it does not come from the serene / which never clouds') wrote Dante in *Paradiso* (XIX, 64–5), and Zanzotto takes this line as a focus for a poem on a literature lesson in an evening class which emblematically signifies the gap between poetry as it is in its 'serene', and ineptly consumerist and didactic readings of it. On the other hand, there is the rich density of signification in poetry which Zanzotto had mythologised in child-language and child-experience and which is not clearly separable from linguistic over-production.

In some of the longer poems Zanzotto takes the risk that the two may coincide or the one cancel the other, and makes language, as it were, pullulate or ovulate. Words stream out in a way that is not quite nonsensical, with some of the sound qualities of *petél*, Zanzotto's baby-talk, and with continual suggestions (especially in the impossibly titled *Pasqua di maggio, Easter in May*) of the themes of birth, eggs, linguistic creation, the emergence of being. But it is a discursive poem which is probably, in the strict sense of the word, the most memorable in the collection. *La Pâsqua à Pieve di Soligo* was written according to Zanzotto's note to the poem in homage to Blaise Cendrars' *Les Pâques à New York*, and, like that poem, it centres on the clash between the traditional meanings of Easter and its modern reality. It is written in a 'failed' poetic form, irregular rhyming couplets of pseudo-alexandrines which re-inforce the violently negative message of the poem – that is, quite simply that Easter, re-birth, language, humanity have been defeated by savagery, rubbish and deceit and that there is no solution.

> e certo dovrei spegnermi e risorgere (rhetorice) col Che
> oggi, signore, prima ben prima che con te;
>
> anche se, mulo, non fido . . .
>
> che vuoi? Va' in analisi, chiunque tu sia, prima di morire per
> me indegno o troppo degno, non saprei, vedi te:
>
> (And sure I ought to fade out and rise up (rhetorically) with

Che / before, well before with you, my lord, today; / even if,
mulish, I doubt . . . / well? Get yourself analysed, whoever
you are, before you die for me / whether I'm worthy or
unworthy I can't say, it's up to you:)

It is a mark of Zanzotto's seriousness that he refuses to make this
remarkable poem a culminating poem in the volume. It is
negative, and in *Codicillo* (*Codicil*), the poem following, he
negates it.

> No, non è vero, più semplice e amico è l'impegno
> qui con umani con divinità.

(No, it's not true, more simple and friendly is the engaging /
here with humans with divinities).

More simple but also it appears more difficult. *Pasque*, unlike *La
Beltà*, ricochets between its alternatives, rather than fuses them.

Since *Pasque* Zanzotto has written some poetry which is more
recognisably 'simple' and 'friendly'. This is the poetry he has
written in dialect, using sometimes the regional dialect (Venetian)
and sometimes the restricted dialect of Pieve di Soligo, although in
both cases Zanzotto has felt free to mix antiquated, present and
neologistic forms as he thinks fit. The adoption of dialect may
seem a curious move which risks reducing the already small
number of poetry readers, since most Italians would find his
language almost as difficult to make sense of as French or Spanish
without the translations and notes that Zanzotto has usually added.
On the other hand the sophisticated reader of *La Beltà* and *Pasque*
may well be surprised by the simplicity of what has been
cumberously deciphered, even disappointed by its lack of bite.

Yet the project is in fact coherent with his previous work, as
Zanzotto himself has made clear. The impulse to write in dialect
came from Fellini, who wanted some verse in Venetian for the
Italian version of his *Casanova*. This verse was to be used for scenes
showing archetypal female figures – the failed attempt to raise the
head of the goddess at the beginning of the film and later the
encounter with the Venetian giantess in London – and Fellini
hoped that it might have some of the sound qualities and
connotations that he found in the *petèl* which Zanzotto had used in
his *Elegia* (as mentioned above), but that it would be in a more or
less intelligible form of the dialect, though not necessarily one that
had ever been spoken. Zanzotto delivered the two chants as Fellini

requested (he said that somehow they already existed) and went on to write a long, discursive poem entitled *Filò* – a dialect word meaning according to Zanzotto 'a peasant evening in company in the stables in winter but also an interminable disquisition that serves to pass the time and nothing else' (*Filò*, 58n). His own *Filò* talks about the cinema, the earth as mother and destroyer (as shown by the earthquakes which in 1976 had just occurred in neighbouring Friuli) and about dialect. Since then have followed at intervals a variety of dialect poems largely about the countryside as it was and about friends and relations from Zanzotto' childhood.

As this chronological summary may suggest, turning to dialect is for Zanzotto a return to a language close to *petél*. As he says in *Filò*, it still has 'in its savour a drop of Eve's milk' ('tu a inte'l tó saor / un s'cip de lat de la Eva'). To write in it is not easy but it is once again to return to, or at least towards, another figuration of the mother who haunts all his poetry, and to another figuration of childhood. Dialect, Zanzotto explains in an essay appended to *Filò*, is for him as for most Italians who are bi-lingual the primary language which has been repressed by the 'official' language, which, inevitably, was learned later. Although literatures have existed in dialect which have imposed some degree of rigidity on them, to remove the weight of Italian is to release a language which is continuously shifting; horizontally any one dialect merges with other contiguous dialects, and vertically it reaches back into the infinite past. It does so because 'it is laden with the vertigo of the past, of the mega-centuries in which language has extended, infiltrated, subdivided and re-composed itself, in which it has died and risen again' (*Filò*, 91). It is a language which both for the race and for the individual, stretches back to a time before writing, before grammar, even before language became a communicative system, a time of 'orality, oracularity, minimal oratory', which at its extremity touches on the biological existence of the individual and the prehistory of humanity. But instead of what might have seemed a desert of vast eternity, Zanzotto finds in the traces of the endless past which dialect rehearses, connections with the majority – the individual, unassuming, unpowerful humanity, lost to official history as to the official language, but which has or has had (notionally) the positive values that he admires. Seen in this light dialect is the repository of real history and to be opposed to the 'imperial, definitive language' (i.e. Italian but tendentially any of the European national languages) which is almost condemned to tyrannise and to fantasise. In dialect it could or should be possible to say simple truths which are not negated by the language which says them – such is the final implication of Zanzotto's essay.

Certainly it is easy to see that at a much less ambitious level what Zanzotto is suggesting may well be true. The dialect writer in Italy takes a step towards a pre-industrial stage of literary production. To write in dialect is to refuse to manufacture a product which the publishing industry markets, and which draws the writer into the cycle that the text in an 'official' language may well pretend to oppose. The dialect writer cannot help but work with a small publishing house for a restricted readership: writer, publisher, and reader (ideally) are intimates in a village of their own which is always outside, before and against the modern metropolis.

And yet it may be that dialect poetry is only for the birds – that is, for the two or three symbolic but also somehow literal birds which, at the end of *Filò*, Zanzotto imagines to have flown away from the shooting and the massacres that all birds are subject to in Italy ('dai sbari e dal mazhelo zoladi via') and to preserve the residues of primal language, in a sense to speak it. It may be the familiar preference for a poetic inferno over a poetic paradise, but, however interesting the logic of Zanzotto's incursions into dialect, the poems themselves, with the exception of the meta-poem *Filò*, seem to me slight, even dull when they are not mystificatory or nostalgic. Perhaps they are indeed private in a way that his other poems are not, but it is hard not to sense in them a cultivated, regressive provincialism of a kind familiar in all the arts in Italy, and which in Zanzotto's case leads to the quietening of the ambiguities that his 'official' poetry dares to call out.

Yet the 'return' to dialect has its effects on Zanzotto's next major collection, *Il Galateo in bosco* (*The Galateo in the Wood*, 1978), which develops some of the suggestions of the *Filò* essay, but mostly in Italian, if with some dialect infiltrations. Once again the centre is local and historical, with prehistoric extremities, but the tone and language are closer to the more difficult parts of *Pasque*. Again, the title is an emblem, which, as in *Pasque*, Zanzotto elucidates in a note. The original *Galateo* was the famous didactic dialogue on the rules for polite social behaviour written by Giovanni Della Casa in 1552–3, when Della Casa was staying in an abbey on one of the hills near the Piave, the Montello, that is in the middle of Zanzotto's region. At that time the hills were covered in ancient woods broken only by the villas that were the retreats of the Venetian aristocracy. What remains of those woods now provide what Zanzotto sees as counterfeits of civilized repose in the form of weekend cottages. But between the Renaissance and the present there has been the tragic absurdity of the First World War, which largely destroyed the woods and turned much of the land into a cemetery, whether officially marked as such or not. According to Zanzotto, at least on the Montello, the cemeteries overlap with the Periadriatic fault in the earth's crust – as if, he seems to suggest, the war corresponded with some crack in the material base of life. From this web of suggestions and associations come the wider implications of the title. 'Galateo in Bosco (if galateos and woods do exist): the extremely fragile rules that keep symbioses and societies going, and the networks of the symbolic, ranging from language to gestures and perhaps to perception itself, balanced like spiders' webs or buried, veiled like filigrees on/in that seething succession of violent outrages which is reality.' And he goes on to suggest that the wood is also the wood of human life and human history, especially the history of waste, sacrifice and war.

What Zanzotto says in this note gives a certain focus to the poetry in the book. Much of it has a quicksilver fluidity which, even more than was the case in previous books, prevents a pinning down of sense, as if Zanzotto is indeed trying to make something as delicate as a spider's web, if anything, something more delicate since what is suggested may only be glimpsed or sensed before it has gone – if it was there at all. Some reviewers who were sympathetic to earlier books have felt that quite often here Zanzotto has not only exceeded limits but in the poems themselves offered few clues to those who might want to follow him. The presence of the note I have just summarised (a note which is far more substantial than the notes to Zanzotto's other collections in Italian) plus a preface, or, as its author calls it 'a viaticum', by the critic Gianfranco 'Contini, are signs enough that the 'wood' of the text does not reveal its paths or clearings lightly. Yet the terms of the note, and of Contini's preface, are also the terms of the poems. Once again what is written about and the way of writing merge with each other, or emerge from each other. A great many poems, some more approachably than others, some more ironically or comically than others, turn on or return to precisely those questions of the 'wood' and the 'rules', especially the rules regulating the life of 'minor' beings, the animals and insects which live in the wood and are terrorized by a violence that refuses to go away. At their most optimistic the poems hazard the possibility of a symbiosis between 'us' and the wood, in which the two ever-changing but apparently opposed systems come together, the cost to 'us' being a surrender of our violence and an acceptance of the violence of the wood, if violence is what it is. At their most pessimistic they posit a total failure to produce anything but the lumpen, cancerous words, the product of a private mania that stifles reality, the self and of course poetry.

Somewhere between the two extremes however comes an attitude which develops from Zanzotto's approach to traditional poetry in earlier books. Instead of seeing poetry as apocalypse or as blindness, in parts of the book there is a willingness to accept the conventions (the *Galateo*) of poetry, and poetry in its bucolic, abstracted, more or less Petrarchan guise. It is a willingness which is always shot through with irony and is commonly self-mocking, but it leads to a remarkable tour-de-force. This is what Zanzotto calls a hyper-sonnet (*Ipersonetto*), consisting of fourteen sonnets each of which stands for one line in a sonnet of normal size, plus two others that act as prologue and epilogue. Zanzotto explains that it is a 'homage to those who wrote sonnets whilst dwelling in the wood', particularly the Renaissance poets, Gaspara Stampa and, once again, Giovanni Della Casa. As a homage it performs the more difficult tricks that Della Casa was capable of with rhyme and structure, but it does so in an idiom that mixes the modern and the Renaissance half-parodically, and also comes close to the incantatory nonsense of *petél*.

> Che pensi tu, che mai non fosti, mai
> né pur in segno, in sogno di fantasma,
> sogno di segno, mah di mah, che fai?
>
> Voci d'augei, di rii, di selve, intensi
> moti del niente che sé a niente plasma,
> pensier di non pensier, pensa: che pensi?

(What do you think, who never were, never / not even in sign, in dream of phantom, / dream of sign, oh of an oh, what are you doing? / / Sounds of birds, of rills, of groves, intense / movements of the nothing that shapes itself to nothing, / thought of non-thought, think: what are you thinking?)

The joke and the seriousness is that of the modern composer who produces a pastiche of Bach. But perhaps the seriousness is greater. It is in this Petrarchan nothingness or insignificance, in what for most of the time since the Second World War has been thought of as the unproductive, unhelpful aspect of Italian literature, that Zanzotto from the middle of the last decade has found (or claimed to find) the positive action of poetry. By simply refusing to accept the historical process and by withdrawing into its own world, poetry performs its historical and human role. As Zanzotto says in an essay on Petrarch (1976b), the Renaissance *littérateurs* who took Petrarch as their model may seem to do no more than ask for indulgence and a quiet life, but 'they work like termites within the structures of violence to diminish its savagery or at any rate its range and move shrewdly between two-faced truths (including linguistic ones), pseudo-acquiescence and moderate effusions of feeling, without ever really losing face.'

To take the Petrarchists as models may be a sign of desperation, or at least of minimal expectations of what poetry can be or do. And certainly Zanzotto would not be alone amongst Italian poets who over the last few years have felt that the only sane demands are impossible ones at the present time and that a going back into the neglected areas of past literature may not only be to go to ground but also to go forward. But of course the choice is not definitive: *Il Galateo* was apparently intended as the first part of a trilogy (of a sort). If they are ever completed the remaining parts will almost surely take Zanzotto into unforseen regions, though once again regions which turn out to be new configurations of recognisable terrain.

BIOGRAPHICAL NOTE

Andrea Zanzotto was born in 1921 in Pieve di Soligo, an isolated but fairly large village in the Veneto not far from Treviso. He took a degree in literature at Padua University but otherwise has lived more or less continuously in Pieve di Soligo, working for a long time as a school-teacher in a secondary school. He participated in the Resistance in the last years of the war and continued to be politically active for some years after as an independent, republican intellectual. Apart from his poetry, which has won him several important literary prizes, he has written a large number of critical articles on literature and the arts and contributed extensively on a range of cultural and sociological topics to newspapers and magazines such as *Il Giorno, Avanti!, Il Corriere della Sera* and *L'Espresso.*

BIBLIOGRAPHY

PRINCIPAL WORKS

Dietro il paesaggio, Mondadori, Milan, 1951
Elegia e altri versi, La Meridiana, Milan, 1954
Vocativo, Mondadori, Milan, 1957
IX Ecloghe, Mondadori, Milan, 1962
Sull'altopiano (racconti e prose 1942-1954), Neri-Pozza, Venice, 1964
La Beltà, Mondadori, Milan, 1968
Gli sguardi, i fatti e senhal, Bernardi, Pieve di Soligo, 1969
A che valse?, Scheiwiller, Milan, 1970
Poesie (1938-1972), ed. Stefano Agosti, Mondadori, Milan, 1973
Filò, Edizioni del Ruzante, Venice, 1976
Il Galateo in bosco, Mondadori, Milan, 1978
Fosfeni, Mondadori, Milan, 1983
Selected poetry of Andrea Zanzotto, ed. and transl. by Ruth Feldman and
    Brian Swann, Princeton University Press, Princeton, 1975

WORKS CITED

Montale, E., 'La poesia di Zanzotto', *Corriere della Sera*, 1 June 1968 (now
    in *Sulla poesia*, Mondadori, Milan, 1976, 337-40)
*Nuvoli, G., *Zanzotto*, La Nuova Italia (Il Castoro), Florence, 1979
Pasolini, P. P., 'Satura, Il pensiero perverso, La beltà', *Nuovi Argomenti*
    21 (Jan-March 1971), 17-26
Zanzotto, A., 'Il *putèl* nel poeta Noventa', in *I metodi attuali della critica
    in Italia*, edited by M. Corti and C. Segre, Einaudi, Turin, 1970, 153-8
—'Infanzie, poesie, scuoletta (appunti)', *Strumenti critici* 20, (Feb. 1973)
    52-77
—'Parole, comportamenti, gruppi', *Studi novecenteschi* 3, (July-Nov.
    1974) 207-35
—'Poesia?', *Il Verri*, 6th series, 1, (Sept. 1976) 110-3, (cited as 1976a)
—'Petrarca fra il palazzo e la cameretta', in Petrarca, *Rime*, with
    introduction and notes by G. Bezzola, Rizzoli, Milan, 1976, 5-16 (cited
    as 1976b)
—Contribution to Bertolucci, Sereni, Zanzotto, Porta, Conte, Cucchi,
    Sulla poesia: Conversazioni nelle scuole, Pratiche Editrice, Parma,
    1981, 63-107

FURTHER READING

Agosti, S., 'Zanzotto o la conquista del dire', in *Il testo poetico: teoria e
    pratiche d'analisi*, Rizzoli, Milan, 1972
Hainsworth, P., 'The poetry of Andrea Zanzotto', *Italian Studies* 37 (1982),
    101-21
Siti, W., *Il realismo dell'avanguardia*, Einaudi, Turin, 1975
Studi novecenteschi 3 (July-Nov 1974) (dedicated to Zanzotto)

John Gatt-Rutter

6 Pier Paolo Pasolini

Il Cuore Diabolico sa
che bisogna essere impopolari: qualcosa
cioè di peggio che deludere!
Bisogna dire verità impossibili (ma verità),
giocare con l'Antipatia come prima
si era giocato con la Simpatia, preparare
con sorda ironia l'ultimo Rifiuto.
                    (*Porcile. Orgia. Bestia da stile*, 270)

(The Diabolical Heart knows / you've got to be unpopular: that's / something worse than disappointing! / You've got to utter impossible truths (but still truths), / play Nasty as you'd earlier / played Nice, you've got to set up / in dead irony, your final No).

These words, which could sum up Pasolini's own career, are almost the last addressed to the fictitious Czech poet Jan, protagonist of Pasolini's play *Bestia da stile* (*Style-horse*). The Father's Ghost then appears and tells Jan that Soviet tanks will sweep into Prague in 1968. Jan replies: 'E tutto qui? Caro padre, / io son saltato giù dal carro da un pezzo, / e, oltre tutto, non per calcolo o interesse' (271: 'Is that all? Dear father, / I got off quite a while ago, / and, when all's said and done, it wasn't out of calculation or self-interest'). The play then ends with an almost symmetrically arranged series of exchanges, eight pages long, in tripping, ballad-like quatrains, between Capital and Revolution. Each claims to contain the other, possessing history, but Capital has the last word.

Bestia da stile is transposed autobiography. Jan's career as a poet involved in a revolutionary movement echoes Pasolini's. His rural Bohemia is the Friuli of Pasolini's youth; his Vltava is Pasolini's Tagliamento. Both experience Nazi occupation and the

Resistance, Jan losing his best friend Karel and Pasolini his younger brother, Guido. Pasolini's father turns into Jan's drink-sodden, Nazi-worshipping mother. The relationship between Jan and his debauched sister represents Pasolini's own split between civic poetry and obsessive sexuality. Jan himself is like enough to Pasolini to masturbate and verbalize copiously in the meadows.

This illustrates the extreme difficulty of separating Pasolini from his works – literary, theoretical, polemical or cinematic. His personality always figured more or less visibly in his artefacts, and the latter kept boomeranging back into his life. He could never help being his own *dramatis persona*, and his audience of interlocutors and persecutors never let him off the stage. Braving social and sexual taboos, outraging conservative norms and mores, attacking settled notions old and new of whatever orthodoxy – right or left, 'advanced opinion' or media consensus – Pasolini's apparent vocation was to be a thorn in everybody's side. Much of his writing, literary or journalistic, was obsessed with Italy's breakneck 'anthropological mutation' ('mutazione antropologica') from a mainly rural early capitalist economy to the advanced capitalism of the economic 'miracle' and after; with the consequent 'homogenization' (*omologazione*) of Italian society into a brave new world of petty bourgeois consumers; and with the 'cultural genocide' of at least two thirds of the Italian people who had until the 1950s retained their pre-capitalist values, especially in the South. Even sex seemed to Pasolini to have lost its authenticity and to have been turned into a consumer commodity, uncoupled from love and responsibility or even from joy – as in entertainment, in pornography and in advertising as a major means of promoting consumption.

As an artist, it was always Pasolini's way to restlessly transform, transcend and discard artistic forms and media. This essay attempts to show how within his evident thematic continuity, each remarkable advance brings a remarkable new creative 'experiment' culminating in the seven quasi-theatrical works conceived in 1966. This boldness can be seen right from his first important work, *Poesie a Casarsa* (1942), where he 'scandalously' uses Friulan dialect not for a lower but a higher stylistic register than that of literary Italian, and where an evanescent rustic Christianity is pervaded by sexuality, outside time, society, history and rational consciousness, in a quintessentially 'poetic', even animistic, world. The religious feeling has nothing to do with faith, morals or Revelation, much less the Church or the priests – not even

Christian love or any other intellectually definable value. Here are some typically elusive though deceptively simple and transparent lines from *Tal còur di un frut* (In a Boy's Heart):

> . Diu al à ciaminàt par ciera
> e sot il So piè la erba
> e sot il So piè la erba
> e Diu sot il So piè la erba.
>
> Diu al à ciaminàt tra li zemis
> e un rosignòul al sigava
> e un rosignòul al sigava
> e a sigavin i rosignoj.

(God has walked the earth / and under His foot the grass / and under His foot the grass / and God under His foot the grass. // God has walked among the tender shoots / and a nightingale called / and a nightingale called / and the nightingales were calling.)

An incantatory, dream-like atmosphere, a tenuous musicality, a luminous rustic freshness are to the fore. Other poems are filled with sweet sinful innocence, frequently associated with a young boy's death. The Friuli and lyricism are associated with the mother, they form an unthinking womb in which Pasolini buries his delicate sensibilities.

A sensuously apprehended metaphysic and a scandalous sexuality were thus Pasolini's first literary keynotes, and he was never to forsake them. As for his exquisite sensibility with words, rhythms and images, his poetic and formal artistry, his aestheticism and irrationalism as of a latter-day *faux naif* decadent – these were to be variously suppressed or transcended, to conflict or to co-exist with new and opposing elements in an increasingly anguished dialogue. In republishing his Friulan poems in *La nuova gioventù* (*Today's Youth*) over thirty years later, Pasolini added bitter new versions of the original poems, sardonic epitaphs on his now vanished 'poetic country', the Friuli. Those thirty years had seen Italy transformed. The new *Ploja fòur di dut* (*Rain Outside All*) reverses the tenor of the original poem:

> Spirt di frut, a plòuf il Sèil
> tai spolers di un muàrt país,
> tal to vis di merda e mèil
> pluvisin a nas un mèis.

Il soreli blanc e lustri
sora asfàlt e ciasis novis,
al ti introna, e fòur di dut
no i ta às pí amòur pai muàrs.

Spirt di frut, al rit il Sèil
ta un país sensa pí fun,
tal to vis di pis e fèil,
mai nassút, al mòur un mèis.

(Boy-spirit, Heaven rains / upon the hearths of a dead
village: / in your face of shit and honey / a rainy month is
being born. // The sun is white and gleaming / over asphalt
and new homes: / it stuns you and, outside all, / you've no
love left for the dead. // Boy-spirit, Heaven's smiling / upon
a village that has no smoke left: / in your face of piss and gall,
/ a month is dying that was never born.)

The poems Pasolini wrote in Italian between 1943 and 1949
(published in 1958 as the collection *L'usignolo della Chiesa
Cattolica, The Nightingale of the Catholic Church*) already show
not only remarkable versatility, but an almost disdainful ease and
profusion. Pasolini uses Italian from the first to range outside the
intensely 'pure' poetic of his Friulan. Some are genuinely and
deliberately prosaic prose-poems, others extend poetic discourse
uninhibitedly and in the most unorthodox ways – empirical or
fantastic – into religious iconography, liturgy, evangelism, sex,
statuary, panoramic vistas, history – but I could go on listing
categories without giving any idea of the poet's capacity for
unpredictable stylistic syntheses. Pasolini clearly knew what he
was talking about when in the 1950s (see Chapter 1, p. 27) he
attacked poetic style ('lingua per poesia'), however versatile, as a
prison, utterly and irredeemably isolated from reality,
corresponding to the poet's 'inner world' which isolates him from
the 'outer world' of other people. So, while the poems of
L'usignolo express Pasolini's devious dealings with Christianity
and his 1949 'discovery of Marx' (though the section so entitled
consists of tiny gems which are *least* indicative of the poetic lava-
flow which Pasolini's newfound Marxist consciousness set off), it
is really their sheer stylistic guile rather than any 'ideas' in them
that hints at Pasolini's future impudence in experiment, his
readiness to take on the whole world in words on the most
unfavourable terms.

The novel *Il sogno di una cosa (The Dream of Something)* belongs to the same period as *L'usignolo* but the version eventually published seems like a joke. In the first place it is a narrative joke in that it falls into five segments unconnected except by the friendship between a group of young Friulan Communist peasants. After the introductory segment showing the group at their rude and rustic merry-making, the next two show them as temporary emigrants, three of them in Yugoslavia and one in Switzerland. In the fourth they are participants in the 1949 agitation by unemployed peasants, and the fifth switches to the girls of a churchy family, variously destined for marriage, widowhood or nunnery. Pasolini uses an idiomatic variant of book-Italian echoing the dialect in which tales would be swapped among the participants themselves. The book also reads like an ideological joke, a tense political issue seen through the eyes of irreverent victims. Sentimentality is the price Pasolini pays for sympathy with his characters. Life, even poverty, is an adventure. Political consciousness is hardly an issue: sympathy and the simple fact of poverty apparently make the choice of communism self-evident, though the religious Faedis family represent a hardly less attractive alternative than Communism. The focussing on an adolescent group, the loose polycentric narrative, the colloquial tone, the presumption of sympathy and the unreflectingness of the protagonists were all to be paralleled at a far more serious level in Pasolini's *Ragazzi di vita (The Ragazzi, 1955)*.

This second novel came after a time of shock and stigma. Pasolini was charged with obscene behaviour, expelled from his post as a schoolteacher and dismissed as local Communist Party secretary. He moved to Rome and his habitat became the tenements and shanties on the edges of the city. No fresh country youths here: Rome's sub-proletarians are born stale, offspring of a warped and soiled environment, neither town nor country. In the Eternal City's eternal - but specifically twentieth-century - poverty, adventure has turned infernal. Thieving, scrounging, card-sharping, prostituting themselves to homosexuals, these youngsters try any ruse except work (which isn't usually available anyway) to get money - only, in most cases, to have it bullied or tricked out of them in their turn. Appalling deaths dictate the rhythm of the narrative. In 'Il Riccetto', Riccetto's mother and his friend Marcello are victims of the collapse of their tenement block. The thug Amerigo dies a lingering self-inflicted death after being arrested in 'Nottata a Villa Borghese' ('A Night at Villa Borghese').

The boy Piattoletta is baited by his friends and playfully burnt at the stake in 'Il bagno sull'Aniene' ('Bathers in the Aniene'). Alduccio, driven beyond endurance, goes berserk and stabs his scolding mother to death in 'Dentro Roma' ('Inside Rome'). And, in the concluding 'La commare secca' ('Death'), Riccetto, almost as casually as he had rescued a drowning swallow in the opening 'Il ferrobedò' ('Ferrobedò'), sees his young friend Genesio drown. Genesio had just announced to his younger brothers that when they were grown up they would kill their unbearable father.

It is the character of Riccetto, weaving in and out of the narrative, that holds these episodes loosely together, and his career anticipates in germ that of Tommaso Puzzilli in the more consecutive *Una vita violenta (A Violent Life,* 1959). This has the same overwhelming, appallingly detailed portrait of the Roman waste-land and its low life, the same predominance of the crude vernacular in the writing, the same lack of awareness within the characters of either self or society, beyond that of the sheer need to survive. But there is a more determined—yet ambiguous—effort to present the emblematic career of a Roman slum boy. From petty thieving and Fascist thuggery, Tommaso is led through a sort of education in social values. He emerges from a spell in prison to find a municipal apartment awaiting him. Full of his own newfound respectability, he seeks clienthood with the Christian Democrat establishment. Then experience of a labour dispute and police repression while he is being treated for tuberculosis in hospital leads him to join the Communist Party. He dies after saving a woman in a flood.

This may sound like exemplary Marxist progress towards becoming politically conscious and a positive hero, but there is not much constructive consciousness in *Una vita violenta.* More than was Riccetto, Tommaso is increasingly tempted by the consumerist utopia of home, family and a steady job—security and respectability. Even before the economic miracle was properly under way, Pasolini seems to have sensed that Italy was moving in that direction and, rather than let Tommaso follow, gave him an edifying death, avoiding the issue.

No wonder that, while the Catholic establishment abhorred and persecuted Pasolini, the Communists found him suspect. His heart seemed to be more with the Roman riff-raff and their anarchic amoralism than with the organized working class where his political loyalties lay. While displaying poverty and squalor in his writing as an indictment of a vicious power-system, he seemed to regard them almost lovingly as the precondition for an instinctual human authenticity, as if a settled livelihood within the new capitalist (or even communist) order were more dehumanizing than guaranteed misery. The same impression emerges from the stories collected in *Alì dagli occhi azzurri (Blue-eyed Ali)* but written around the end of the 1950s: 'Accattone', 'Mamma Roma', 'Mignotta' ('Whore'), 'La notte brava' ('Crazy night'), 'La ricotta' ('Cheese') and others – many of them made into films – are film-scripts as literature, bare dialogues, uncompromisingly cast in the slang of Roman low life. Here the dizzy wheeling of fortune and the fantastic, deadly gaiety of Pasolini's desperadoes always eventually crystallize as fatalities combining tragedy with squalor, pathos and grandeur.

This was not what the Italian literary left meant by Neo-realism. Pasolini's ultra-realism in dialogue, description and narrative is highly selective. He never dignified the workers or the bourgeoisie with empirical representation. His 'experiments' crashed through the notion of Neo-realism. Astoundingly self-aware and articulate, Pasolini admitted his gut-attachment to the unselfconscious populace, the sub-proletariat, rather than the people in their conscious historic role. He declares his 'oscuro scandalo della coscienza' ('obscure scandal of conscience') addressing the ashes of Gramsci in the long poem and book of that title (*Le ceneri di Gramsci*, 1957):

> Lo scandalo del contraddirmi, dell'essere
> con te e contro te; con te nel cuore,
> in luce, contro te nelle buie viscere:
>
> del mio paterno stato traditore
> – nel pensiero, in un'ombra d'azione –
> mi so ad esso attaccato nel calore
>
> degli istinti, dell'estetica passione;
> attratto da una vita proletaria
> a te anteriore, è per me religione
>
> la sua allegria, non la millenaria
> sua lotta: la sua natura, non la sua
> coscienza . . .

(The scandal of contradicting myself, of being / with you and against you; with you in my heart, / in the light, against you in the darkness of my guts; / traitor to my paternal state / – in thought, in a shadow of action –/ I know I cling to it in the heat / of instinct, of my aesthetic passions; / drawn to a proletarian life / from before your time, my religion / is its gaiety, not its age-old / struggle: its nature, not its / consciousness . . .)

Le ceneri di Gramsci – and most of his subsequent poetry – dramatizes in Pasolini's own person the ambiguities and contradictions of our contemporary human condition: the conflicting pulls of atavistic instinct and forward-looking project; of tradition, of nostalgia for a vanishing rural and provincial past, and a motorized, cosmopolitan, affluent society; nature and history; the private and the public; *popolo*, the unreflecting populace, and *partito*, the party or the organized working class. This collection of poems and the three following represent an extraordinarily rich articulation of this difficult material. The first person singular – the real Pier Paolo Pasolini, down to the shirt he is wearing and the troublesome contents of his trousers – is always the centre of consciousness of his poetry, probing itself as a locus of the contradictions of Italian society while showing us, in massive discursive-descriptive poems, the grandeur and misery of Italy in historical zooms, geographical panoramas, animated scenes of Italian urban life (especially Rome's teeming outskirts). Other poems are satirical epistles or epigrams, vigorously colloquial, yet culturally and intellectually sophisticated.

So Pasolini brings about the most important innovation in Italian poetry for over a quarter of a century by involving it, desperately, with the real world and by making extended discourse once again possible, demolishing the poetic prison of hermetic first-person poetry. Systematically and repeatedly he desecrates the prison-house of language so that it cannot look like a holy shrine. He makes poetry as impure as possible, and his poetic achievement lies in turning his own eloquence and proven virtuosity (the 'estetica passione' of the poem to Gramsci) against themselves. First of all, he made rational enquiry the heart of his poetic enterprise – especially when 'reason' itself, and the irrational and pre-rational, were the object of that enquiry. The 'impure' language of discourse, as well as that of everyday phenomena and experience even at their most sordid or shameful, thus rules his poetry and makes it hard to distinguish from prose. Verbal bravura – whether descriptive or analytical, evocative or witty – is thrown off almost tongue-in-cheek, as deliberate pastiche or kitsch, and devalued by the underlying urgency of the inquisitorial stance, which may be sardonic but is never cold.

Prosodic skills are no less deliberately thrown away. In the 1950s Pasolini wrote mostly in tercets of rhyming couplets or blank verse. But rhyme, rhythm and syllabic count all become more and more loose as Pasolini's delicate ear guards against the acoustic prison-walls of style. He moves towards an ever more anarchic form of free verse, which becomes his *only* verse-medium after *Poesia in forma di rosa (Poem in the Form of a Rose)* of 1964 (apart from the palinodes of *La nuova gioventù*). All this makes Pasolini's an extensive rather than an intensive style with a corresponding breadth of reference or socio-historical allusiveness, so that it does not lend itself to localized sampling and analysis under a critical magnifying-glass, but could be adequately treated only in a separate essay. Something of its character can, however, be gauged from the quotations given in this essay as illustrations of thematic points.

The interval between *Poesia in forma di rosa* and the last book of new poems, *Trasumanar e organizzar (To be Transfigured, to Organize*, 1971), is filled by plays, films and militant journalism. *Bestia da stile*, with which I opened, is one of six plays which, together with the quasi-novel *Teorema (Theorem)*, Pasolini began in April 1966 while convalescing from a stomach ulcer. The other five are *Calderón, Pilade (Pylades)*, *Affabulazione (Your Life as Fable)*, *Porcile (Pigsty)*, *Orgia (Orgy)*. *Teorema* – book and film – came out in 1968. A modified *Porcile* was filmed in 1969. *Calderón* was published in 1973. Pasolini went on tinkering with all the plays except *Calderón* until his death, but even those which never reached definitive forms can be read as organic and complete works.

The works conceived in 1966 have been on the whole neglected, but, despite the great abundance and richness of the rest of Pasolini's extremely varied output, they are a kind of summation of his long and tumultuous endeavour to communicate with himself and the world, and collectively fill a crucial gap in his crowded career. His poetry, however open and 'impure', remained, as monologue, imprisoned within the form of direct discourse. The same applied to his numerous cultural and theoretical essays, beginning with those published in the Bologna journal of the later 1950s, jointly edited by Pasolini, Fortini, Roversi and Leonetti and pointedly entitled *Officina (Workshop)*. His polemical journalism, too, though it won the attention of a much wider readership, was still limited to a first-person delivery. His narrative fiction was in its different way limited by a localized plebeian language and the outlook and experience that went with it. In order to communicate more directly with all his fellow-Italians (and others), Pasolini turned to the cinema. Here, the first person singular could disappear and the medium provided fertile creative opportunities which Pasolini abundantly exploited: but it also placed constraints on the messages that could be conveyed, and was more readily exploited in the interests of induced consumption and socialization (entertainment and edification) – the very things Pasolini was fighting against – than popular enlightenment. Impressive as his achievements were in all these fields, Pasolini evidently felt that they could not adequately enact *the* central drama of our time.

In his 'nuovo teatro', on the other hand, Pasolini was able to get his own person out of the way (or at least distance it in autobiographically based characters) and directly dramatize the workings of blood and brain, religion and capital, power and the sexual-existential self, bourgeois alienation and historical processes, revolution and modernization. The forms he invented enabled him both to verbalize and, at one and the same time, to enact abstract issues while firmly rooting them but not *limiting* them to their specific empirical (i.e. historical) circumstances. He freed himself from naturalism or realism without escaping into Surrealism or the Absurd or subjectivism. Rather he struggled to retain and share with the reader a rational control – no matter how problematic and elusive – of the real world and of the historical moment and of the literary artefact itself and of language as a communicative last resource. His language and conceptual framework remain, if anything, over-explicit, even peremptory and reductive. Many startling and baffling things in the plays defy the limits of theatre; the plays are disconcerting and paradoxical in both development and conclusion. And yet the reader is always aware of a purposeful, questing, transforming, shaping mind that does not attempt the aesthetic disappearing act of hiding its intentions but carries the dynamic of this very peculiar strain of drama through its own unfolding.

The final dialogue between Capital and Revolution in *Bestia* illustrates this naked dramatization of the author's conceptual categories and points to some of the anti-theatrical audacities of the 1966 plays: it is a stand-up debate between personifications identifiable only as named. Even more extreme is the sequence of ballad-like utterances, ten pages long, in Episode II, by a whole procession of 'characters', singly or in groups, thirty-four in all, beginning with Penumbra, Sense of Penumbra, Charon, The Rustic World, The Ante Literam, and Bisons, and including various groups of Bureaucrats (Orthodox or Heterodox), various tradesmen, a succession of more or less obscure (named) sociologists, Fate, A Mother, The Ravens of Fate, The Year 1938 and Humanism.

As if this were not enough, the play consists almost entirely of monologues, often many pages long, many of them addressed to a silent Jan. The logic of this is spelled out by the Chorus (villagers of Semice, or ordinary Czech citizens) in Episode VI. Their 'religion of revolution' makes them unaware – so they say! – that all dialogue is impossible: 'Nothing: we say nothing at all. / And so, this act of the tragedy / can't consist of anything else than two monologues: / the workers' monologue, / and the poet's monologue / – one after another.' (240–1). Which also illustrates Pasolini's anti-naturalist scripting: the Chorus directly state their unconscious and define the literary artefact of which they are a substantive part. Earlier they had defined themselves as peasants unaware of their own presumption of an unchanging world; later (after the revolution), they say they are petty bourgeois unaware of being such. The playwright thus paradoxically uses unselfconscious characters to make explicit their own historical transformation. Characters in other plays similarly define themselves in terms of Pasolini's analytical and critical categories as they could not do in the real world. Pasolini's quest for reality thus brushes realism contemptuously aside.

The same Chorus open the play with a comment on the verse-medium used: 'Versi senza metrica / Intonati da una voce che mente onestamente / Vengono destinati / A rendere riconoscibile / L'irriconoscibile / / Liberi versi non-liberi / Ornano qualcosa che non può essere che disadorno.'(197: 'Verse without metre / Intoned by a voice that tells honest lies / Is meant / To make recognizable what is unrecognizable / / Free verse without freedom / Adorns something which can only be unadorned'). This both defines and exemplifies the style of all the plays, as well as that of most of Pasolini's verse from the 1960s onwards, including the verse-sections of *Teorema*. It is a verse barely distinguishable – except typographically – from the drabbest prose: yet, as in the passages so far quoted, it is a language subtly heightened by paradoxical word-play or wit, by verbal economy, by elusive rhythms cunningly counterpointed against the Italian reader's conditioned reflex to the flow and ebb of such classic measures as the hendeca- and heptasyllable. It is in fact a style which hides considerable muscle, capable of relating, as in these plays, bed-linen with metaphysics, meadows with sado-masochism, Spinoza and a piggery, gas-chambers with Velazquez. It is a synthetic style in both senses of the adjective. It is prose enough to adhere to anything, appropriating it; poetry enough to estrange and alienate. As such it is a prime instrument of the 'teatro di parola' theorized in Pasolini's 'Manifesto per un nuovo teatro' ('Manifesto for a New Theatre', 1968), dramatic work envisaged to be read rather than staged, and read only by a select few – revolution-conscious 'gruppi avanzati della borghesia' ('advanced groups of the bourgeoisie'). The plays offer the producer a formidable challenge and have rarely been performed.

As modern Mystery Plays they are effective on the page, and even weirdly theatrical. All variously pit the self – reason and libido – against contemporary history from the Nazi horror to what Pasolini saw as the New Nazism, the totalitarianism, of consumer homogenization. The 'Manifesto' demanded an open-ended drama, and these plays in fact fail to sustain free selfhood against this historical process or any facile political perspective. Whilst their *meaning* is always predetermined by the very conceptual categories which they dramatize and verbalize (as in Christian works like the Miracle and Mystery Plays and Dante's *Divine Comedy*), those concepts themselves, as will be seen, are subject to dramatic and dialectical transformation.

All the 1966 works are precisely located in history within the contemporary bourgeois hegemony. *Affabulazione* and *Orgia* dramatize bourgeois familial sexuality, in deliberately generic abstraction. Characters are simply called Father, Mother, Son, Girl-Friend. They lack individual identity or psychology and are only abstractly and generically related to the wider world. (In *Porcile* Julian and Ida make a game out of the interchangeability of names and identities). Contemporary history therefore broods over these plays (like God in the Mystery cycles) mainly in its abstractness – a condition (bourgeois or petty-bourgeois) which irremediably defines the characters. And, apart from their sexuality, it is the *only* thing that defines them.

Porcile bears more directly on the specifics of history. Two rival German industrialists – Klotz, from an old-established dynasty, and Herdhitze, who came up through the Nazi system – are trying to blackmail each other. Herdhitze has Nazi crimes to hide, while the skeleton in Klotz's cupboard is that his son Julian mates with pigs. Klotz and Herdhitze agree on a merger, while Julian, after meeting Spinoza (representing Reason, which, in rationalizing God, has explained itself away) in a pigsty, is devoured (off-stage) by his pigs. The Italian immigrant farm-workers report to Herdhitze that not a trace of him is left, not even a button. Herdhitze's reply closes the play: 'Allora, sssssst! Non dite niente a nessuno.' ('Then – shhhhhh! Don't say a thing to a soul.') Julian, the authentic, unassimilated individual, has dropped away and the new phase of capitalism is secure in its suppression of the truth.

Porcile is the closest Pasolini cares to come to a conventionally 'well-made' play, with mannered, tongue-in-cheek dialogue, interaction between characters, and slyly linear plot. Yet it displays Pasolini's direct and spontaneous moral sense. The shock of living under Nazi-Fascism in Northern Italy in 1943 and 1944 and the horror of the death-camps do not lose any of their sharpness and conviction in his repeated treatments of the motif, even when, as in *Porcile*, they are obliquely and almost flippantly referred to. Pasolini deliberately interweaves this sense of moral outrage with a display of scandalous sexuality in which guilt and glory are combined in varying proportions from play to play. In *Porcile*, Julian's proud secret is a direct response to the values of his father's world which reach their apotheosis in the deal with Herdhitze. By it he asserts his 'difference' like Pasolini himself and his other protagonists. Julian neither obeys nor disobeys, but loves pigs, unlike the sons of other fathers, who either obey or disobey but, either way, conform and comply with history. Even in protest they serve the dialectic of capitalist progress.

History holds the stage as analogue in *Pilade*. This is Pasolini's sequel to the Oresteian trilogy of Aeschylus (which he had translated). The judgement of the new goddess Athene has sanctioned the bourgeois democratic revolution which Orestes has brought to Argos in the name of justice, reason, progress and economic growth and change (industrial revolution) against the dark, atavistic, irrational forces of tradition (religion and Fascism), represented by the Furies, who have now been tamed, integrated into Orestes' new order and given an honourable but subordinate position as Eumenides, consolers. This is in keeping with the spirit of Aeschylus and with the historical reality of Periclean Athens, but viewed sardonically. Orestes identifies Athene with metropolitan Capital: '. . . her worship / doesn't require secluded shrines far out amid the fields: / she dwells rather in market-places, squares, / banks, schools, stadiums, harbours, / factories'; and he dwells at great length on the peculiarity of Athene's birth straight from her father's brow without gestation in a mother's womb. So he concludes: 'No memory of the impotent flesh / has been deposited within her, then. / She has no memories: / all she knows is reality. / What she knows – that is the world.' (*Affabulazione. Pilade*, 121–3).

The Chorus of citizens of Argos open Episode II with a description of Athene's industrial revolution, and Episode VIII, bringing the historical process up to date, eloquently describes the 'economic miracle' or 'modernization' of the Second Industrial Revolution:

> In a short space of time – overnight! – the city grew / more than it had grown through all the centuries / of its existence. Work bore sudden fruit. / Towering buildings, factories, bridges sparkled / with bright materials never seen before. New / technologies were born. / The character of everyday life altered. / It seemed as if it weren't so much a new idea of man / as a new idea of life / had got into people's heads.

Pylades, who had helped his friend Orestes carry through his revolution in the name of Athene and Reason, now, to the scandal of the Chorus, leads the peasants and workers in another revolution, this time against Orestes and the capitalist order which he embodies. Reason has turned against Reason. New historical configurations follow as Orestes makes a succession of compromises with Electra, who has remained attached to the old dark cult of the Furies. These are analogues to Italy's successive Fascist and Christian Democrat periods. Against these configurations, Pylades stands out as 'la Diversità fatta carne' ('Difference made flesh': 145) – parallel to Jan in *Bestia*.

And with this parallel between Pylades and Jan we approach something central in Pasolini's consciousness. Jan's Sister in Episode VIII of *Bestia* accuses her brother of having extruded his sexual compulsion upon her when he opted for the role of civic poet. With the Revolution achieved, its shortcomings and disappointments necessitate a reintegration of Jan's nature, divided between himself and his Sister, the civic and the sexual. She asserts: 'So we are one and the same Person / (Dissociation is the structure of structures: / the Split of one character into two / is the greatest of literary inventions). / I have taken upon myself the shameful role / and left the glorious one to you.' (*Porcile. Orgia. Bestia da stile*, 268-9).

Analogously, Pylades, carrying on his revolution in the name of something that is civic and rational, comes up against the instinctual and the sexual within himself, the dark urge that will not be denied. This - if I interpret Pasolini correctly - is not irrational, but pre-rational. To suppress it in the name of civilized progress (as Freud demanded) is to distort our own nature, sublimating a false and mutilated Reason and erecting a corrupt and mystified civilization whose real name is Power. Pylades - as Pasolini himself often does - begins to doubt his own sincerity, and his reintegration comes only in Episode VII when he 'scandalously' falls in love with his opposite, Electra, with a passion in which spirit and flesh are one (211-9). Through various historical configurations, the sophistries and contradictions underlying the 'Reason' for which Orestes stands are gradually brought to light. Athene, in defining her own function to Orestes, suddenly appears to lose her voice (190), but then gives a horrifically graphic and detailed 'HUMOROUS DESCRIPTION' (Pasolini's emphasis) of the dismembered and chopped up limbs and organs of a boy being boiled in a pot - symbolic of the obscene sacrifices demanded by Reason as it takes the world into a 'new Pre-history' (another of Pasolini's recurrent notions, hinting at the hideous repression of the struggling peoples of the Third World) (195-7). The circle is complete as Reason becomes synonymous with barbarism. Pylades abjures Athene: 'YOU, REASON, ARE ALWAYS AND ONLY SOLACE' (Pasolini's emphasis). Reason, he now realizes, is but a rationalization of Power: 'But, in listening to you, I've struggled for nothing else / but to seize power! / And now I know that that is the guiltiest of guilts. / The mere idea of seizing power / (even if it isn't on one's own behalf) / is the guiltiest of guilts . . .' (236-8).

The other plays focus not on the protagonists of bourgeois revolution as such, but on bourgeois individuals seen as victims of the power they themselves sustain. *Affabulazione* and *Orgia* show the bourgeois and petty-bourgeois condition as irremediable. The repressed instinctual and sexual levels can only destroy those who attempt to release them. The Father in *Affabulazione* has a dream of God ('Our Father, Who art in Heaven') and is set in turmoil by the impulsive need for existential - that is, sexual - sharing with his Son. The Ghost of Sophocles informs him that the Son is a mystery beyond the reach of Reason, his life to be contemplated as a theatrical performance rather than possessed in the way the Father is impelled to possess it. The Father consults a Fortune-Teller, whose crystal ball shows him among other Fathers planning thermonuclear war and – as is in the nature of bourgeois fathers – the sacrifice of their own sons. The Father then has a lascivious vision of the pitiful naked victims of the Nazi extermination camps before he stabs his own son to death.

The Prologue to *Orgia* also refers to Auschwitz as a product of the petty-bourgeoisie gone mad. It is a long monologue delivered by the protagonist who, now that he has hanged himself, is able to explain the tragedy of his own one-dimensional petty-bourgeois existence. He has enjoyed the perfect freedom of utter conformity by serving the interests of power and avoiding all issues of conscience, commitment of any kind. The play re-enacts the process that has led him to his suicide. Petty-bourgeois neurosis – nostalgia for the lost innocence of the rural past and for a world of meaningful communication – leads husband and wife to try the natural language of the body but produces only the perversions of sado-masochism and fetishism. Repression exacts its revenge: the wife drowns her children and kills herself; the husband, left alone, tortures a prostitute before hanging himself.

These two bourgeois tragedies, like *Teorema*, contemptuously ignore such bourgeois conventions as 'realism', 'psychology' or 'morality'. For the empirical self (the 'individual') of bourgeois tradition, Pasolini substitutes the anthropological *person*, the Everyman or Everywoman underlying the empirical contingencies that condition and constrain each human existence in each specific human situation. *Calderón* shows Everywoman's transformations across a series of different social situations, dazzlingly exploiting an idea from *Life is a Dream* by Calderón. Pasolini's Rosaura wakes up three times to three different realities in Franco's Spain in 1967–8, each of which she experiences as a dream. Each time she fails to recognize, or rejects, her surroundings and society and insists that she belongs to some other time or place. The first time, she awakes as daughter to the upper-class Don Basilio and Doña Lupe; the second time, as a prostitute in a Barcelona slum; the third time, as a middle-class housewife married to Basilio, when her 'maladjustment' has turned into aphasia. Throughout Rosaura resists attempts to socialize her by psychotherapy or the Church.

In each case she is in love with an upper-class revolutionary: first the cultured and sophisticated Sigismondo, who, we learn, is her real father; second the teenage rebel Pablo, who feels himself a predestined outcast, labelled by society 'Virgin, pederast and bastard', and who turns out to be her son; third Enrique, one of the revolutionaries of 1968.

As ever, Pasolini has no interest in a representation of bourgeois living. His characters act out a critique of their condition. Rosaura is the naive subject, the victim of the depersonalizing pressure towards conformity. The rebels or quasi-rebels, Sigismondo, Manuel the psychotherapist, Pablo and Enrique – whether worldly-wise, opportunistic or idealistic – provide a critical discourse that can be absorbed and exploited by the power-system and turned to account in perfecting its own evolution. This is the real theme of the play. Not only does the power-system incorporate every individual into itself, but it engenders its own internal antitheses in order to achieve a new, more advanced configuration, more perfect in its appropriation of the whole of human reality.

Basilio (whose name in Greek means 'king') continuously ordains people's 'dreams' (that is, their reality) from the other side of the looking-glass through his allegorical agents Melainos and Leucos ('black' and 'white'). The representatives or adherents of Power themselves define the situation – its origins, its process, its final goal. Rosaura's sister Stella defines her father Basilio as a burgeoning neo-capitalist: 'Yes, we are rich, Rosaura, our father / owns round about Madrid enough land / to build another Madrid; and building / plots go up in price day / by day; time is working for us; / innovations, however opposed / to our habits, increase our capital.' (14). Doña Lupe's friend, Doña Astrea, after dwelling on the advantages of being Catholics and the therapeutic value of confession, remarks: ' . . . but we're bourgeois, too, / (I mean in culture, as our blood / is patrician and feudal, while it pleases God)' – and recommends Freud. Lupe remarks that Himmler would have done well to exterminate that ignoble Jew along with all the rest. Astrea reproves her: such sentiments must be dissimulated under the forthcoming liberal-industrial consensus of the post-Franco era (22–3).

All this is elegantly articulated in extended discourse – defiantly and drily sociological and contrary to naturalistic verisimilitude – which figures also slyly in *Porcile* and wryly in *Teorema* and which holds *Calderón* together. Characters repeatedly view themselves in a sociological mirror, and the mirror becomes a controlling image of the play. The Speaker introduces the second chorus stanza by explaining that the following scene is to be understood as set within the frame of the mirror within which Velasquez painted *Las Meninas*. The effect is to reinforce the theme of the continuity of Power through its various historical transformations, for the scene shows Basilio and Lupe as King and Queen (vainly) urging Rosaura to confess her guilty love and conform: 'Dove regna l'ordine, regna l'unicità. / E l'unicità ci da la più grande delle consolazioni: / quella di vivere realmente la vita.' (39: 'Where order reigns, there reigns oneness. / And oneness lets us have the greatest solace of all: / that of living in reality.')

Reality is what Rosaura rejects. In her various incarnations ('dreams'), the phallus of her incestuously desired male stands, as the ultimate taboo, for the negation of reality. Her anguished and repeated howl voices the crisis of bourgeois existence in this as in all Pasolini's 1966 works.

Basilio reveals himself to be fully aware of what the bourgeoisie is about. In the concluding scene Rosaura describes a dream which, Basilio ordains, is her ultimate reality – to be one of the living skeletons in a Nazi extermination camp. As elsewhere, Pasolini stresses in Rosaura's final monologue the complicity of the victims in their own dehumanization: '. . . we are left with only one freedom: that of betraying one another. / . . . / We want to be our murderers' / foremost assistants . . .' (181).

But that is only the first part of the dream described by Rosaura. It is followed by liberation. To glorious strains of revolutionary music and the waving of red flags and neck-scarves, a great tide of workers brandishing hammers and sickles and sub-machine-guns swarms into the death-camps, restoring their inmates to health and liberty. Basilio's words end the play: 'A lovely dream, Rosaura, truly / a lovely dream. But I think / (and I'm in duty bound to tell you this) that this / is the very moment when the real tragedy begins. / Because, of all the dreams you've had or will have, / you could say they could also be realities. / But as regards this dream about the workers, there's no doubt: / it's a dream, nothing but a dream.'

Teorema can be called a novel, though only for lack of a better word. It flouts even more literary presuppositions than *Calderón*. It is described rather than narrated. The present tense is used, and the scientific procedure denoted by the title provides the framework for the whole: the opening sections are presented as 'data', and 'corollaries' and 'appendices' follow. Where the plays took theatre itself as a metaphor for existence, this work uses the theorem as a metaphor for knowledge. There is virtually no direct speech except that the bourgeois family quartet singly speak out their alienation in soliloquies couched in typically profuse Pasolinian free verse – a brilliant farrago of sex, politics and metaphysics.

The structure of *Teorema* also befits its title, being deliberately schematic. An 'angel' (as Pasolini calls the telegraph messenger) announces the arrival of a visitor to the house of a Lombardy factory-owner. The visitor, who is male and yet androgynous, with a gentle light shining in his face, comes upon the servant Emilia just as she is gassing herself in the oven. Overcome by his manner, she offers herself to him. The four members of the family likewise mate with him. He departs, but the experience he has given them shatters their bourgeois existence. Each of them fails to transcend the bourgeois condition. Paolo, the Father, after giving away his factory to the workers, strips naked in Milan railway station, 'FULL OF A QUESTION WHICH I CANNOT ANSWER' (198), ratiocinating lengthily about his howl of existential anguish. Emilia by contrast goes back to her village and turns silent saint, weeping continuously, levitating and eating nothing but nettles. She dies and is buried beneath a development site, from which her tears continue to flow as a miraculous stream of healing waters. Pasolini strenuously makes the point, both by these symbolic means and discursively through highly stylized press-conferences included in the text, that the transition from peasant society to the bourgeois order has involved the loss of the sense of the sacred.

Teorema defies any notion of either narrative or natural time. The water-meadows and poplars of Lombardy which are being encroached upon by industrial development could denote, indifferently, both at the beginning and at the end of the work, either spring or autumn, the text tells us. It also affirms that there is no significant sequence of events. There is no empirical 'before' or 'after'. Yet *Teorema* is anchored firmly in history. The 'action' takes place during the economic miracle of the 1960s, and there is a tight network of references to contemporary and recent events and personages of the 20th century, often with dates. Once again Pasolini is concerned with the analytical and conceptual categories of his own personal kind of contemporary historical anthropology, his view of the species man undergoing change, and not with psychological or existential (that is, merely individual) case-histories. His bourgeois 'characters' are object not subject for him. He uses them unceremoniously as ventriloquist's dummies –

and very loquacious ones. By contrast, the pre-bourgeois Emilia is silent.

In all the 1966 works, then, theatrical and narrative 'situations' are really a device for articulating the author's own reflections. Pasolini is thus stripping down literary conventions and revealing what every author is up to in using characters, setting and material objects to conduct his argument for him but fostering the illusion of their autonomy by dressing them up in the garb of concrete and specific individuality. Such an author is in effect conveying the super-message of individuality as his own overriding value and mode of apprehension of being. This Pasolini – particularly from 1966 onwards – refuses to do.

He presents such individuality as being itself, despite appearances, an abstraction, an inauthentic rationalization, an ideology, which suppresses the reality – especially the fleshly reality – of the human person. The terms 'individual' and 'person', in contra-distinction the one with the other, may therefore perhaps be used to interpret and define the results of Pasolini's literary works (and, I think, of his *oeuvre* as a whole). The 'individual' is seen as an interchangeable part in the machinery of production and in the manipulations of Power, whereas the unassimilated 'person' – in a sphere which, through Pasolini's successive works, grows increasingly more notional – resists the pressures of a dehumanizing 'Reason'. His 1966 works are tragic in showing that, once the bourgeois transformation has taken place, the fleshly 'person' buried in each 'individual' can emerge only at the cost of annihilation. His journalistic articles spell out the empirical evidence for this in our day-to-day history.

In our bourgeois being, we may doubt that our alienation is as terrible as Pasolini makes out, that it is any worse than that of pre-consumerist society, that our individuality is so illusory, or that Power is so cold-bloodedly in control. The totalitarianism of everyday life with its pleasures, its pressures and its compulsions, and the resulting totalitarianism of everyday people (such as ourselves) may be perhaps an imminent danger rather than a present and permanent apocalypse such as Pasolini shows us. But I remember being taken, as an uncomprehending sixth-former in the late 1950s, to a cultural exhibition at the U.S. embassy and receiving a glossy brochure entitled *Consumer Capitalism in Action* announcing economic miracles on the conveyor belt. Bretton Woods, the IMF, GATT, the World Bank were all instruments of the new economic order to which capitalism struggled to give birth after the Second World War. The miraculous era came and – too late for Pasolini – has possibly gone. With Pasolini, we, the lucky ones, may debate how or whether the human race has benefited from that miracle.

BIOGRAPHICAL NOTE

Pier Paolo Pasolini was born in Bologna in 1922. His father was an impoverished infantry officer from Ravenna, his mother a village school-teacher at Casarsa della Delizia in the Friuli. His father's military career involved the family in many moves, but Pasolini grew strongly attached to his mother's world. In 1942 he published *Poesie a Casarsa*. He escaped there from military service in 1943. In 1945 his younger brother Guido was killed by Yugoslav Communist partisans in an internal feud within the Resistance. After the war Pasolini became a teacher in Casarsa and local Communist Party secretary. In 1949 he was accused of a sexual misdemeanour, removed from his teaching post and expelled from the Party. He moved to Rome with his mother and lived in poverty for some years. The success of *Ragazzi di vita* in 1955 brought financial relief but led to a campaign of judicial prosecution for immorality, the first of many to which Pasolini was to be subject throughout his life. He was one of the founders of the journal *Officina* in 1955. *Le ceneri di Gramsci* (1957) and *Una vita violenta* (1959) confirmed his success as a writer. He produced his first feature film, *Accattone* in 1960, and went on to make a number of others, including *The Gospel according to St Matthew* (1964), *Uccellacci e uccellini* (*Hawks and Sparrows*, 1966), *Oedipus Rex* (1967), the 'Trilogy of life', based on *The Decameron*, *The Canterbury Tales* and *The Arabian Nights* (1971–74) and *Salò, or the 120 Days of Sodom* (1975). In the last four years of his life he was particularly active as a newspaper-columnist, fiercely critical of the country's social and economic system and its political leadership. He was found battered to death early on 2 November 1975 on some waste land near Fiumicino. Giuseppe Pelosi claimed to have killed Pasolini accidentally in self-defence and was convicted of manslaughter.

BIBLIOGRAPHY

PRINCIPAL WORKS

Poesie a Casarsa, Landi, Bologna, 1942. Included in *La meglio gioventù* and *La nuova gioventù* (ed. cited) (see below)

La meglio gioventù, Sansoni, Florence, 1954

Ragazzi di vita, Garzanti, Milan, 1955; (transl. E. Capouya) *The Ragazzi*, Grove Press, New York, 1968

Le ceneri di Gramsci, Garzanti, Milan, 1957. Included in *Le poesie* (ed. cited) (see below)

L'usignolo della Chiesa Cattolica, Longanesi, Milan, 1958

Una vita violenta, Garzanti, Milan, 1959; (trans. B. Kupelnick) *A Violent Life*, Garland, New York, 1978

Passione e ideologia (1948-1958), Garzanti, Milan, 1960

La religione del mio tempo, Garzanti, Milan, 1961. Included in *Le poesie*

Il sogno di una cosa, Garzanti, Milan, 1962

Poesia in forma di rosa, Garzanti, Milan, 1964. Included in *Le poesie*

Alí dagli occhi azzurri, Garzanti, Milan, 1965

'Manifesto per un nuovo teatro', *Nuovi Argomenti*, January-March 1968

Teorema, Garzanti, Milan, 1968

Pasolini on Pasolini: Interviews with Oswald Stack, Thames and Hudson, London, 1969

Trasumanar e organizzar, Garzanti, Milan, 1971. Included in *Le poesie*

Empirismo eretico, Garzanti, Milan, 1972

Calderón, Garzanti, Milan, 1973

La nuova gioventù, Einaudi, Turin, 1975

Scritti corsari, Garzanti, Milan, 1975

Le poesie, Garzanti, Milan, 1975. This includes the previous volumes *Le ceneri di Gramsci*, *La religione del mio tempo*, *Poesia in forma di rosa* and *Trasumanar e organizzar* and some 'Poesie inedite'

Lettere luterane, Einaudi, Turin, 1976; (transl. Stuart Hood), *Lutheran Letters*, Carcanet New Press, Manchester, 1983

Affabulazione. Pilade, Garzanti, Milan, 1977

Porcile. Orgia. Bestia da stile, Garzanti, Milan. 1982

Amado mio, including *Atti impuri*, Garzanti, Milan, 1982

Poems, (transl. Norman MacAfee and Luciano Martiengro: dual text), Random House and Vintage paperback, New York, 1982.

FURTHER READING

Anzoino, T., *Pasolini*, La Nuova Italia (Il Castoro), Florence, 3rd ed. 1974

Betti, L. (ed.) *Pasolini: cronaca giudiziaria, persecuzione, morte*, Garzanti, Milan, 1978

Fernandez, D., *Dans la main de l'ange*, Grasset, Paris, 1982

Ferretti, G. C., *Letteratura e ideologia*, Editori Riuniti, Rome, 1964

—, *Pasolini: l'universo orrendo*, Editori Riuniti, Rome, 1976

Groppali, E., *L'ossessione e il fantasma: il teatro di Pasolini e Moravia*, Marsilio, Venice, 1979

Mannino, V., *Invito alla lettura di Pasolini*, Mursia, Milan, 1974.

*Martellini, L. (ed.), *Il dialogo, il potere, la morte – Pasolini e la critica*, Cappelli, Bologna, 1979

Rinaldi, R., *Pier Paolo Pasolini*, Mursia, Milan, 1982

Siciliano, E., *Vita di Pasolini*, Rizzoli, Milan, 1979; (transl. J. Shipley) *Pasolini*, Random house, New York, 1982

*Snyder, S., *Pier Paolo Pasolini*, Twayne, Boston, 1980. (On P.'s films, with English bibliography)

Lino Pertile

7 Dario Fo

Dario Fo is hardly a writer and is not at all literary. His work is not amenable to the critical methods usually brought to bear on literary texts. Indeed, over the years, he has developed in a distinctly anti-literary direction. In part, this corresponds to his aspiration to be author-cum-actor-cum-director-cum-political militant, but it is also a response to a public thoroughly at ease with the mass media and indifferent, skeptical, even hostile to literary activity. So Dario Fo has broken with the venerable Italian tradition of the theatre as high culture. Instead, he has applied his unequalled artistic ability and critical awareness to evolving a kind of theatre where the act of writing has been demoted to being just one of several elements in the complex process of communication.

At least two further factors discourage a literary-critical approach to Dario Fo. First, his texts are extremely fluid and undergo continuous modification in performance. No printed version can even begin to convey their extra-literary character. Second, before being a writer-actor-director, Fo is a 'theatrical animal'. That is, his very teeth, his nose, eyes and voice, his arms and legs speak in the biological code of the born actor. No written language, and no amount of training can master it. The first functions of this primordial language are to establish, and nourish, a non-verbal contact between stage and auditorium. The verbal function is constantly modified by a phatic counterpoint – an astonishing range of gestûres, nods, winks and grimaces – which creates, from the outset, an atmosphere of magical complicity with the public. To put it briefly, Fo does not 'recite' his texts, he uses them to create shows, and for that reason, we may not

---

I should like to thank the British Academy for a generous grant that made possible much of my research in Italy for this chapter and Angus G. Clarke for translating it from Italian. L.P.

pin him to these texts.

So far we have distinguished Fo from other writers, but not from other performers equally able to generate this pre-verbal, pre-rational flow of empathy in the theatre. Fo stands out from the latter, for his earnest attempt to give this flow an ideologically directed rational charge, so that the performance refers beyond itself and encourages the spectators to become aware of themselves and their roles in society. Thus Fo's work unfolds between two poles: on the one hand, it is drawn to a preconscious but reductionist enchantment which naturally appeals to all classes, and on the other hand, there is an increasing determination as years go by to render that enchantment rational, to channel it into didactic ends and – after 1968 – into political propaganda. I think that all Fo's theatrical effectiveness hinges on the resolution of this difficult polarity and accordingly I shall discuss his artistic career in terms of it.

Whatever his antagonism towards intellectuals and *littérateurs*, there is no doubt that Fo too is an intellectual – though one who, perhaps, has come to reflect more clearly than many the painful changes Italy has experienced in the last thirty years. Indeed, it is only a slight over-generalization to say that while literature since the mid-50s has tended, in a variety of ways, to distance itself from social realities, Fo has gone in the opposite direction. Whether as the frivolous satirist of social behaviour, or the ardent political provocateur, he is an eye-witness to the cultural, social and political vicissitudes of his country. While writers and thinkers were increasingly coming to concern themselves with the human condition in general, irrespective of specific historical factors, Fo anchors his dramatic strategy to the contingent issues of the moment. He proposes on the one hand to unmask the 'cultural colonialism' of the ruling class, and on the other, to contribute to the contemporary Italian political and social struggles by disinterring the fertile and irrepressible identity of the working class. Rather than merely a dramatist, Fo intends to be what Gramsci calls an 'organic' intellectual – a sobriquet frequently adopted by Fo himself – an intellectual of the people whose work questions the value to modern Italy of the traditional type of writing which is largely the subject matter of this book. This particular essay will be largely concerned with examining how successful Fo is in realizing his intentions.

Fo's first important job was with RAI, the State broadcasting corporation, in 1952 at the age of 26. He broadcast a series of grotesque monologues, in a mixture of Italian and Lombard dialect, centering around the figure of *Poer nano* (*Poor git*), the poor wretch disregarded by establishment historians. These monologues consisted of an idiosyncratic re-examination of history and literature in the popular culture mode of the world upside-down. So, for example, in the retold version of David and Goliath, the good-natured giant lets himself be killed so that no-one could say he took advantage of his opponent's weakness. Recasting the stories of Cain and Abel, Caesar and Brutus, and Othello and Iago, Fo puts on the shoes of the 'bad guys' and overturns the clichés enshrined in the establishment culture.

In a recent reappraisal of *Poer nano*, Fo has claimed to find the elements of a critique of conventional morality in favour of the dispossessed victims of bourgeois historiography. This ideological interpretation of what was originally simple entertainment would not be very convincing were it not for the fact that, despite very high audience ratings RAI interrupted the broadcasting of *Poer nano* after the eighteenth episode. Clearly Fo had gone beyond the joke and someone had noticed. The importance of this experience for Fo was that it demonstrated the effectiveness of the theatrical formulae which he was to use thereafter.

Meanwhile, success on the radio and in revue brought Fo to the cinema. The Carlo Lizzani film *Lo svitato* (*The Screwball*, 1956), with Fo in the title role, was comprehensively slated by the critics. And with reason; but nevertheless the film made the rounds of all the provincial and hinterland cinemas, and introduced Fo's name to the large and undiscriminating public – not yet reached by television – which he was to try and capture twelve years later, in radically different social circumstances and with changed ideological intentions.

So, when Fo set himself up independently in 1959, he had a solid experience of writer-acting and could count on a good degree of popularity. An important contribution to this popularity was made by Franca Rame – married to Fo in 1954 – herself an exceptionally experienced 'daughter of the stage'. Franca Rame deserves more space than we can spare here. Briefly, the development of her stage persona in Fo's theatre parallels the evolution of that theatre. During Fo's bourgeois period, the beautiful Rame, a versatile actress with great comic talent, played the dumb blonde whose magnetic sex-appeal was exploited to the full with exiguous costumes and saucy poses. In the years of the economic miracle she became the incarnation of the wildest erotic fantasies of the typically repressed, mother-smothered Catholic man in the street. Indeed it is hard to tell whether the audiences were more attracted by Fo's daring jokes and astounding performances or by Rame's seductive presence on the stage. Whatever the case, this formula – one consumed with particular avidity by audiences of the 1960s – brought Fo and Rame considerable success, televised and live. The disingenuous exploitation of the dumb blonde ended in 1968 when Rame began to explore new personas within the context of the feminist movement. This process culminated in 1978 with her *Tutta casa, letto e chiesa* (*Just Home, Bed and Church;* adapted in English as *Female Parts: One Woman Plays,* 1981), a series of monologues on the condition of women in contemporary Italian society.

In September 1959, the newly-formed 'Compagnia teatrale Dario Fo – Franca Rame' gave its first performance of *Gli arcangeli non giocano a flipper* (*Archangels Don't Play Pinball*) at the Odeon in Milan. This was followed at yearly intervals by *Aveva due pistole con gli occhi bianchi e neri* (*He had Two Guns with Black and White Eyes*) and *Chi ruba un piede è fortunato in amore* (*He Who Steals a Foot is Lucky in Love*). All three are well-produced and basically conventional light comedies. Compared with the brief, explosive absurdity of the *Poer nano* monologues, these comedies are wittier and more inventive, but also more drawn-out. The 'world-upside-down' formula is taken to its limits in a frenetic succession of situations, parodies and ridiculous double entendres generated by rapid-fire verbal association. Fo's protean personality dominates these pyrotechnic performances – by turns actor, mime, dancer, clown and *maschera*, he can raise a laugh from nowhere, in an apparently easy and spontaneous recitation that is however pervaded with disturbing satirical allusions.

Clearly the tension between 'theatrical animal' and moral commitment is not yet posed in a disciplined and conscious way. Even the satire, usually a minor element in these comedies, arises not so much from a particular programme of criticism, as from Fo's own effervescent love of life and theatre, his desire for recognition and success. The comic structure is still conventional, so too the content, despite a certain daring suited to the liberal audiences in the capital of the on-going economic miracle. The reality of the situation was, however, that despite his vitriolic darts against national scandals, corruption and the hypocrisy of the bourgeoisie, such theatre could only play the establishment's game. This was because Fo was speaking to a cultured bourgeois audience in the register of bourgeois theatre. To present corruption in the highest places in farcical terms could legitimize corruption in the ordinary bourgeois citizens who were his audience – far from feeling threatened they felt absolved.

It was in these conditions that in 1962 Fo and Rame were invited to produce, direct and present *Canzonissima*, the most popular television programme of the day. This was the ultimate accolade from the Italian show-business world, and Fo had achieved it within only ten years. It was his triumph for the present and an assurance of future success. *Canzonissima* was broadcast every Saturday between October and January each year at peak-viewing times. Linked with a national lottery it offered a selection of new pop songs (in the old Italian sentimental style) from which the public had to choose the most 'canzone', the 'canzonissima'. And the invitation to Fo came at a moment when, with the cautious 'opening' of the government to the Socialist Party, even some DC fiefs, like RAI-TV, seemed prepared to give space to opinions and forms of expression which were not directly controlled from the centre.

It was against this background that Fo appeared on television, with a fairly broadminded programme of songs, satirical sketches, sallies aimed at one or another prominent personage, and comic renderings of typical (but not stereotyped) Italian situations. The mixture was intended to stimulate thoughtful viewers to question the cultural value of this kind of entertainment. The first programme opened, according to a well-tested Fo formula, with a song whose words were slightly unusual:

> People of the miracle, of the economic miracle, oh magnificent people, champions of freedom. Free to move, free to sing, to sing and to counter-sing, from the chest and in falsetto. Let's sing, let's sing, let's not think in case we argue, let's sing. Let's make the orphans sing, and the widows who weep and the workers on strike, let's get them all to sing . . .

This was followed by irreverent and anticonformist sketches parodying other programmes, satirising the police, the bureaucracy, and in one grotesque and openly allusive instance, the worker who toadies to the boss. So keen was he not to stop the mincing machine, that he had to take home the 150 tins containing his aunt who came to visit him in the factory and ended up in the cogs of industry.

Howls of indignation went up from the conservative press, and even in parliament. Heavy censorship was imposed on Fo's texts and he was forced to resign after the seventh episode. Clearly, while the country was ripe for Fo's invigorating anti-conformism, its institutions were still living in the times of De Gasperi. The only victors of this furore were Fo's enhanced reputation and the increased sales of televisions. But the *Canzonissima* experience was crucial for Fo, burdened as he was with censorship and at loggerheads with ETI (the Italian Theatre Council). It revealed the truly conservative character of the apparent leftward opening in the DC – like *Canzonissima* it was a manoeuvre to soothe the opposition into the system. It helped him to identify his resolve not to compromise with the dominant conformity. The Fo who emerges is more aggressive, more aware of his strengths and of the contradictions inherent in his cultural environment, more demanding too about the forms and contents of his own shows. His success would now serve a more rigorous and systematic political satire.

Over the next three years Fo produced three new comedies, first shown, as usual, at the Odeon in Milan and then doing the ETI circuit: *Isabella, tre caravelle e un cacciaballe* (*Isabel, Three Caravels and a Bamboozler*, 1963), *Settimo, ruba un po' meno* (*Seventh, Steal a Bit Less*, 1964) and *La colpa è sempre del diavolo* (*It's Always the Devil's Fault*, 1965). Compared with his previous work, this group of plays was characterised by more complex and interwoven structures, without digressions from the main plot, and an attempt to bring social and political satire to the forefront, though without in any way slowing the pace or diminishing the entertainment value. Fo managed to combine moral fervour and dramatic interest, depicting raw and disturbing actuality with the limited possibilities of the farcical. In short he succeeded in harnessing the instincts of the 'theatrical animal' without compromising his mission as anti-conformist intellectual.

Isabella is a grotesque and symbolic version of the story of Christopher Columbus in which he flirts with power, is corrupted and ends up a poor wretch in dire straits. This plot is an obvious metaphor for the condition of the intellectual in Italy under the centre-left regime. Some technical devices new to Fo's theatre are introduced, notably the theatre-within-a-theatre. The play is also notable for the body of research and historical documentation on which it draws. Where this procedure differs from that of *Poer nano* is that here the past is systematically desecrated in accordance with an ideological interpretation of the present.

The last chorus of *Isabella* closes thus: 'The real smart alec is the straight guy, not the opportunist. It's the guy who at all costs stays always and only on the side of the poor sods, of the fair men.' This moralising conclusion is a bridge towards the following show, *Settimo*, certainly the best of Fo's bourgeois period and one of his finest works. The plot is too complex to summarize here. Suffice it to say, each scene aims to unmask and pillory some aspect of endemic national corruption. At the end the exhilarating crescendo is brusquely interrupted by some worthy political personage – a genuine *deus ex machina* – who silences everything, thus brutally frustrating the audience's desire to see justice done if only on the stage, and thereby entrusting it with the responsibility for seeing justice done off-stage. The settings – a cemetery, and a bank/convent/lunatic asylum – are a transparent allegory of alienated and 'miraculous' Italy, and the alliances of its ruling classes. For the first time Fo directly confronts the reality of Italy and analyzes it in a grotesque register. A bunch of grave-diggers from the cemetery – which is about to be cleared to make way for a colossal illegal building project – watch an off-stage clash between police and strikers, some of whom are killed. For the first time the Italian public is being exposed to scenes like this. The song of the lunatics is hardly less provocative:

> Nearly once every day they give us electric shock treatment because we're psychopathic, not to mention neurotic, and being endocephalic we're outside society . . . But at the last elections the nuns helped us to vote, to vote with the little cross, holding our hands, singing us a story, and all for the glory of this civilisation . . . And thanks to the well-known method of conditioning in this convent, we're more normal now . . . We're still psychopathic, tainted endocephalics, but we know the rules of conventional thinking: he who wants things to stay the way they are is wise, and he who complains about the little he hasn't got is mad.

A novelty in this show was the creation of a substantial character – the gravedigger Enea – around whom the whole action revolves freely. Enea is more than a variation on the sterotype – dear to comedy and to Fo – of the simpleton. She is a kind of Fellinian Cabiria, innocent and unsmirched by the corruption around her; a character whom the author looks upon with ill-concealed tenderness, capable of eliciting the uncharacteristic lyricism which was to reappear in the later 'committed' works. The most delicate and magical moments occur when Enea meets other creatures, imagined and real, from an honest, pre-industrial world; the whore who gives Enea the street-woman's outfit she had so long wanted; her dead father, still drunk even as a ghost; the cherubim who speak in *grammelot*, described by Fo as 'a series of sounds without apparent sense, but so onomatopoeic and allusive in their cadences and inflections as to allow their sense to be intuited'. At the end she is the only one to save herself from the rampant alienation of bourgeois society. But the force of this character is completely moral, rather than political. There is some way to go before we reach class-consciousness.

The next farce, *La colpa è sempre del diavolo*, is almost too rich in inventiveness and somewhat undeveloped satirical sallies. At the politico-historical kernel of the play is the struggle between the Holy Roman Emperor and the Cathars, the communitarian and evangelical sect wiped out for heresy in the late thirteenth century. Here too, the allegory is obvious. The Cathar communards stand for the Italian communists, the Imperial forces represent the USA which, at the time, was stepping up its commitment in Vietnam. An interesting pointer to the later Fo is his attempt here to disinter authentically revolutionary episodes from the history of popular culture, especially those involving pre-Reformation evangelical religion, which challenges the corrupt and reactionary orthodoxy from an, as it were, left-wing point of view.

It was works like this which highlighted the absence of a coherent ideology uniting Fo's theatre and its audiences. Otherwise, what was the point of recreating forgotten popular uprisings for the bourgeois audiences in the Milan Odeon? In a vain attempt to fill this ideological void Fo was pushing the ambiguities of farce and theatricality to their limits. But he was knocking on an open door. While his farces were getting more and more daring, his public had become broader-minded. In industrialized Italy the middle class (and no other class went to the theatre) was as liberal and permissive as any of its European counterparts, and it needed more than a Fo farce to shock it. Fo realized that he had become 'court jester' to the bourgeosie. On top of this, there was a ferment of fresh ideas. The Living Theatre had arrived and new dramatic forms were being discussed especially in youth and left-wing intellectual circles. The wind of change reached even that pop music business which Fo had castigated so ferociously for its ability to take genuinely popular art forms, make them banal and use them against the masses. Something of this sentiment inspired the 'Nuovo Canzoniere Italiano', a group of young, left-wing musicians and musicologists who were beginning to exhume – with scrupulous historical and philological rigour – the inheritance of authentically popular songs, old and new, which still preserved the pristine intensity of the people's rage against the injustice and greed of its rulers. Fo and the 'Nuovo Canzoniere' group collaborated – not without dissensions – on a new show, *Ci ragiono e canto* (*I'll Think and Sing about It*, 1967). If the popular songs here lose a degree of philological purity, there is a more than adequate compensation in terms of dramatic, hence didactic, intensity. Fo's idea had been to recreate the context of gestures from which the songs had emerged, the gestures of the workers in the fields, on the rivers, in the factories.

These were not the only avenues Fo was investigating at this time. In September 1967 he offered his middle-class audience something quite different, *La signora è da buttare* (*Madam is Disposable*), a free-wheeling satire of capitalist America consisting of a series of political vignettes staged by clowns and acrobats in a vertiginous whirl of witticisms, somersaults, jokes and acrobatics. The audience was perplexed by the unusual show and by the vitriolic attack on America. The police, for once without a definitive text with which to indict Fo, were alarmed. Eventually Fo was threatened with arrest and cautioned for jokes 'offensive to the head of a foreign state' (Lyndon B. Johnson). It was the end of Fo's bourgeois era. At the peak of his professional success Fo decided to leave ETI, to leave the official theatre circuit and its guaranteed full houses, and instead to put his theatre to work for the people. In order not to be the court jester of the bourgeoisie he was prepared to start all over again.

In 1968 Dario Fo and Franca Rame set up the 'Associazione Nuova Scena' with the declared intention of putting their skills 'to work for the revolutionary forces, not to reform the bourgeois state with opportunist politics, but to encourage the growth of a genuine revolutionary process which would bring the working class to power' (Binni 1977, 46). This new association abolished the hierarchical power-structures typical of conventional theatre companies. It also proposed to create an alternative theatre circuit. This would lean heavily on the resources of the Italian Recreational Culture Association (ARCI), which was the cultural wing of the Italian Communist Party, and its network of co-operatives and *case del popolo* (working people's recreational clubs). The new audiences were to be drawn from the working classes, the mass of workers and their families who had never been in a theatre. And one of the new circuit's advantages was that since it consisted of private clubs it lay outside the jurisdiction of the censor, and police interference.

It was no coincidence then that 1968 saw in Fo's work a new quality which had been previously conspicuous by its absence. There was now a mature political awareness. The themes he chose could be analyzed in an ideologically coherent and committed fashion. To put it simplistically, Fo based his ideas on the concept of the class-struggle (and we should recognize here a degree of influence from Franca Rame, who had joined the PCI in 1967). Henceforth all his works were to revolve about this basic premise. Now the challenge was to bring all the resources of his theatre to bear on the political and cultural issues of the day. This meant tackling them together with the audience – another novel element – and sweeping away the last vestiges of the 'fourth wall' by means of which the theatre had traditionally been able to neutralize cathartically the most disturbing events on the stage. Fo concentrated more on the audience's reactions – indeed he positively invited its participation. He also instituted the 'third act' a period of discussion which followed the show. By reconstituting traditional street-theatre in the light of his newly forged ideology, Fo nudged the spectators out of their passive voyeurism and made them participate in the production as well as the performance of the show. Technically speaking that meant an increasing recourse to improvisation, pantomime and gesture – Fo's natural forte. But paradoxically, this new praxis required of the actor-author an even greater intelligence and mastery of the medium, if the message was not to be submerged in banalities. While it was enough just to entertain, or at the most, provoke a middle-class audience, when dealing with a proletarian audience the need to raise laughs could not be allowed to obscure the over-riding didactic requirement. Gesture and pantomime could no longer be gratuitous, but had to be invested, à la Brecht, with social meaning.

Undoubtedly the most committed product of this most intense phase in Fo's career, and probably his most original work altogether is *Mistero Buffo* (*Comic Mystery Play*), first put on at the Cusano Milanino *casa del popolo* in October 1969, and then performed all over Italy and abroad in modified and expanded versions. It is a collage of mediaeval texts, some original, some altered, some even made up by Fo on the basis of a variety of historical inspirations. These texts are presented critically, then interpreted, by Fo who – in a dark sweat-shirt and trousers – remains alone on the otherwise empty stage for the entire show.

The interest in research, which had led Fo to excavate mediaeval history to find material for his theatre, comes to its finest fruition in *Mistero buffo*. More recently Fo had been very impressed with the experience of *Ci ragiono e canto*, re-done in 1968 in a politically revamped version. Shows like these gratified Fo's 'court jester' vocation, but allowed him to put his all-round acting skills to serve his ideological convictions rather than to entertain the bourgeoisie. For Fo, the jester was the incarnation of the creativity of popular culture at a time when it was still distinct from, even antagonistic to, the culture of the aristocracy.

> Since the tenth century – Fo maintains – the jester has gone from town to town reciting his clowneries, grotesque tirades against the authorities. Even a reactionary historian like Ludovico Antonio Muratori admits that the jester came from the masses, and that it was their rage he was giving back to them through the medium of the grotesque. For the masses, the theatre has always been the principal means of communication, of provocation and agitation. The theatre was the spoken and dramatized newspaper of the people.
>
> (Valentini 1977, 124)

So *Mistero Buffo* was not an operation of archaeological recovery (not an unknown phenomenon in the cinemas and theatres of the sixties), but an attempt to restore to the figure of the jester the actuality and significance he once enjoyed as spokesman for a pristine popular culture, not as yet contaminated and perverted by the cultural colonialism of bourgeois society. The aim of this operation was to give the contemporary worker back his history, his identity, and the dignity of his world-view. Only on this basis, Fo thought, could a new future be founded. There is here an obvious appeal to Gramsci, often quoted by Fo:

> To know oneself means to be oneself, to be master of oneself, to individuate oneself, to emerge from a state of chaos, to exist

as an element of order – but of one's own order and adherence
to an ideal. This cannot be achieved without knowing others,
their history, the sequence of efforts they have made to
become what they are, to create the civilization they have
created, and which we seek to replace with our own.

(Gramsci 1972, 25)

In becoming historian and court jester to the people, in trying to
show the masses the identity, priority and continuity of their
culture, Fo adopted an enormous variety of materials. They range
from standard school texts such as the thirteenth-century *Contrasto*
by Ciullo d'Alcamo, relieved of its conventional bourgeois-
idealistic overlay by means of a sociological analysis, to original
drafts *(canovacci)* like *The Morality of the Blind Man and the
Cripple* by Andrea della Vigna and *The Birth of the Jester or The
Birth of the Villein* attributed to the jester Matazone da Caligano.
There are texts reconstituted entirely out of suggestions found in
ancient chronicles, like the story of *Boniface VIII*, or taken from the
Gospels, like *The Wedding at Cana* and *The Raising of Lazarus*.
The protagonists of these pieces are always the oppressed – the
villein, the jester, even Christ – struggling against the arrogance of
power. There is also the heretic – seen as the mediaeval
revolutionary – establishing alternative communities and living
his faith as a social as well as a spiritual revolution, until he is
exterminated. Using the formulae of the *commedia dell'arte*, each
story juxtaposes the two characteristic themes of popular culture:
on one hand the gross realities of physical life, and on the other the
primitive popular spirituality and its perennial obsession with
social justice. On stage Fo breathes life into this mass of material
using a specially developed Lombardo-Venetian idiolect. Its low
register and archaic flavour contrast with the literary language of
bourgeois theatre and with the insinuatingly paternalistic use of
dialectal forms, especially Roman, much encouraged by the mass
media. In any case the meaningfulness of the spoken word counts
far less than that of gesture, which Fo's performances invest with
an all-pervasive power of suggestion. *Grammelot* and pantomime
become increasingly the principal media of communication with
the public.

How does Fo prevent his extraordinary talent for mime from
becoming a dazzling end in itself? How does he prevent the
political message from being relegated to the background? *Mistero
buffo* operates in two registers. One is that of contemporary reality,

which Fo alludes to in his commentary, in Italian, on slides
showing his mediaeval characters. The second register – his
Lombardo-Venetian 'dialect' – is used for the actual stories. Fo's
aim is to exploit his virtuoso ability to pass from one register to
another – to interrupt the performance to respond to the audience
or to discuss some contemporary issue and then to slip
imperceptibly back into the recitation. Thus he hopes to guide his
audience by acting as a spectator of his own creations. By
estranging himself from his dramatic selves he sets an example.
But this chameleon ability to shift from past to present, from
register to register, becomes itself a spectacle. The danger is then
that the magical attraction of his solitary presence on the stage
distracts the spectators from the lesson Fo wishes to impart. It is as
if for dramatic theatre he substitutes epic theatre and ends up
producing a variety of the bourgeois theatre that he had
repudiated. To be sure, Brechtian theory proposes to avoid the
danger of catharsis by employing, among other things, the
grotesque register, but the very foundations of the production of
popular culture had changed irreversibly by the 1960s and 1970s,
and it is not impertinent, I think, to ask whether this use of the
grotesque in the theatrical praxis of the time does not lead to a
trivialization of content. We will come back to this later. For the
moment it is enough to suggest that there was something counter-
productive in Fo's efforts, partly because he was a victim of his own
myth, partly because his audiences were neither those of Brecht nor
those of the piazzas of mediaeval Italy.

Fo put together two other productions in this period. *Legami
pure che tanto io spacco tutto lo stesso* (*Tie Me Down as Much as
You Like, I'll Still Smash Everything Just the Same*) consists of
two one-act plays on the theme of the exploitation of the workers.
The first, *Il telaio* (*The Loom*) is a stinging indictment of black
labour and cottage industries. The second, *Il funerale del padrone*
(*The Funeral of the Boss*), examines industrial accidents and closes
with the grotesque proposal to kill a worker in order not to upset
the accident statistics. Instead of the worker a live goat is brought on
stage and a genuine professional butcher makes ready to cut its
throat. But the audience protests, the tension mounts, the lights go
up and a debate opens as to whether the unfortunate animal should
be killed or not, that is, whether things should be done properly
instead of just being talked about. And so the audience is drawn
into direct contact with the real.

Apart from their technical innovations, these one-acts are

interesting for their criticism, from a left-wing point of view, of the PCI, which is accused of collusion with the bourgeoisie and reminded of its radical revolutionary duties at exactly the moment when it was widening its power-base towards the centre and evolving the concept of the national path to socialism. The other show to do the ARCI circuit in the same season, *L'operaio conosce 300 parole, il padrone 1000: per questo lui è il padrone (The Worker Knows 300 Words, the Boss Knows 1000: That's Why He is the Boss)* decisively underlined Fo's political extremism. The central theme here is the utter indispensability of culture to the proletarian struggle. This discovery is made by a group of workmen dismantling the library in a *casa del popolo*, as they linger over passages from Mao, Gramsci, the Gospels and Majakovsky. Reading yields to discussion and they decide to replace the books instead of throwing them away. The overall impression is somewhat confused, due to the variety of settings, in place and time, and the ambiguity of the registers employed. What do emerge clearly, however, are Fo's increasingly Maoist views – views not easily tolerated by the PCI. Italy at the time was undergoing a number of crises: the bombing in Piazza Fontana, the expulsion of the far-left Manifesto group from the PCI, the proliferation of extra-parliamentary groups on the left and right, daily confrontation in factories, universities and schools, and commotion in the streets. In this period of 'contestation' the audiences in the *case del popolo* and *camere del lavoro* (district headquarters of the left-wing Trades Union Confederation), who would normally follow an orthodox PCI line, interested Fo less than a new public of militant workers and, mainly, students with intensely critical, if not provocative, views. Daggers were out between Fo and the PCI (not to mention part of the 'Nuova Scena' group):

> We wished to put our work – Fo states – at the service of the class movement. For us, however, 'at the service of' didn't mean filling a neat, prepackaged slot, being 'the artists of the left' who leave all policy-making to the Party and accept its directives and compromises. We had decided to contribute to the movement, to be present, to collaborate personally in the struggles. To be, that is, revolutionary militants.
>
> (Valentini 1977, 116)

Hence the break with the PCI and ARCI. 1970 sees the beginning of Fo's most militant phase.

The splintering of the 'Associazione Nuova Scena' led to the formation of the 'Collettivo Teatrale La Comune', which remained faithful to the aims of the former. In solving the urgent organizational problem of creating a network of theatres and centres separate from the bourgeois organizations and from those of the established parliamentary left, by now suspected of revisionism, the new group relied largely on the burgeoning, militant ultra-left. In this period, Fo's most successful synthesis of the, by now, urgent tension between art and politics came in *Morte accidentale di un anarchico (Accidental Death of an Anarchist)*.

Morte accidentale cannot be understood without reference to the dramatic events of the time. On 12th December 1969, at the end of the 'hot autumn' four bombs were exploded in Rome and Milan (Cf. Chapter 1, p. 11). One, in the Banca dell'Agricoltura in Piazza Fontana, Milan, left sixteen dead and eighty-eight injured. Police investigations were directed exclusively at the extra-parliamentary left. An anarchist, Pino Pinelli, was arrested in Milan. Three days later another anarchist, Pietro Valpreda, was arrested. In the middle of the night of 16th December Pino Pinelli 'fell' from the window of the fourth-floor room in the police head-quarters where his interrogation was taking place. Despite ambiguous evidence, the police maintained that Pinelli had com-mitted suicide and that both he and Valpreda were guilty of the Milan bombing. The media adopted this version. While the police were shelving the Pinelli papers, a counter-investigation into his death, published as *La strage di stato (Massacre by the State)*, ad-vanced the hypothesis that the bombings were part of a wider plot – involving police, secret services and judiciary – to isolate the working classes and to extirpate the vanguard of left-wing militants be means of police repression. There was a public outcry. The editor of *Lotta Continua* – the group which had produced the book – was subjected to a protracted trial. Precisely at this juncture, when the official account of events was beginning to come under fire from a wide variety of commentators, Fo wrote and performed *Morte accidentale*.

The text of the play is based on the Comune group's painstaking researches into the bourgeois and alternative presses, collecting all the most improbable contradictions that had emanated from police and judiciary since the death of Pinelli. But while the consensus of public opinion – including the PCI, which sat conspicuously on the fence – was that the Pinelli affair was a disgraceful example of police mismanagement, Fo, along with the entire new left, maintained that it was an emblematic reaction of the ruling class towards the first stirrings of popular militancy. The success of *Morte accidentale* rests, I believe, on its ability to put across a revolutionary message while still being irresistible as theatre. The technical means of achieving this, though primarily designed to avoid the rigours of censorship, has a determining effect on the play's didactic efficacy. At the beginning of the play, Fo informs us that he intends to tell the story of Salsedo, an Italo-American anarchist who 'fell' from the fourteenth floor of the New York police headquarters in 1921. The account will, however, be set in contemporary Milan. This device allows Fo to present data from the Pinelli case in an allusive fashion so that the audience must decipher them itself. If on the one hand it substantiates the *strage di stato* thesis of the counter-investigation, the constant oscillation between history and current events also sidesteps the problem of over-topicality by stressing the historical continuity (the 1920s in America and the 1960s in Italy) of capitalist repression and class struggle. The outcome makes for remarkably didactic theatre – of a Brechtian inspiration – resting on the solid foundation of Fo's artistic experience, especially bourgeois farces like *Isabella* and *La colpa è sempre del diavolo*. The farcical register also harks back to these last named; the protagonist of *Morte accidentale* is neither Salsedo nor Pinelli, but a madman of hallucinatory metamorphic abilities. Fo transmutes tragedy into farce: this triumph of the popular-grotesque in its most extreme form expunges the last trace of pathos and the last possibilities of catharsis. In fact, it is the madman himself, under arrest for the latest of his interminable fraudulent impersonations, who has the idea of conducting a counter-investigation into the death of the anarchist. The interrogation room happens to be that of the defenestration. One after another, the madman assumes a series of socially significant roles – psychiatrist, judge, forensic investigator, bishop – hyperbolic incarnations of power in its academic, judicial and clerical guises. Via innumerable *coups de théâtre* and grotesque gags, the truth of the Pinelli case is slowly revealed with all its ramifications and obscure interconnections – until the madman himself is unmasked. At that point he plunges his hand into the enormous bag from which he has been pulling out the props required by his incredible metamorphoses throughout the play, and produces a bomb. He threatens to blow everybody up and is thus allowed to escape. He takes with him a tape-recording of the entire proceedings which he will send to politicians and the papers.

Scandal will erupt – scandal which is 'il concime della democrazia' ('the manure of democracy') and 'the best antidote to the worst poison, the coming to consciousness of the people'. That scandal would erupt is the madman's greatest ambition:

> So that the Italians, like the Americans and the English, can become social-democrats and can honestly say: 'It's true we're up to our chins in shit, and that's why we walk with our heads held high'.

This apparently contradictory finale anticipates, while exposing its reactionary mechanism, the subsequent evolution of the Pinelli case one year later when the anarchist's innocence came to be widely believed and attention turned to the subterranean activities of the Neo-fascists. In other words, as the madman left the stage promising to kindle the scandal of all time, the audience had to realise that scandal was not enough. Scandal operates in bourgeois society like a belch after the worthy citizen's dinner. It was essential that the audience went home more angry, more committed to the struggle, more willing to counter bourgeois power with pro-letarian violence. Fo puts it this way:

> We don't want to relieve our audience of their indignation, we want their anger bottled up and we want it to stay bottled up and to become consciously effective at the moment in which we come together and channel it into the struggle. If we do shows where everyone can unload themselves – you know: 'Look at all these murderous bastards running around' and we shout – then they just walk out at the end oohing and aahing. It's the polite belch, through the nose. Everything which should stay inside comes out; the anger and the hate have to become conscious actions shared with, and for, others, instead of an impotent, individualistic outlet.
>
> (Binni 1975, 311)

Despite the moralising tone of the last half-hour, *Morte accidentale* is certainly Fo's best achievement in the vein of dramatic topicality. Differing from the more broadly didactic *Mistero buffo*, it captures the moment of direct intervention, when popular awareness, restored to the people by the jester, is enlisted into the daily praxis of class struggle. And it captures, more vividly than any literary work of the time, the enthusiasm, the agitation, the anxiety and fear which swept Italy. All the same, this adherence to contingent political reality is also a limitation, as every new performance means that the author-actor has to bring the news up-to-date, to cut out narrative deadwood, and graft in the latest ramifications.

These were the years of Fo's greatest popularity in Italy and abroad, particularly in Scandinavia, Germany and France, where he was a resounding hit with critics and public alike. In Italy strikes, factory occupations, demonstrations and trials of ultra-left activists were supported by Fo's frenetic on-the-spot improvised shows. His condemnation of the PCI grew even more bitter. 1971 saw *Morte e resurrezione di un pupazzo (Death and Resurrection of a Puppet)* in which Togliatti, the historic leader of the party, appeared in clerical vestments. But theatrical activity was not enough to alleviate the frustration of the Comune group. The disused hangar, adopted as headquarters of the Fo organisation in Via Colletta, Milan, became a nerve-centre for left-wing activism. There was, for example, *Soccorso Rosso (Red Aid)* – founded by Franca Rame to help comrades in trouble, especially political detainees. But police harassment and right-wing counter-militancy were intensifying. *Soccorso Rosso* was indicted, La Comune was evicted from Via Colletta, Fo and Rame were evicted from their home, Rame was kidnapped by Fascists and beaten up, and Fo was arrested and kept overnight in a cell in Sassari. He had protested against the presence of the police – ostensibly checking the suitability of the premises – during a rehearsal. La Comune itself was riven by dissensions and finally broke up in the summer of 1973. The split with the PCI and ARCI repeated itself; this time Fo broke with *Avanguardia Operaia (Workers' Vanguard)*, the ultra-left group which had tried to restrict him to artistic activities alone. So Fo and Rame had to begin once more from the beginning, founding the 'Collettivo La Comune diretto da Dario Fo'. It was a period of 'open-air services', improvised shows, on the lines of the 'Teatro Campesino', for country people who had never been to the theatre.

The first of these new shows was *Guerra di popolo in Cile (The People's War in Chile)* which came out a month after the assassination of Salvador Allende, while the Italian left was still convulsed by events in Chile. The notable and provocative novelty here was the interruption of the show by a series of extremely realistic devices designed to make the audience think that a *coup d'état* was happening in Italy. The intention was obvious. A prefatory note to *Guerra di popolo* explains it as:

a political intervention which denies the audience its passive role, forcing it to realize that here in Italy the basic mechanisms of colonialism and capitalism are identical to those which gave birth to the bloody counter-revolution and military takeover in Chile. The historically proven fact is that ruling classes do not relinquish power peacefully. The Chilean experience teaches us that when capitalism feels threatened it does not hesitate to use bloody violence in its defence.

The two basic modes of research and expression run unchanged through the theatre of this period, but their synthesis, from the point of view of the critic, becomes increasingly problematic. On the one hand Fo continues to reappraise popular culture, as in *Mistero buffo* which he modifies as current events dictate; on the other he is always ready with prompt propagandist contributions to the political struggle – so prompt that his theatrical contrivances sometimes anticipate events, instead of vice versa. Meanwhile he was satisfying his aspiration to independence by occupying, in 1974, the Palazzina Liberty in Milan. Despite the efforts of the City Council this was to remain the general headquarters – a real alternative workshop – of the new Collective for years. This renewed contact with a less politicized public tended to push Fo into the older theatrical forms whose popular appeal he could rely on. An instance of this is *Non si paga! Non si paga! (We Can't Pay, We Won't Pay!)*, a farce about spontaneous popular price-cutting in response to the spiralling cost of living. Equally farcical was *La marjuana della mamma è la più bella (Mummy's Dope is the Best, 1976)*, despite the fact that the growing use and abuse of hard drugs by young people was turning out to be far too serious an issue for such a reductive and simplistic treatment. And in fact the juxtaposition of the farcical and the moralistic was somewhat indigestible. Another topical show was *Il Fanfani rapito (Fanfani Kidnapped)*, put on to mark the 1975 local government elections and again for the general election in 1976. In this blistering satire, the current secretary of the DC, reduced to the stature of a dwarf, dreams of being kidnapped, dying and then revealing all the back-stage machinations of the party to Christ, the Madonna and the Lord God Almighty, who, disguised as terrorists, put him on trial. He awakens to find he has been genuinely kidnapped by his rival Andreotti who hopes in this way to arrest the party's catastrophic decline. The play's admitted relevance to the moment could not make up for its fragility. When the poor electoral performance of the Christian Democrats relegated – temporarily – Fanfani to the rearguard, the play quickly became outdated. This notwithstanding, Fo must be credited once more with anticipating events, as the kidnapping and assassination of Aldo Moro was to show three years later.

By the mid-1970s, the intimate connection between Fo's artistic activities and political militancy had led him into an impasse. His theatre no longer stood in any kind of dialectical relationship either with bourgeois culture or with the broad mass of the working classes which continued to follow the PCI. Never had Fo preached so blatantly to the converted. His plays functioned mainly as celebrations, or consolations. They merely confirmed in simplified terms what his petty-bourgeois audience of intellectuals, informed workers and militants already understood in its full complexity. Even the range of his language was circumscribed: on one hand it increasingly adopted the slogans of the ultra-left, on the other its insistence on low registers merely reflected the process of cultural degradation happening in Italy. The triumph of his political narcissism was matched by a plebeian narcissism, which became less incisive and effective as it spread. Isolated from the genuine political currents of the day, Fo found himself preaching a kind of left-wing *qualunquismo* which none of his subsequent work – notably the return to the farcical – could redeem.

When in 1977 the higher-brow Second Channel of RAI-TV invited Fo to present a retrospective of his theatrical work on television, he was quick to accept. Fourteen years after his exile from the small screen, the invitation was a personal triumph and, for the militant in him, the chance to reach an enormous audience. So Fo emerged from the ghetto of the ultra-left to enter the overwhelming majority of Italian homes, there to sow the seeds of his vision of the world, of history and of society. In fifteen hours of air time between spring and autumn Fo presented three of the old bourgeois comedies (*Settimo, Isabella* and *La signora è da buttare*), two versions of *Mistero Buffo* and of *Ci ragiono e canto* and a new work, *Parliamo di donne* (*Let's Talk about Women*) which, a year later, was to develop into Franca Rame's *Tutta casa, letto e chiesa*. Despite the omission of the most provocative works, like *Morte accidentale*, and notwithstanding the ire of the church and criticism from left and right – polemics which were to spread out of all proportion – Fo's return to television was a resounding success.

In an interview with the Italian edition of *Playboy* (December

1974) Fo had said: 'If television were to let me do what I want, it would mean that the state, the government, everything had changed'. With the advantage of five years of hindsight, we can see that the television which gave Fo carte blanche in 1977 was very different from the one which had ejected him in 1962. Television had changed – it had learnt to deal more sensitively with alternative culture – because Italy had changed, radically. The Italy of 1977 had democratically chosen divorce, abortion, regional autonomy and a pact between the PCI and the DC which revitalised the state's fight against terrorism. Student unrest was still raising dust but the alliance of student and worker movements was foundering in the new climate of recession and austerity. The most effective civil reforms were being initiated by the Radical Party and the ultra-left was reduced to the isolation that was both cause and symptom of its recourse to armed militancy. Within a single decade the nation had developed the extraordinary capacity to absorb violence which it was to show in the Moro affair. Even if the social and political order had not changed, 'mores' had, irreversibly and radically. To borrow Pasolini's apt expression, it had been an 'anthropological mutation' which had occurred day by day in pursuit of the mirages of consumerism, and the affirmation of the individual over the common weal. The forces which had propelled Italy from economic backwater to major industrial power had also swept away the foundations of the country's moral habits. In a single generation Italy had become more liberal and 'social-democratic' than many other Western countries.

So when Fo was called to the television screen in 1977, it meant only that the country had grown sufficiently flexible for it to absorb the destructive impact of his work. Given this, it seems more accurate to talk not of Fo's undoubted success but of his mummification by the cultural apparatus which the television represented. The 'Fo case' was consumed just as avidly as any other harmless product of the system, though with a voracity equal to the reputation for scandal and outrageousness which followed him. This is confirmed by his gradual disappearance from the cultural scene. None of the new shows – *Tutta casa* in 1976, *Storia della tigre* (*The Story of the Tiger*) in 1979, *Clacson, trombette e pernacchi* (*Horns, Hooters and Raspberries*) in 1981 – nor his increasingly frequent participation in congresses and round tables in Italy and abroad has done anything to slow or reverse this process of disappearance.

To trace the history of Fo's theatre is to trace the history of Italian popular culture from the Catholic provincialism of the 1950s to the permissiveness, world weariness and pessimism of the present. It is the history of a lost opportunity. At the outset there did exist the preliminary conditions for an authentic moral and social evolution which would not jettison the old popular culture of Italy. But now these conditions have been utterly destroyed and there seem to be no viable alternatives to the prefabricated myths of consumerism and materialism. Thanks to his inexhaustible determination, his phenomenal talents, his courageous and polemical non-conformism, Dario Fo's theatre generated a radical renewal of theatrical activity in Italy. So effective was his critique of Italian society, he came to stand in a dialectical relationship with that society. But Fo was betrayed by his natural ability, and led down the blind alleys of extremism and wishful thinking. In the frenzy of his sincere but naive revolutionary aspirations to serve the people, he failed to come to terms with the real and complex needs of the people as Italy emerged from the pre-industrial circumstances of the 1950s. Once the public had refused to apply the extreme solutions which Fo had been proposing for more than a decade, what remains of his theatre which is more than mere entertainment? The justification for Fo's reductivism was always his didactic intention to transmute the tepid spectator into a burning revolutionary, willing to share the burden of dismantling the capitalist system. But that, it had been clear for some time, even to the PCI, was not what the Italian people intended to do. While Fo had put the political struggle first, the audiences chose instead to be entertained, and especially by the simplistic, anti-intellectual slant of his treatment of major contemporary issues.

We may well wonder whether Fo did not, despite himself, pander to the lowest cultural denominator of the farce, the belch and the raspberry, and thus promote, or at least contribute to, the blight of counter-productive vulgarity which is the bane of recent Italian popular culture – and all this despite his ambition to heighten the political consciousness of the working masses. The superficiality of Fo's propaganda became propaganda for the superficial and his theatre was its first victim.

This conclusion, while provisional as far as Fo's career is concerned, is definitive as regards his political strategy, and is, I think, unavoidable. Fo, the 'theatrical animal', always redeems himself by his exceptional and irrepressible talents, but many of the titles of Fo, the playwright, have slid into obscurity. Of those that remain, *Mistero buffo* and *Morte accidentale di un anarchico* are landmarks in the evolution of contemporary Italian culture, and in the history of modern theatre. Despite the linguistic prevarications of the former, and the propagandism of the latter, these two have best stood the test of time and will no doubt be reckoned among the most important artistic contributions to the difficult years of protest.

BIOGRAPHICAL NOTE

Dario Fo was born in 1926 at S. Giano (Varese), near Milan. He attended the Fine Arts Academy of Milan and later studied at the Polytechnic, though without graduating. His main interest at the time was painting – an interest which he has kept up ever since. His career as comedian started in 1952 with Italian Radio and he continued in show-business, producing in collaboration with F. Parenti and G. Durano a number of successful light shows: *Cocoricò* (*Cockadoodle*, 1952) *Il dito nell'occhio* (*The Finger in the Eye*, 1953) and *Sani da legare* (*Sane as Nutters*, 1954). In 1954 he married Franca Rame with whom, except for a short spell in the cinema (1955-57), he has worked ever since, first producing two more revues, *Ladri, manichini e donne nude* (*Robbers, Mannequins and Naked Women*, 1958) and one year later *Comica finale* (*Afterpiece*). In 1959 they established together their own theatre company.

BIBLIOGRAPHY

PRINCIPAL WORKS

Le commedie, Einaudi, Turin, Vol. I, 1966 (Includes: *Gli arcangeli non giocano a flipper*, *Aveva due pistole con gli occhi bianchi e neri*, *Chi ruba un piede è fortunato in amore*)

Le commedie, Einaudi, Turin, Vol. II, 1966 (Includes: *Isabella, tre caravelle e un cacciaballe*, *Settimo: ruba un po' meno*, *La colpa è sempre del diavolo*)

Morte accidentale di un anarchico, Bertani, Verona, 1970; ed. cited: Einaudi, Turin, 1974

Pum, Pum! Chi è? La polizia!, Bertani, Verona, 1972

Mistero buffo, Bertani, Verona, 1973; ed. cited *Le commedie*, Einaudi, Turin, Vol. V, 1977 (Includes: *Mistero buffo*, *Ci ragiono e canto*)

Guerra di popolo in Cile, Bertani, Verona, 1974

Non si paga! Non si paga!, Bertani, Verona, 1974; trans. L. Pertile, *We can't pay? We won't pay!*, adapted by B. Colvill and R. Walker, Pluto Press, London, 1978

Il Fanfani rapito, Bertani, Verona, 1975
Le commedie, Einaudi, Turin, Vol. III, 1975 (Includes: *Grande pantomima con bandiere e pupazzi, piccoli e medi, L'operaio conosce 300 parole il padrone 1000 per questo lui è il padrone, Legami pure che tanto io spacco tutto lo stesso*)
La marjuana della mamma è la più bella, Bertani, Verona, 1976
Le commedie, Einaudi, Turin, Vol. IV, 1977 (Includes: *Vorrei morire anche stasera se dovessi pensare che non è servito a niente, Tutti uniti! tutti insieme! Ma scusa quello non è il padrone?, Fedayn*)
F.Rame and D. Fo, *Tutta casa, letto e chiesa*, Bertani, Verona, 1978; trans. M. Kunzle and S. Hood, *Female parts: one woman plays*, adapted by O. Wymark, Pluto Press, London, 1981
Storia della tigre e altre storie, La Comune, Milan, 1980

WORKS CITED

Binni, L., *attento te. . . .! il teatro politico di Dario Fo*, Bertani, Verona, 1975
— *Dario Fo*, La Nuova Italia (Il Castoro), Florence, 1977
Gramsci, A., *Scritti giovanili 1914-1918*, Einaudi, Turin (3rd ed.), 1972
Valentini, C., *La storia di Dario Fo*, Feltrinelli, Milan, 1977

FURTHER READING

Artese, E. *Dario Fo parla di Dario Fo*, Lerici, Cosenza, 1977
Dort, B. *Théâtre en jeu. Essais de critique 1970-1978*, Seuil, Paris, 1979, 201-215
Joly, J. 'Le théâtre militant de Dario Fo', *Travail théâtral*, 14 (1974)
Jungblut, H. *Das Politische Theater Dario Fos*, Lang, Frankfurt-am-Main, 1978
*Meldolesi, C. *Su un comico in rivolta. Dario Fo, il bufalo, il bambino*, Bulzoni, Rome, 1978
Puppa, P. *Il teatro di Dario Fo. Dalla scena alla piazza*, Marsilio, Venice, 1978
Quadri F. (ed.) *Il teatro del regime*, Mazzotta, Milan, 1976
Sogliuzzo, A.R. 'Puppets for Proletarian Revolution', *The Drama Review* 16 (1972), 71-77

Judy Rawson

8 Dino Buzzati

Buzzati's chief field was prose narrative. He had a particular flair for the really short story, a typically Italian genre which often features on the third page, the cultural *terza pagina* of many Italian daily newspapers. He also wrote several novels, a few plays, a few children's books, together with poetry and opera librettos. And he was a painter of some note. His profession was journalism which he pursued with great distinction all his life in the offices of the *Corriere della Sera,* Italy's most prestigious newspaper. In fiction his speciality was a certain *frisson* which lies somewhere along the axis between the fantastic and the allegorical.

His first novel, *Bàrnabo delle montagne (Barnabo of the Mountains,* 1933*)* was set in high mountains resembling the Dolomites with their sheer faces, startling colours, eternal snows and their mystery. Buzzati was a mountaineer and he had a particular feeling for this world of silence, danger and purity. The chief character Bàrnabo is more anti-hero than hero. He is a Lord Jim figure who fails his fellow forest wardens when they are under attack from bandits. He retreats to the tame peasant life of the plains, but returns finally to make good in his own unspectacular way as the solitary warden of an outpost in the high mountains near the frontier. Frontiers and crossing points are an essential part of Buzzati's landscape. Death, the fear of death and the inexorable passage of time are his paramount preoccupations. The mountains are at once a danger, a challenge, a mystery and a spiritual refuge. Buzzati, like the short story writer that he basically was, captures Bàrnabo at his finest hour:

> Strano che il cuore non batta. Bàrnabo quasi si meraviglia di sentirsi tanto tranquillo. Molte cose sono cambiate. È questa la sua grande ora che non gli dovrà sfuggire. Ma adesso, nel

grande silenzio, il suo sguardo si fissa alle creste che si innalzano vertiginose. Da una cengia all'altra i suoi occhi vanno su, per le azzurre scanalature, per le rossastre pareti, fino agli ultimi picchi che non sembrano nemmeno veri, cosi bianchi contro il cielo profondo.   *(Bàrnabo, 84)*

(Strange that his heart is not pounding. Bàrnabo is almost surprised to feel so calm. Many things have changed. This is his finest hour which must not escape him. But now, in the great silence, his gaze is on the mountain crests which rise up to dizzy heights. His eyes climb from one ledge to the next, along the blue gulleys, over the reddish walls, to the topmost peaks which hardly seem real, so white are they against the deep sky.)

It is rare for Buzzati to use colour so explicitly. He is abandoning his habitual monochrome to signal that this is a unique occasion. In fact Bàrnabo will feel so much in control of the situation that he allows the brigands to escape for this last time but now out of magnanimity and not through fear. The last image is one of a crown of snow in the mountains and we know that Bàrnabo is fulfilled.

Il deserto dei Tartari (The Desert of the Tartars, 1940) is Buzzati's best known novel. It takes place again at a frontier in the mountains where Giovanni Drogo is a young officer doomed through his own ignorance and bad luck to spend his career in the fortress waiting for a probably mythical enemy to attack across the Northern desert. Buzzati catches Drogo as he tries to write home but finds he cannot confess his dark fears sincerely even to his mother. Then while Drogo is sleeping, Buzzati gives us in allegorical form a picture of the span of Drogo's, or any young man's, life with its promise and its inevitable disappointment. It is a moment similar to one of Joyce's epiphanies, of which the reader is aware but not the character.

Giovanni Drogo adesso dorme nell'interno della terza ridotta. Egli sogna e sorride. Per le ultime volte vengono a lui nella notte le dolci immagini di un mondo completamente felice. Guai se potesse vedere se stesso, come sarà un giorno, là dove la strada finisce, fermo sulla riva del mare di piombo, sotto un cielo grigio e uniforme, e intorno né una casa né un uomo né un albero, neanche un filo d'erba, tutto cosí da immemorabile tempo.   *(Deserto, 68-69)*

(Giovanni Drogo is sleeping now inside the third redoubt. He dreams and smiles. These are the last times that sweet images of a completely happy world will come to him in the night. It is just as well that he cannot see himself as he will be one day where the road ends, standing at the edge of the leaden sea, beneath unbroken grey sky and not a house, not a man, not a tree, not even a leaf of grass around him, just like that from time immemorial).

The story is one of waiting and unacknowledged fear lulled by habit. Others make their stands. Drogo's friend Angustina has a gentle brush with the enemy over a boundary dispute between survey teams in the high mountains. In order to make his presence felt he allows himself to die of exposure. Drogo's moment does not come, however, and when the longed for battle finally seems imminent, he is too old and too ill to be anything but a liability. He has to be ordered to let himself be taken ignominiously down towards the city in a carriage. Drogo's last waiting and his death in total solitude and yet in dignity sum up Buzzati's main preoccupations.

Two years later Buzzati published both his first play, *Piccola passeggiata (Little Walk)*, and his first collection of stories, *I sette messaggeri (The Seven Messengers)*. In the play there is a figure of Death in the guise of an Old Professor who, says Buzzati, must 'come over as symbolic and human at the same time', a comment that may usefully be applied to Buzzati's characters in fiction too. And in the final scene it is interesting that a sense of 'anguish, the passage of time and a hidden menace', is to be given by a three- or four-beat motif repeated incessantly as background noise. This idea of menace, the threat of the abyss which Drogo dimly senses but glosses over in his early years, is present in many of the stories of *I sette messaggeri*: from flooding in 'Eppure battono alla porta' ('And Yet They are Knocking at Your Door') to leprosy in 'Una cosa che comincia per elle' ('Something Beginning with L'). Best known is probably 'Sette piani' ('Seven Floors'), which Buzzati later transformed into a play with the title *Un caso clinico (A Clinical Case)*. Camus liked it and translated it into French as *Un Cas Intéressant*. The play had more success in Paris and earned Buzzati a mention among the writers of the Absurd (Esslin, 1961). In fact the short story has a greater impact by reason of its brevity and small range of characters. The threat here is the fear of death through illness but it is expressed also through the fear of falling, an idea already implicit in the challenge of the mountains in

Bàrnabo delle montagne. Buzzati said in his conversations with the French critic, Yves Panafieu, that mountains give one the feeling 'of the abyss, of the precariousness of the situation' (Panafieu 1973, 223). In 'Sette piani' the falling process is protracted over a patient's stay in a seven-storey hospital. Giuseppe Corte arrives at the smart clinic with a slight illness. He is put on the seventh floor. He learns that the clinic has one strange quirk in its organization; patients are allotted to different floors according to the gravity of their complaint. When this is coupled with an understandable unwillingness of the part of the doctors and nurses to worry a patient with the negative aspects of his illness, there emerges what looks like a conspiracy to send a man down by lingering degrees to a certain death on the ground floor. The dramatic version of this story adds, among other characters from Corte's home and office, a strange female figure of death who haunts the office and the hospital, not unlike the Professor in *Piccola passeggiata.* The figure was unnecessary in the short story, but once seen on stage she immediately reminds one of the tradition of Strindberg's *The Ghost Sonata.* Of Strindberg, James McFarlane has said, 'The figures in the plays, poised between the substantiality of "characters" and the abstraction of personified concepts, become the differentiated images of a tormented humanity' *(Modernism,* 526). This description is valid for Buzzati's characters both in the theatre and in his fiction. It also helps us to understand why they are so little 'characterized' in any realistic sense. They are already aspects of the human mind.

However, as we have seen in the cases of Bàrnabo and Giovanni Drogo, there is room for grace in Buzzati's overall vision. The title story of *I sette messaggeri* leaves room for an unexpected hope, the motion is no longer that of a vortex but rather of a widening spiral. A king's younger son sets out to seek the boundaries of his father's kingdom. The exploration takes many years and gradually the links maintained with the capital city, by means of the messengers, are broken; there is a change from looking back with nostalgia to looking forward with expectancy. There is a final sense that the boundary may not exist or that if it does, it may be crossed without anybody being aware of it.

Buzzati started writing under Fascism. Nor did he find himself at odds with the regime. By temperament, training and conditioning, he had nothing in common with realist or Neo-realist writers. He was of the upper middle class, from a Veneto family transplanted to Milan, which looked more to Central Europe than to the

Mediterranean. He was a very private person both in his social and his literary life. When he wished to figure forth certain areas of human experience it came naturally to create an inner world rather than to recreate an external world. Nevertheless such a private world, admitting both the allegorical and the fantastic, and often based on vivid dream experiences, was a more suitable means of expressing under Fascism those fears and aspirations which could not comfortably be discussed under a repressive regime. This is not to say that Buzzati's fantasy was a screen for any revolutionary purposes. He was not a political animal. He was by no means a 'committed' writer and he did not believe that politics had any place in literature.

However, a writer who already had a bent for allegory and the exploration of hidden fears and anguish, which people normally preferred to keep hidden, naturally found the Fascist world provided congenial subject matter and attitudes. A story from the collection *Paura alla Scala* (*The Scala Scare*, 1949) is a useful illustration. In 'Una goccia', ('A Drop') set in a huge, endless block of flats, the only item of interest is a drop of water that is disconcertingly climbing up the stairs. The setting is symbolic of the powerlessness of the individual. It is on a par with the military machine of *Deserto* or the smooth-running train of 'Qualcosa era successo' ('Catastrophe').

Non siamo stati noi, adulti, raffinati, sensibilissimi, a segnalarla. Bensí una servetta del primo piano, squallida piccola ignorante creatura.

(*Sessanta Racconti*, 171)

(We sophisticated, sensitive grown-ups were not the ones who reported it. No, it was a little maid on the ground floor, a common, uneducated little creature.)

The drop comes up at night. Night fears, one of humanity's common denominators beloved of the romantic story-tellers, are Buzzati's special province. And the drop comes up from the bottom of the stairs which are 'umidi sempre, ed oscuri di abbandonate immondizie' ('always dank, and dark with forgotten refuse'). Damp, darkness, depth, desertion, filth: everything that civilized humanity rejects is recognized by an ignorant, perhaps drunken servant girl and not by her well-organized tidy-minded employer. It is obvious that Buzzati wants to face his reader with a truth, a reality as stark and perturbing as any that a Neo-realist writer might have in mind. He is merely going about it in a totally different way. That he is aiming at the discomfort of his reader is apparent at the end of this story when the narrator picks up the reader's attempts at an interpretation. Is this an allegory? Does it symbolize death, some danger, the passage of time? Or more subtly dreams, hopes, something poetic? Or places farther off, that we will never reach? No, it is not a joke, there are no double meanings, it is simply a drop of water coming upstairs at night – 'E perciò si ha paura' ('And that is why we are afraid').

A later piece 'Il senso recondito' (from *In quel preciso momento, Just at That Moment*, 1963), dwells more explicitly on the nature of the teasing 'hidden meanings' that Buzzati liked to couch venomously in his little tales. Here the writer confesses in an imaginary conversation that the 'little stories' are innocent allegories that appeal just because the ordinary reader does not understand them. Then underneath the allegories there is a maxim or moral law, and underneath the maxim 'c'è pure un significato più sottile, non accessibile a molti, che può riuscire disagevole a chi non è abituato' (295: 'there is an even subtler meaning that not many people can grasp which might prove uncomfortable for those who are not accustomed to it'). The mind of the 'reader' has been blunted by habitual lies for so long that he will never discover the truth behind the little present prepared for him, which nevertheless teases and attracts him. Here we find Buzzati experimenting with his readers in the position of tormentor and hoodwinker. But allegory and hidden meanings are essential to the overall effect of Buzzati's stories and they are not simply contrivances born of the need to avoid political censorship. To deal with those whose minds have been blunted by habitual lies, unrecognized, illogical fears that have been forgotten at the bottom of the stairs of one's mind must be brought to life again so that they can be confronted. Perhaps Drogo in *Deserto* would have been a slightly different person, or led a different life if he had been able sincerely to face and express his 'unknown fears' on that crucial night at the end of his youth. This confrontation with fear, whether it is scotched or allowed to proceed to its logical conclusion, provides one of the unexpected pleasures of reading Buzzati, Later in *Poema a fumetti (Comic-Strip Poem*, 1969) Orfi's song to the dead consists entirely of a calculated rehearsal of a random selection of man's fears of death. The dead are held spellbound by the pleasurable nostalgia for those fears to which they are now perforce no longer subject.

This is not to say that Buzzati subscribed to any school of psychology. Of Freud, he said that he admired his writing in terms of his prose style, but thought that his psychology was not to be taken seriously. This was how he answered Panafieu who was questioning him on his life-long love of mountains (1973, 55). Mountains could of course have connotations in terms both of the return to the mother principle and of male sexual prowess. Buzzati, having lost his father as a boy, had a very close relationship with his mother throughout his life and continued to live at home with her until she died.

He did not marry until 1966, shortly after her death, and women seem to have played a relatively small part in his life until his later years. Certainly they have very little place in his early fiction. His later novels, on the other hand, though not so much his short stories, all depend for their plot on man's search for woman. In *Il grande ritratto* (*Larger than Life*, 1960) he made an excursion into the realm of science fiction, and used this as the fantastic element which would allow him to turn a clearer eye on the human condition. The motif is in the tradition of Mary Shelley, Hoffmann and Poe. A mad scientist has availed himself of the cold war to create in a military zone in the Alps a vast complex of electronically controlled buildings in which he has trapped the soul of his first wife (named Laura in the best Petrarchist tradition) after she and her lover have died in a car crash. In this way he hopes to synthesize all knowledge and so control the world. Jealousy between his second and his first wife brings the experiment to an end. Death which was usually feared in Buzzati's earlier fiction is seen here as a natural freedom and release for the enigmatic and tormented figure of 'Laura'. The area of fear explored here through the medium of science fiction is that experienced particularly acutely in the 1950s by man faced with the atomic scientist during the Cold War, or the technologist or the computer programmer, all of whom threatened the individuality and unity of the human personality. Calvino dealt with the same matter in his trilogy *I nostri antenati (Our Ancestors*, 1960) where divided or separated man tries to affirm himself as a human being (cf. Chapter 11, pp. 261-267). But the fact that the separated figure in the mountains is that of a woman, and not Bàrnabo or Drogo in their man's world, brings in a new dimension. The woman is feared because of her destructive powers but pitied at the same time for her defencelessness and there is a growing sense throughout the novel that for Buzzati, woman has two roles: mistress and mother.

This understanding is worked out and fulfilled in *Un amore (A Love Affair*, 1963) which is a much more successful novel. It describes the disastrous humiliating love of a Milanese architect, Antonio Dorigo (as Mignone points out the name shows some kinship with Giovanni Drogo) for a brash young call-girl Laide (*laido* means 'foul', 'obscene' in Italian). In *Un autoritratto* Buzzati explained how this type of all-consuming love came to him in fact very late in life, and the novel is to some extent autobiographical. It catalogues the humiliations and the jealousy Laide inflicts on Dorigo, and tells how in perseverance, and even some anti-heroic dignity, he finally comes to terms with her. At first sight the plot of the novel might seem eminently suitable for the normal Neo-realist treatment of the immediate post-war period. However, we soon realize that Buzzati's solitary world of mystery and challenge is simply being brought to bear now on the city, the call-girl system and the woman herself rather than on the mountains and the frontier. Laide represents for him mystery and the unknown: 'Antonio aveva la sensazione di varcare un confine vietato . . . In compenso, però, c'era il mistero' (31: 'Antonio had the feeling that he was crossing a forbidden frontier . . . But in return there was mystery'). Both Laide and he are repeatedly presented as children. When he first meets her in Signora Ermelina's boutique 'soprattutto colpivano i capelli neri, lunghi, sciolti giù per le spalle. La bocca formava, muovendosi, delle graziose pieghe. Una bambina' (28: 'he was particularly struck by her long black hair falling over her shoulders, and the pretty shapes formed by the movements of her mouth. A child'). Later, Laide, whom Antonio has taken to a flat borrowed from a smart bachelor friend 'girava curiosando, tutta contenta come una bambina che stia cercando i regali nascosti' (88: 'went poking around completely happy, like a little girl hunting for hidden presents'). The bed is like a big toy for her.

As for Antonio himself:

> anche a cinquant'anni si può essere bambini, esattamente deboli smarriti e spaventati come il bambino che si è perso nel buio della selva. L'inquietudine, la sete, la paura, lo sbigottimento, la gelosia, l'impazienza, la disperazione. L'amore!
>
> (*Amore*, 93)

(even at fifty you can be a child, just as weak and lost and frightened as the child who is lost in the dark of the forest.

Worry, thirst, fear, fright, jealousy, impatience, despair. Love!)

The simile of the dark wood before the list of adult abstracts has a peculiar Dantesque ring. At the end Dorigo realises that his preoccupation with Laide has allowed him to forget for two years 'la più importante di tutte le cose' (269: 'the most important thing of all') '. . . la velocità il precipizio gli avevano fatto dimenticare l'esistenza della grande torre inesorabile nera' ('the speed, the fall had made him forget the existence of the inexorable dark tower'). But against death is Laide, the strong but weak, ongoing feminine principle which can challenge death, white against the dark:

> è una cosa giovane piccolissima e nuda, è un tenero e bianco granellino sospeso pulviscolo di carne, o di anima forse, con dentro un adorato e impossibile sogno . . . È la sua ora, senza che lei lo sappia è venuta per Laide la grande ora della vita e domani sarà forse tutto come prima e ricomincerà la cattiveria e la vergogna, ma intanto lei per un attimo sta al di sopra di tutti, è la cosa più bella, preziosa e importante della terra. Ma la città dormiva, le strade erano deserte, nessuno, neppure lui alzerà gli occhi a guardarla.
>
> (*Amore*, 270)

> (She is a tiny naked young thing, she is a tender little white grain, a suspended speck of flesh, or a soul perhaps, with an adored, impossible dream inside . . . Now is her hour, without her knowing it Laide's hour has come and tomorrow everything may be as before and the bitchiness and shame will begin again, but meanwhile for a moment she is above it all, the most beautiful, the most precious, the most important thing in the world. But the city was sleeping, the streets were deserted, nobody, not even he, will lift up his eyes to look at her).

This is the positive side of the coin that we have already been shown in the similar reverie over the sleeping body of young Giovanni Drogo in *Il deserto*. Here, however, the way out is posited in terms of the child who, at least in the imagery, has haunted so much of the novel so far. And the dark tower and even the evil and vulgarity of the future are negated by the spiritual truth of love and its consequence.

In two of his later works Buzzati examined this dark side of life or death. At the end of *Il colombre* (*The Colombre*, 1966), he has a

'Viaggio agli inferni del secolo' ('Journey to the Hells of the Century') which brings up to date the Dantesque descent into Hell. It grew out of a story he was asked to cover for his newspaper, the *Corriere della Sera*, when the new underground was about to open in Milan. The reporter Buzzati stumbles across the door into Hell. Doors, like frontiers, always held a particular fascination for him. He finds there a city 'much like' Milan, and in fact uses his fantastic mode merely to satirise the pace of life and the moral attitudes of the big twentieth-century city. There are some telling moments when one recognises the inventiveness of Buzzati's imagination, for instance the vision of Hell as an interpenetration of cities. Or there is the driver who becomes the 'Beast at the Steering-wheel' because 'qui all'Inferno mettono sui volanti delle auto una speciale vernice che è una droga simile a quella famosa che scatenava i torbidi istinti del dottor Jekyll' (441: '. . . here in Hell they put a special paint on the steering wheels that is a drug like the famous one that unleashed the gruesome instincts of Doctor Jekyll'). But the initial motif of a variety of Hells on earth is never really transcended. Later in *Poema a fumetti*, however, where he combines his artistic and literary skills to deal again with a descent into Hell in the persons of a modern Orpheus (Orfi) and Eurydice (Eura), the negative and static elements of Hell are redeemed by the very fact of the passage of time in life, man's suffering and feeling, the sharpness itself of experience in living. For the visitor realizes that the souls in Hell envy the living their capacity for fear, longing, suffering and hoping. So that the fear of death itself can be made more terrible but at the same time can be experienced as an indulgence only of the living. The child is adumbrated again as a solution:

> La carne è il Paradiso
> solo perché ciascuno lasci
> un altro dietro a sé
> e così al termine
> della divina congiunzione
> l'uomo si vedeva intorno
> la palude sterminata nel crepuscolo.
>
> (*Poema*, 164)

(The flesh is Paradise / only so that each one can leave / someone behind him / so at the end / of the divine conjunction / man saw / the endless marsh around him in the dusk. . .)

So love and finally God are found wanting and Orfi's song stops 'sopra un altro ricordo contenente la grande idea fatale' (178: 'on another memory containing the great fatal idea') expressed in the cartoon as a huge dark rock dwarfing a smaller one on the mountain side. The 'Poem' ends after the revelation that all this has been a dream, belied to some extent by Orfi's clutching the dead Eura's green ring. The dead sleep quietly in nothingness. Meanwhile the fantasy opens out into eternity:

> In quel preciso momento sulle creste della gran Fermeda
> turbinava la tormenta con le sue solite anime in pena.
> Gli ultimi re delle favole si incamminavano all'esilio
> e sul deserto di Kalahari le turrite
> nubi dell'eternità passavano lentamente.
>
>   (*Poema*, 220-222)

(Just at that moment on the crest of the Great Fermeda / the whirlwinds screeched with their usual souls in torment./ The last kings of story set off into exile / and the towering clouds of eternity / passed over the Kalahari Desert.)

Story and narrative were in fact the very essence of Buzzati's concern, so it is not surprising to find 'i re delle favole' taking pride of place at the end of *Poema a fumetti*. Already in *Bàrnabo delle montagne*, Bàrnabo's victory implies immediately 'il racconto meraviglioso. Il racconto, proprio il racconto. Egli ci tiene a poterlo narrare ai compagni; ed 'e tutto qui, c'è poco da dire' (84: 'the marvellous story. The story. Just the story. He is looking forward to being able to tell his friends; and that's all, there's no more to it'). Calvino describes a similar initiation into fiction through the real tales of the partisans at the end of the war. (*I nostri antenati*, ix-x.) Even within Buzzati's stories one finds him making up subsidiary stories as similes or metaphors. The train that does not stop even though it is thundering North towards some catastrophe goes like 'il soldato onesto che risale le turbe dell'esercito in disfatta per raggiungere la sua trincea dove il nemico già sta bivaccando.' (*Sessanta racconti*, 259: 'the honest soldier who makes his way back up through the hordes of the routed army to reach his trench where the enemy is already bivouacked'). The reader sensing a hidden meaning in a tale is like '. . . chi sa l'orsatto imboscato nel macchione ma non riesce a vederlo e gira intorno aprendo con le mani le frasche perimetrali per guardare dentro ma non scorge niente e comincia a pensare che la bestia sia scappata eppure ha sempre la sensazione che sia acquattata là, tra le piante, a due tre metri da lui'. (*In quel preciso momento*, 295: 'someone who knows the bear cub has gone to ground in the thicket but cannot see it and circles around opening the outer branches to look inside but can make nothing out and begins to think that the animal has escaped and yet still has the feeling that it is lurking there among the bushes two or three metres away from him'.)

Ponzio, in his introduction to a collection of Buzzati's articles, speaks of his 'constant concern to capture the great essential moment', a comment which is valid for Buzzati's fiction as well as for his journalism (*Cronache Terrestri*, viii). We have witnessed moments of this kind in his novels, but of course the ideal form for such observations is the short story, and it is this form at which Buzzati particularly excelled. Some of his short pieces are very short. 'Una goccia' is four pages, 'Qualcosa era successo' six. His stories are very carefully structured with a strong sense of progression which is sometimes even numerically monitored. There is a very definite turning-point which brings about a heightened sense of awareness and leads sometimes through change, and often through a reinforcement of the situation, to an inevitable conclusion. Half way through 'Qualcosa era successo' frightened travellers aboard the express for Milan watch the station platforms on the opposite line filling up with refugees as they flash by.

> E tutti avevano la stessa direzione, scendevano verso mezzogiorno, fuggivano il pericolo mentre noi gli si andava direttamente incontro, a velocità pazza ci precipitavamo verso la guerra, la rivoluzione, la pestilenza, il fuoco, che cosa poteva esserci mai? Non lo avremmo saputo che fra cinque ore, al momento dell'arrivo, e forse sarebbe stato troppo tardi.
>
> (*Sessanta racconti*, 257)

> (And they were all going in the same direction. They were going South, escaping from the danger while we were going directly towards it, at a crazy speed we were careering towards war, revolution, pestilence, fire, whatever could it be? We would not know until we arrived five hours later and then perhaps it would be too late).

The story ends with a shriek resounding under the empty vaults of Milan railway station. In 'Il colombre', the title story of the collection of 1966 mentioned above, the 'maxim or consideration' is spelled out half way through the story at the point when the hero makes his fatal decision to go to sea despite the threat of his own personal destiny waiting for him there in the shape of a mysterious shark. 'Grandi sono le soddisfazioni di una vita laboriosa agiata e tranquilla, ma ancora più grande è l'attrazione dell'abisso' (13: 'Great are the satisfactions of a hard-working, comfortable and settled life, but still greater are the attractions of the abyss'). Stefano Roi is going to end up as a skeleton in a small boat clutching a white pebble which may or may not have been the Pearl of the Sea handed to him by his Shark, the 'colombre'. The progression is a particularly suitable scheme for Buzzati's short fiction because it represents a repeated turning of the screw and so gives the spiralling motion or vortex which perfectly expresses certain of his themes. 'I sette messaggeri' for example, is built around the geometrical progression produced by the distance ridden by the messengers as they carry letters between their explorer prince and his father's court.

Only in two novels did Buzzati use the more traditional forms of fantasy literature. *Il grande ritratto* relied on some science fiction situations such as the mad scientist, the trapped soul and the machine out of control. In his second novel, *Il segreto del bosco vecchio (The Secret of the Old Wood*, 1935) the fantasy belonged more to legend and fairy tale relying as it did on tree spirits disguised as foresters, talking birds and mice, and rival winds. In neither of these novels is he outstandingly successful. His own brand of fantasy seems to require something subtler and less removed from normality. In *Il segreto* one finds it playing delicately with the very recognizable wireless which functions perfectly only when someone has come to mend it. Most often the situations for his fantasy are normal except for one thing. It is like a children's game of 'Just supposing'. One of the stories in *Il Colombre* is called 'E se' ('And if'). It is a title he could have used over and over again. So in 'Una goccia' we are in a normal, though vast, block of flats, but the drop of water is going upstairs not down. The hospital in 'Sette piani' is perfectly credible except for its sinister organization.

Before Buzzati died, critics had started to take an interest in the nature of fantastic or anti-realistic fiction. He himself was rather flattered to have been considered a writer of the Absurd (particularly in France after the appearance of the dramatic version of 'Sette piani'), although he did not feel that the word really applied to him. He felt that he 'broadened or compressed an idea to the utmost in order to get the greatest meaning from it' (Panafieu 1973, 233), and that the fantastic was used in order to intensify the 'expression of certain ideas' (176). In answer to a questionnaire published in *Le Monde* in August 1970 on the occasion of the appearance of Todorov's *Introduction à la Littérature Fantastique* Buzzati found the definition of the fantastic there too subtle and limited. 'I will put things more simply: in fantastic literature one fundamental element (the plot, the atmosphere, the characters) appears more or less unrealistic.' (Lagoni-Danstrup 1979, 83) Very often the fantasy element has to do with a stoic resolve in the face of threat: the flood that nobody believes in, the blighted career that nobody rights, the train that nobody stops - but then ' i treni come assomigliano alla vita' ('how like life trains are'), for this is again Buzzati's central theme of life as a waiting for death. Rosemary Jackson argues that 'the emergence of such literature in periods of relative "stability" (the mid-eighteenth century, late-nineteenth century, mid-twentieth century) points to a direct relation between cultural repression and its generation of oppositional energies which are expressed through various forms of fantasy in art.' (1981, 179). This means that Buzzati's relationship to the Fascist ethos should be considered, particularly what Tannenbaum calls 'its boastfulness and its scoffing at death' (1973, 247). It was natural that this required stance of Fascist *menefreghismo* should generate a fear of death which would then find expression in a fantasy preoccupied with the idea of death. That this fear is a central human preoccupation naturally means that Buzzati can speak out of this experience to a very much wider audience.

Buzzati's approach to his subject via the fantastic is not limited to his creative writing. We can find it also in his journalism. Indeed the inspiration for 'Viaggo agli inferni del secolo' was a real assignment to cover the opening of the Milan underground for his newspaper. At a conference dedicated to Buzzati Indro Montanelli, the historian and journalist, recalled how Buzzati was sent as a war correspondent with the Italian navy during the Second World War. The difficulty was that only victories could be reported and these were few and far between. 'The only one who managed to write even about the lost battles was Buzzati. Why? Because you could not understand where they had happened, which century they had happened in, or who was fighting.' (*Il Giornale*, 9 March, 1977). Indeed if we look at *Cronache terrestri* we can now find his description of the 'Battle of the Mediterranean', of April 1941 (17-

27). This is the Buzzati we know announcing what must have been losses:

> Le ultime parole che troviamo sui nostri fogli di note sono le seguenti: "Ore 22.28 Lampeggiamenti all'orizzonte". Come formule di un drammatico enigma, questi fuochi lontani il cui riverbero sorgeva al di là dell'ultimo mare, accesero nei cuori di tutti un'ansia che non si può dire. Poi, andando la nostra nave nella notte, sempre più rari e lontani si fecero i misteriosi lampi. Finché il buio e una cupa tranquillità regnarono sul mare chiudendo il segreto di tanto eroismo.
>
> (*Cronache*, 27)

(The last words we find on our notepads are the following: "22.28 hours. Flashes on the horizon". Like the clues to a dramatic puzzle, these distant fires whose glow rose above the edge of the sea roused an *indescribable anxiety* in everybody's minds. Then as our ship went on into the *night* the *mysterious* flashes grew rarer and further off until darkness and a *grim tranquillity* reigned over the sea enclosing the *secret* of so much heroism.)

My italics show that the world of Drogo is not far away. Psychologically it is the same. The same battle recalled six years later gives more specific details such as the names of the ships, the *Sunderland* and the *Vittorio Veneto* among others, and their position south-east of Gaudo off Crete making towards Alexandria. But in addition to these particulars now freed from censorship there is a superior vision of the whole battle whereby it seems to be dominated by an infernal machine changing gear with each turn of Fortune. At the appearance of the *Sunderland* before the Battle of Matapan 'La molla della infernale macchina aveva cominciato a caricarsi' (75: 'The spring on the infernal machine was beginning to be wound up'). And once the *Vittorio Veneto* had been put out of action by bombs and torpedoes and was lying stationary with her steering gone, 'Tac, la molla della diabolica macchina aveva fatto un altro giro.' (77: 'Click, the spring on the diabolical machine had completed one more turn'.) So a fantastic dimension is added and we have a foretaste of the devils in Hell with their stress machines.

In 1949 Buzzati covered the round-Italy cycle-race, the Giro d'Italia for the *Corriere della Sera*. Before the race had even begun we find him moving from a comparison of different racing speeds to a higher level of discourse to discuss the nature of time. 'How many years and months and days have I seen time racing amongst us men changing our faces little by little; and although we do not check its fearful speed with a stopwatch, I suppose it is much faster than any average clocked up by a cyclist, racing driver or astronaut since the world began!' (*Dino Buzzati al Giro d'Italia*, 28). And one of the officials goes around grumbling 'looking like a sulky bulldog. I watch him with great pleasure and wonder how long it was since I saw such a happy man.' Buzzati the journalist also worked with fantasy and those 'considerations' or 'maxims' he mentioned in 'Il senso recondito'.

Given the element of the fantastic in the plot of a story, the treatment must be the most realistic possible. 'The more fantastic the theme is, the more precise the language must be'. (Panafieu 1973, 169). So like Calvino in his fantastic fiction, Buzzati uses a very precise vocabulary, sometimes giving lists of nouns, or verbs, or even proper names. (See 'Enumerazioni' in *Siamo spiacenti di . . .*, 87). And he takes great care over places and dates, even though like Gogol's 'Diary of a Madman' they may feature such oddities as the 37th April.

We have seen how 'Viaggio agli inferni del secolo' had its origins in an assignment for the *Corriere della Sera*. This gives a clue to the voice behind the stories Buzzati tells in the first person, which are many. The character of the narrator in fiction is of course not an easy one to fix and is particularly important in short fiction where every element in a story has to be finely balanced. Pirandello's narrator figure is a case in point. And Calvino's Qfwfq has a very special task in the 'science fiction' stories. But from his profession as a journalist Buzzati had, as well as ready access to the original stuff of 'story', a ready-made tone of voice. That he was not dealing with normal realistic material only enhanced the impact he made. For him the writer's craft and journalism were the same. The aim was, he said in the conversations published as *Un autoritratto (Self-portrait)*, 'to tell things in the simplest possible way, the most dramatic or even the most poetic way possible' (Panafieu 1973, 165). Later in those conversations he went on to discuss poetry explaining that, like Leopardi, he felt mystery was at the root of poetry. 'It is poetry when someone is saying something and suddenly something else flashes upon you, something completely different and profound and painful, which has sprung from the first thing without anyone being able to say how' (190). And of Leopardi he says '. . when he told how as a child he used to write in his little room in the evening by lantern light, he was saying very, very ordinary things, but in such a way that they grew to take in the whole drama of his life and of the lives of many people like him' (188). When Buzzati says that a journalist and a fiction writer must both write as 'poetically' as possibly, it is this notion of poetry that he has in mind: the 'idea', platonic as it may be, emerges from the particular situation whether it be expressed in poetry or prose, and can bear a fruitful meaning for each individual reader. The process he felt had in it the *meraviglioso* (marvellous) that Leopardi required in poetry. A passing from the particular to the general is a feature of many of Leopardi's greatest *Canti* (in this particular instance *Le ricordanze*). It is also a feature of many of Buzzati's pieces and one of the chief reasons for his special appeal.

This question of a universal appeal on a poetic level together with Buzzati's overall preoccupation with death takes on a particular importance when one considers the period in which he began his career as a journalist and writer of fiction. We have seen how his allegorical approach was suitable for the Fascist period, although it was not specifically invented in order to avoid censorship. Edward R. Tannenbaum has described the conditions of censorship under which journalists were expected to work:

> The most frustrating experience for Italian journalists was not having to say things about the regime which they knew to be exaggerated, but having to keep quiet about many kinds of real news . . . The rationale for censoring news about train wrecks, flood and other public calamities was the following: "The exaggerated and alarmist reporting of such events could give the false impression that the Italian people has not yet reached that level of maturity which would allow it to face reality with a strong and virile spirit". Most crime news was also to be strictly censored – from muggings to embezzlement. Finally, in order to keep the public from knowing about censorship, orders concerning it were to be transmitted orally to the newspaper editors and the reporters. (1973, 259)

Here, of course, the very stuff of journalism was being tampered with. A journalist was being denied access to his 'story' at a fundamental level. Further to this, however, is the consideration that 'train wrecks, floods and other public calamities' are the very stuff of Buzzati's fiction, or more precisely it is the fear of such calamities which he works through until it is finally exorcised.

The reality of those calamities was more the province of the Neo-realist writers who were able to react so strongly against the Fascist prohibitions immediately after the war. In other words both the Neo-realists' art form and Buzzati's fantasies were reactions to the inhibiting nature of Fascist repression of a fundamental human need to face certain truths and fears. But just like other writers who were revolting against the blinkered Fascist culture, Silone and Carlo Levi for instance, Buzzati found a recipe that went beyond the Fascist overlay and penetrated to basic human problems. Silone and Carlo Levi discovered that Fascism had merely aggravated a fundamentally unjust situation that had been perpetuated in the South over the centuries since the Middle Ages or even Roman times. Buzzati, retreating into inner landscape, found that the insidious Fascist censor was merely reinforcing a human tendency to repress fears and not to face up to unpalatable facts. Death is not a problem that existed only under Fascism, but the problem was aggravated and sent underground by the scoffing attitude of the black-shirts with their skull-and-cross-bone flags. Courage and an acceptance of responsibility in the face of death or a moral challenge also take on a much greater importance when the fact of death is faced squarely as in the cases of Bàrnabo and Drogo. Naturally this could be done only in terms of allegory under Fascism. Buzzati was not so far from Vittorini who had recourse to the soldier's ghost in *Conversazione in Sicilia* when he wanted to refer to Italian casualties in the Spanish Civil War, and tellingly uses the cryptic 'Ehm', a 'parola suggellata' ('sealed word') to convey his hero's censored understanding and complicity with his dead brother.

So we can say that Buzzati's writing both as journalist and as narrator has its source in the basic human impulse to formulate experience into story and from there to extrapolate to some further 'maxim or consideration'. The first impulse in this direction came at a time when repression favoured his own bent to fantasy and allegory. It is easier for us now to recognize that these too can be methods not of escape but of a particularly searching form of self-knowledge, possibly because they speak more directly to the reader's own springs of creativity. Certainly they belong to that area of 'poetry' which in Buzzati's terms can just as well be expressed in the simple prose of the journalist or the short-story writer.

BIOGRAPHICAL NOTE

Buzzati was born at San Pellegrino near Belluno, in 1906. The family lived in Milan. His father, who died in 1920, was Professor of International Law at Pavia. After taking a degree in Law, Buzzati joined the *Corriere della Sera* in 1928. He visited Ethiopia in 1939 as foreign correspondent with the Italian navy. He won the Napoli Prize for *Il crollo della Baliverna* in 1957 and the Strega Prize for *Sessanta racconti* in 1958. Also in 1958 he held his first exhibition of paintings in Milan. He visited the U.S.A., Japan and Brazil on assignments for the *Corriere della Sera* and accompanied the Pope to India. Shortly after his mother's death he married in 1966. He died in Milan on 28 January 1972.

BIBLIOGRAPHY

PRINCIPAL WORKS

Bàrnabo delle montagne, Treves-Treccani-Tuminelli, Milan-Rome, 1933; ed. cited Garzanti, Milan, 1965

Il segreto del bosco vecchio, Treves-Treccani-Tuminelli, Milan-Rome, 1935; ed. cited Garzanti, Milan, 1965 (with *Bàrnabo delle montagne*)

Il deserto dei Tartari, Rizzoli, Milan, 1940; ed. cited Mondadori, Milan, 1970; (trans. S.C. Hood) *The Tartar Steppe*, Secker and Warburg, London, 1952; Farrar, Straus and Young, New York, 1952

I sette messaggeri, Mondadori, Milan, 1942 (including also 'Sette piani', 'Eppure battono alla porta', and 'Una cosa che comincia per elle'); ed. cited *Sessanta racconti*, Mondadori, Milan, 1961

La famosa invasione degli orsi in Sicilia, (for children, with illustrations by Buzzati), Rizzoli, Milan, 1945; (trans. F. Lobb) *The Bears' Famous Invasion of Sicily*, Pantheon Books, New York, 1947

Paura alla Scala, Mondadori, Milan, 1949, (including 'Una goccia'); ed. cited *Sessanta racconti*, Mondadori, Milan, 1961; (trans. C. Jolly) 'The Scala scare', *New Writers* 1, 145 – 187, 1961

In quel preciso momento, Neri Pozza, Vicenza, 1950; 2nd ed. Mondadori Milan, 1963 (including 'Il senso recondito'); ed. cited Mondadori, Milan, 1974

Il crollo della Baliverna, Mondadori, Milan, 1957 (including 'Qualcosa era successo'); ed. cited *Sessanta racconti*, Mondadori, Milan, 1961

Sessanta racconti, Mondadori, Milan, 1958 (including stories from *I sette messaggeri*, *Paura alla Scala* and *Il crollo della Baliverna* and others); ed. cited Mondadori, Milan, 1961. Some of these stories were translated into English in *Catastrophe, The Strange Stories of Dino Buzzati* (trans. J. Landry and C. Jolly), Calder and Boyars, London, 1965

Esperimento di Magia, Rebellato, Padua, 1958

Il grande ritratto, Mondadori, Milan, 1960; (trans. H. Reed) *Larger than Life*, Secker and Warburg, London, 1962; Walker, New York, 1967

Egregio Signore, siamo spiacenti di . . . , Elmo, Milan, 1960; ed. cited
    Siamo spiacenti di, Mondadori, Milan, 1975
Un amore, Mondadori, Milan, 1963; ed. cited Mondadori, Milan, 1970;
    (trans. J. Green) *A Love Affair*, Farrar, Straus, New York, 1964; André
    Deutsch, London, 1965
Il colombre, Mondadori, Milan, 1966 (including 'E se?', 'Progressioni'
    and 'Viaggio agli inferni del secolo')
La boutique del mistero, Mondadori, Milan, 1968, (an anthology of earlier
    stories)
Poema a fumetti (strip cartoon by Buzzati), Mondadori, Milan, 1969
Le notti difficili, Mondadori, Milan, 1971
Cronache terrestri, ed. Domenico Porzio, Mondadori, Milan, 1972; ed.
    cited 1980
Teatro, ed. Guido Davico Bonino, Mondadori, Milan, 1980

WORKS CITED

Bradbury, M. and McFarlane, J. (eds.), *Modernism*, Penguin, Harmonds-
    worth, 1972
Calvino, I., *I nostri antenati*, Einaudi, Turin, 1960
Esslin, M., *The theatre of the Absurd*, Doubleday, New York, 1961;
    Penguin, Harmondsworth, 1968
Jackson, R., *Fantasy: The literature of subversion*, Methuen, London and
    New York, 1981
Lagoni-Danstrup, A., Dino Buzzati et la rapport dialectique de la
    littérature fantastique avec l'individu et la societé, *Cahiers Buzzati* 3
    (1979), 75–115
Marabini, C. (ed.), *Dino Buzzati al Giro d'Italia*, Mondadori, Milan, 1981
Mignone, M.B., *Anormalità e angoscia nella narrativa di Dino Buzzati*,
    Longo, Ravenna, 1981
Panafieu, Y. (ed.), *Dino Buzzati: un autoritratto*, Mondadori, Milan, 1973
Tannenbaum, E., *Fascism in Italy: Society and Culture, 1922–1945*, Allen
    Lane, London, 1973

FURTHER READING

*Arslan, A.V., *Invito alla lettura di Dino Buzzati*, Mursia, Milan, 1974
Bertacchini, R., Dino Buzzati, *Letteratura italiana; I contemporanei*,
    Marzorati, Milan, 1963, 1395–1411
Biasin, G.P., 'The Secret Fears of Men: Dino Buzzati', *Italian Quarterly* 6
    (1962), 78–93
Carlino, M., *Come leggere il Deserto dei Tartari di Dino Buzzati*, Mursia,
    Milan, 1976
Debenedetti, G., Dino Buzzati, *Novecento: I contemporanei*, ed. G. Grana,
    Marzorati, Milan, 1979, 5633–5670
Gianfranceschi, F. *Dino Buzzati*, Borla, Turin, 1967
Lagona Gion, A., 'La réalité existentielle sous le fantastique chez Buzzati',
    Cahiers Buzzati 3 (1979), 20–70
Pietrosi, L., 'Dino Buzzati', *Italica* 42 (1965), 391–402

9 Elsa Morante

Elsa Morante celebrates the miseries and splendours of the imagination with the passion of a devotee and the resolution of a proselyte. It is no exaggeration to say that the imaginary is the very stuff of which her characters live. What we know of them is their dreams, hopes, desires, fears, the barely articulate underside of consciousness. When they speak it is not to engage in the niceties of social exchange, but to find a way of giving voice to the obsession which governs their lives. When they are given a physical shape and physical attributes on the page, it is not as flesh-and-blood characters to whom things happen, but as the coalescing of sensations that are the physical manifestation of intense emotion. They and their author inhabit a world more amenable to mythical than to scientific explanation, where history is the surface rumbling of an obscurer cycle and human life in its essentials is not distinguishable from that of all other animals. To penetrate this world you must be prepared to draw on the metaphorical reserves of legend, dream and the imagination of children. Omniscience in Morante's narrators is not a question of positive knowledge, of being able to read off the facts of the case like an all-seeing eye, but rather of a kind of divination, the state of 'lucid insomnia' which is the main medium of the narrator's perception in her first novel. Rather than representing some abstract objectivity, the omniscient narrator in Morante is quite transparently the embodiment of her or his author's imagination.

So when Morante describes herself as 'having begun in the writer's art as soon as she learnt the alphabet' (1969, 5) she is using the word 'writer' very differently from how many of her contemporaries use it. It is fashionable to utter the word 'writer' with the same tone of respect for professional accomplishment with which one might say 'microbiologist', or 'juggler'. But in

Morante, the name of writer or poet or artist has religious connotations, and conveys a sense of vocation and mission. 'The *novel* may be defined,' she wrote in 1959, in reply to a magazine inquiry, 'as any poetic work [long or short, in verse or prose] in which – through the invented narration of exemplary events (chosen by the author as the pretext, or symbol of human relations in the world) – the author gives *entire* his or her own image of the real universe (that is, of humanity in its reality)'(1959, 18). It is enlightening to compare Italo Calvino's definition of the novel in reply to the same inquiry: 'a narrative work which may be used (*fruibile*) and which signifies on many intersecting planes' (Calvino 1959, 9). The technicizing objectivity of the latter definition contrasts forcefully with the prominence given to subjectivity in Morante's approach, and the impression it conveys of the total immersion of the author, his or her personal commitment, in the work. And if we were to extend the comparison to the practice of the two writers, it could be said that, while both are masters of style, in Calvino elements of style are used kaleidoscopically, to produce innumerable combinations and to underline the relativity of perspective, while in Morante they are more like pieces of a mosaic, or threads of a carpet, each single one inseparable from the overall design.

Morante's cult of the imagination is nothing new in Western literature, even where imagination touches on magic and madness. Its roots lie deep in Romanticism, and it has continued to be fed by the author's wide reading in anthropology and epic and sacred writings, and by her travels and contacts with other, non-Western cultures. But the immediate sources of Morante's writing are to be found in the period between the wars, in Kafka and surrealism, and, more locally, in the 'magic realism' (*realismo magico*) which Massimo Bontempelli put forward in 1927–28 as the epitome of the avant-garde under Fascism: the combination of precise realistic detail and an atmosphere of 'lucid stupor', for which Bontempelli saw analogies in Quattrocento painting. The assimilation of art (or poetry) to magic is complete in Bontempelli: '. . . [Art] has all the characteristics of enchantment (*incantesimo*) and all its modes: it is the calling-up of dead things, the making visible of distant things, the prophecy of future things, the subversion of the laws of nature, brought about by the imagination alone' (Bontempelli 1974, 29). Morante would not dissent from this view: the imagination, invested with this power, is the writer's only means of reaching the reality of things which it is his or her duty to represent. Where Morante parts company from Bontempelli is over the fact that he is in it for excitement: 'magic realism' on inspection turns out to be a kind of heightened awareness that restores a sense of adventure to dull suburban life, making the reader believe there is something else there, whether there is or not. In Morante, there is no trip, no journey into the unknown. It is the job of the writer to 'restore reality to others' (1968, v) through language. We should therefore think of a Morante novel not as an adventure of the imagination through time but as an enclosed and dark space – to use an image dear to the author – empty at first, or flickering with insubstantial shadows, but receptive and filling, till at the end of the novel it is totally occupied by the intricate truths which the imagination has managed to recover.

The posture of the writer as the scribe of the imagination is one of hunched concentration: 'Thus, at the moment of his greatest attentiveness to real things (the moment when he begins to write) the writer must create silence all around him, free himself from all the screens put up by culture, from all fetishes, from all the vices of conformism. His consciousness, proven and mature, must at that moment draw in upon itself and focus on one single point: the real object he has chosen that it might confide in him its own truth' (1959, 26). But such absorption in no way excludes the reader. On the contrary, the other moment of this absorption is expansiveness: the truth is that Morante does everything possible to make her vision communicable to the readers. The narrative form itself is a vehicle of 'exemplary' events; and the focus of the imaginative effort is on deep symbolic vocabulary of universal validity. But Morante's communication with her readers is assured not so much by these structural components, important though they are, as by her particular style of narrative prose. At first sight it is a difficult language, or at any rate a learned one, rich in adjectives, steeped in the archaic and Latinate forms of the literary tradition going back to Boccaccio, subtle, almost mannered in its discrimination of meanings. This lexical refinement, however, is supported by a syntax which, while it is not exactly simple (much depends on the artful placing of clauses in apposition), is for the most part linear, avoiding any too complex subordination, and readable. It is the language of a great realist: precise in every detail yet carrying the reader forward without hesitation.

This implicit criterion of communicability in its turn implies some limitation on the operations of the imagination, in the sense that, for the novelist (as distinct from the private person Elsa Morante), only what is in the last resort communicable can be imagined. This is the writer's defence against the obscure, the sentimental and the pathological, and also against the excesses and blind alleys of her characters. In some of her early stories – especially 'Il gioco segreto' ('The Secret Game', 1937) – Morante appears to be testing the forces of the imagination, marking out the limits in which she as a writer will perform. But it is her first novel, *Menzogna e sortilegio* of 1948 (translated as *House of Liars*), that presents the fullest exploration of the ambiguities of the imagination and the equivocal stance of the sorcerer's apprentice who serves it.

The apprentice is Elisa, the twenty-five-year-old narrator who, alone in the world, begins to reconstruct the story of her family, painstakingly separating fact from fiction, truth from legend. It begins with her maternal grandmother, Cesira, ambitious and narrow-minded, a teacher up from the provinces in search of a good marriage, whose life with Teodoro Massia, a seductive but ageing and impoverished nobleman, will prove an inferno for both parties. The only consolation for Teodoro is the birth of their daughter Anna, a girl of fiery temperament who is as morbidly attached to the father who dotes on her as she is contemptuous of the mother who sees in her the symbols of her own humiliation. After Teodoro's death, Anna's love is concentrated on her cousin, the golden Edoardo, scion of the wealthier and socially more elevated Cerentano side of the family, who appears to her as a kind of sun-god, capricious, wilful and dangerous, and who, as far as his infinite selfishness will allow, loves her too, in a possessive and tyrannical fashion. What one owns one can also give away, and thus after an illness, Edoardo arranges for Anna to be married to his new-found friend, Francesco De Salvi, a young and eager law-student from the country who is both convinced of his own aristocratic origins, though he is in fact the illegitimate son of a peasant-woman and the Cerentanos' bailiff, and committed, at least verbally, to a radical socialism. The pieces are assembled from which will be produced Elisa, the only child of Anna and Francesco, and it is through her recollections of her childhood that we witness the final stages of her family's drama and decline. Ten years after her marriage, after a chance encounter with his demented mother, Anna learns that Edoardo has died, but she refuses to accept the idea, and joins with the old woman in an elaborate pretence that her lover is still alive by writing a series of letters purporting to come from Edoardo on his travels. Francesco, who in the meantime has taken up again with his old flame Rosaria, a vivacious working-class prostitute loved by both him and Edoardo, is gradually drawn into this game while unable to understand or accept that Anna's love for her cousin, dead or alive, is total and exclusive. The child Elisa witnesses her father, with whom she is sullen, become incapacitated through drink and her mother, whose indifference to her she repays with servile adoration, spin away into raving lunacy. The degrading death of both parents leaves Elisa to be brought up in another town by her 'second mother' Rosaria, with whose own death the story opens.

This rapid plot-summary comes only half-way to indicating on what a treacherous terrain the novel is set. The lies and deceits, the incantation and wizardry, alluded to in the Italian title, are not only those practised with varying degrees of success and varying degrees of malevolence by nearly all the principal characters, but also those of which the narrator herself is the protagonist and victim. For Elisa, the figures of her narrative are neither wholly fictional entities existing 'out there' in a realistic setting created by her, nor are they entirely 'remembered' from her own past and reconstructed on the page. They are suspended somewhere between these two relatively solid structures of narration, in the physical setting of the southern Italian town of P. (presumably Palermo, though with traces of Rome in the later sections of the novel) during what we take to be the early years of this century – a time and place that are recognizable in a general way (and particular attributes of which are carefully described), but which are never precisely located. Although the narrative is presented in the form of a sober chronicle, its assumptions are visionary: half-remembered, half-imagined, but more accurately evoked, like ghosts, the actors in the family drama move in a space occupied pre-eminently by insomnia, fantasy and day-dream.

Thus the first thing that the reader notices about *Menzogna e sortilegio* is the degree of concentration with which each character is presented, as though spotlighted in centre-stage. In this way, even relatively minor characters are given all the space they need to act out their inner life, their fantasies, expectations, fears and frustrations. The external world becomes little more than a hazy background to a drama of pure consciousness, in which the real protagonists are not so much people as the images that they create of themselves, the ways in which they see themselves reflected in others, what others do effectively make of them. So the stage is also a prison, or a cloister, or a little room, or a hall of mirrors – all metaphors of enclosure that are repeated through the novel.

Fantasy also bears upon society itself and social relations – and its deployment in the novel may be seen as a form of social critique. On the part of those characters who are socially inferior – particularly Francesco and Anna – their dreams of advancement (or indeed of already achieved status) are manifestly inadequate instruments for dealing with the more mundane reality in which they find themselves. Thus Anna, already at the age of seven, is enslaved simultaneously to the myth of Edoardo (instilled by her father) and to the dream of propulsion into the aristocracy (encouraged by her mother):

> In segreto, a bassissima voce, e piena di timore, pronunciava talvolta questo nome: e le pareva che il dire: Edoardo, la investisse d'un'arcana autorità. Subito, a quel nome misterioso, le si spalancavano le porte, ed ella veniva assunta alle regioni, per lei sovrumane, dei signori che andavano in carrozza sul Corso e abitavano i palazzi. A questo punto, si ripeteva, quasi a confermarselo: *Siamo cugini,* e tale verità la colmava d'uno sbigottimento ineffabile: simile a quello d'un povero pastore che ignora le proprie origini e infine, da un genio, apprende d'essere un semidio, figlio di dei.
>
> (*Menzogna,* 72)

> (In secret, very softly, and filled with fear, she would sometimes pronounce this name: and it seemed to her that to say "Edoardo" invested her with an arcane authority. As soon as she had uttered the mysterious name, doors would fling open wide before her and she would be taken up into what for her were the more-than-human realms of the gentlefolk who went in carriages on the Corso and dwelt in palaces. At this point, she would repeat, as if to make sure of it, "We are cousins," and this truth filled her with unspeakable confusion: like that of a poor shepherd ignorant of his own origins until one day he learns from a guardian spirit that he is a demi-god, a son of the gods.)

On the part of those characters who are socially strong, on the other hand, and Edoardo is the outstanding example, the imagination is symbolic of the inequitable luxury in which they live: they have too much of it and they spend it recklessly. Edoardo uses his to tantalize, tease and torment Anna with stories of other affairs and journeys and power, and finally to humiliate and mutilate her, to no purpose but the satisfaction of his own vainglory. Yet this apparent purposelessness points also to the other principal function of the characters' fantasizing, as a form of psychological compensation, as for example when Francesco as a young man, feeling betrayed by life and by Rosaria in particular, turns his mind to Anna, his future wife:

> [Francesco], tuttavia, non poteva in nessun modo intendere di rivolgersi alla sua vera madre, Alessandra, la quale, per vari motivi, come già s'è accennato, gli faceva onta. E in luogo di costei, la madre che venne in suo soccorso fu una che spesso, in simili casi, consola i giovani un poco vili e immaturi: voglio dire, l'Immaginazione. La quale assunse, com'è suo costume, le sembianze più adatte a risollevare Francesco dalle sue tristezze: le sembianze, cioè, di Anna. Non certo della vera Anna, ma di un'Anna assolutamente fantastica, altrettanto limpida e benigna per quanto la vera si mostrava nuvolosa e scostante.
>
> (*Menzogna*, 353)

(There was, however, no way in which Francesco could think of turning to his real mother, Alessandra, who, for various reasons, as we have said, made him feel ashamed. The mother who came to his aid instead was one who often in these cases brings comfort to rather feeble and immature young men: I mean, Imagination. Which appeared, as is its wont, in the features most likely to lift Francesco from his sorrows, namely Anna's. Not of course the real Anna, but an entirely imaginary Anna: one who was as bright and kind as the real one was gloomy and unwelcoming.)

Only one other person in the book has the privilege of acquiring a 'second mother', but unlike Francesco's, who misleads him no less than the first had done, Elisa's second mother, Rosaria, the only major character who does not suffer from the mania for fabrication that infests the other characters, leads her adoptive daughter at least towards the principle of reality. Only Elisa, both character and narrator, has the possibility of change, even though when her parents die – this we learn from the narrator's 'Introduction to the story of my family' at the beginning of the novel – she suffers the common fate of all her family: that of constructing fantasies. As a *child*, her development in the real world is arrested by submission to the fantasies of the parents (as Edoardo was worshipped by his mother, Anna relieved of having to think about the future by the imaginary journeys she and her father would undertake together, and Francesco protected from his true social origins by the stories that his mother made up). As an *adolescent*, she compensates by entering a fantasy-world of her own, making up stories about her family, in an endless, self-generating 'stramba epopea' ('weird epic', 25) in which the characters take on more and more substance, to the point of becoming 'quasi delle anime incarnate' ('almost souls incarnate', 25). The purpose of these inventions is clear enough to the critical mind: to 'vendicarmi [. . .] dei miei amori non ricambiati, [. . .] saziare i miei segreti orgogli' ('to avenge my unrequited love and satisfy my secret pride', 26). Gradually, however, Elisa loses control of her fantasies which with their 'poter stregato' ('bewitching power', 27) become increasingly more real than real life and real people. But with Rosaria's death and Elisa's total solitude thereafter, a new opportunity presents itself for her to break out of the circle of fantasies and lies that beset her family.

The act of narration itself is posited as a liberation from the ghosts and traumas of childhood, a passage into adulthood, achieved by seeing the other adults' actions and fates in their true perspective (their 'legend' as a 'petty-bourgeois drama', 19) and refusing the childish consolation of fantasies. The adult task is seen to consist in the shaping and ordering voice of reason, which exorcizes the ghosts of the past and chases away nightmares. A kind of bargain is struck in *Menzogna e sortilegio:* the disordered experience of the characters' imaginations (including Elisa's as a character), which is the subject of the narration, is balanced by the regular structure and relative calm of the narration itself. To achieve the necessary balance between imaginative freedom and communicability, Morante delegates these different functions to her characters on the one hand, and the narrator on the other. She keeps to this bargain throughout her subsequent writing, where the authority and lucidity of the narrative voice is never in doubt, even when it belongs to someone who speaks in the first person and is directly involved in the action, in short who is also a character. And at the same time the narration serves to distance the author and the reader from material which is frequently volatile: it is the crust of an emotional volcano.

The drama which Morante's players act out is that of exclusion, set primarily in the relation between child and parents, though the theme also has mythical (religious) and historical (political) dimensions for the author as we shall see. *Menzogna e sortilegio* introduced the theme, particularly in Elisa's story of her own childhood: it was expanded in 'Lo scialle andaluso' ('The Andalusian Shawl'), a long short story written in 1951, which focussed on the possessive love-hate of a boy for his actress mother. Since then Morante has devoted two novels, separated by a gap of twenty-five years, to male protagonists whose lives are marked by a childhood trauma of rejection: *L'isola di Arturo (Arturo's Island, 1957)* and *Aracoeli (Aracoeli: Altar of Heaven, 1982)*. Because of the thematic link between these two books, I propose to override the chronological sequence of Morante's production and consider them together. At the end of this chapter, however, I shall return briefly to *Aracoeli* in the light of the other two important works which immediately preceded it.

The rejected males desperately seek attention, approval and love, but are destined to a submissiveness which the Elisa of the first novel seemed at least capable of overcoming. The pain of this recurrent scene is made more acute precisely by the fact that it is narrated, that is, in Morante's terms, made conscious. Indeed, this is consciousness in a colder and crueller light than in Elisa's rationalist enterprise: here nothing is left to the mercy of the unexpressed.

Even so, *L'isola di Arturo* begins with the same strange silence as that with which *Menzogna* ended. Just as we do not finally know whether, by telling her story, Elisa has succeeded in breaking from her isolation, so in the second novel, which is a recollection of childhood and early adolescence, we do not know how old the first-person narrator is: in fact we know nothing at all about him as an adult. The present from which he looks back is blank and he himself without qualities. Childhood is evoked not as a preparation or as a stage in a progressive history, but as an experience entire in itself, separated from adulthood by a line which cannot be rubbed out. From the very first paragraph of the novel, the recollection of this special time is suffused in intimations of myth and legend:

Uno dei miei primi vanti era stato il mio nome. Avevo presto imparato [. . .] che Arturo è una stella: la luce più rapida e radiosa della figura di Boote, nel cielo boreale! E che inoltre questo nome fu portato pure da un re dell'antichità, comandante a una schiera di fedeli: i quali erano tutti eroi, come il loro re stesso, e dal loro re trattati alla pari, come fratelli.   (*Isola*, 21)

(One of my earliest boasts had been my name. I had soon learnt [. . .] that Arthur is the star Arcturus: the quickest and brightest in the constellation of Boötes in the northern sky! And furthermore that this name was borne by an ancient king who led a band of loyal followers: who were all heroes, like the king himself, and treated by the king as equals, like brothers.)

Mythical references such as these colour the entire narrative and highlight the extraordinary situation of the protagonist. Arturo grows up on the island of Procida (near Naples) virtually an orphan. His young mother dies giving birth to him: he cultivates a respectful memory towards her. He is nursed in his earliest months on goats' milk by an adolescent boy, Silvestro, who then disappears from his life only to reappear at the end of the novel as the agent of Arturo's departure from the island. Arturo inhabits a rigorously masculine world. The rule that 'L'autorità del padre è sacra' ('The father's authority is sacred', 47) is the first of the Absolute Certainties which form the moral code which as a child he has culled for himself from his sporadic reading. His actual father, Wilhelm, is for the boy a marvellous and mysterious being. Frequently away on journeys, he is a stranger among the other islanders; fair-featured like Edoardo Cerentano, he is, like that character, arrogant, disdainful, cruel, and dominating. Arturo is his willing slave: 'La mia infanzia è come un paese felice, del quale lui è l'assoluto regnante' (41: 'My childhood is like a happy country, of which he is absolute ruler').

This male paradise is broken when Wilhelm unexpectedly brings home a second wife, Nunziata, a girl from the slums of Naples. Arturo's maturation takes place through his evolving perception of Nunziata, as a rival for his father' affections, as the usurper of his mother's place, but also as a companion of almost the same age, a playmate, a sister. He tries to establish his ascendancy over her by playing on her superstitions and mocking her ignorance. But even from the beginning his feelings towards the intruder are not unalloyed. Arturo needs affection, and Nunziata, human, warm and generous, seems ready to provide it. Her very presence on the island marks a kind of betrayal of Arturo by his father. The pages in which Arturo's confused emotions struggle to the surface as he spars on and off with Nunziata during her first afternoon and evening on the island (*Isola*, 115-147) are among the very best that Morante has written. Within a short time, Arturo also begins to see her as a lover. Three times he tries to possess his step mother sexually, three times she rebuffs him: on the third occasion he will leave the island. By this time, however, Arturo has learnt that his father's legendary journeys take him no further than Naples and that the band of faithful followers with whom he would one day take Arturo off to see the world is the homosexual circuit that he frequents in the city. Denounced as a 'parody' by a former lover who is now blackmailing him, Wilhelm can no more function as a model in Arturo's life than the mother who is dead or the stepmother who cannot replace her.

The departure from the island with which the novel ends can in a sense be seen as a liberation: Arturo, like Elisa before him, is freed of his fantasies. Certainly, the novel recounts a progressive disillusionment and a corresponding initiation into adult life as gradually Arturo's primal beatitude is disturbed and broken into. The hero crosses a series of threshholds and arrives on the brink of life in the grown-up world. But here we are faced with the problem of the blank after the narrated events which I mentioned at the beginning of this description. Progress into what? This is not a novel of 'sentimental education', in which the hero is gradually socialized and can therefore be left at the gate of life entirely prepared to enter. Arturo's experiences do not prepare him for the social world which he will encounter on leaving the island and which is as much a mystery to him at the end of his years there as it was at the beginning. Indeed, on one of the rare occasions on which the narrator comments about his actual present, it is precisely to say that he is still waiting:

> Io, da quando sono nato, non ho aspettato che il giorno pieno, la perfezione della vita: ho sempre saputo che l'isola, e quella mia primitiva felicità, non erano altro che una imperfetta notte; anche gli anni deliziosi con mio padre, anche quelle sere là con lei! erano ancora la notte della vita, in fondo l'ho sempre saputo. E adesso, lo so più che mai; e aspetto sempre che il mio giorno arrivi, simile a un fratello meraviglioso con cui ci si racconta, abbracciati, la lunga noia.
>
> (*Isola*, 225)

(Since I was born, all I have been waiting for is the fullness of
the day, the perfection of life: I always knew that the island,
and my former happiness, were nothing but imperfect night:
even the wonderful years with my father, even those evenings
there with her! were still the night of life, deep inside I always
knew it. And now, I know it more than ever; and I still wait
for my day to come, like a marvellous brother to hug and talk
together of the long dullness.)

So the accumulation of Arturo's experiences cannot be seen as
progressive in the sense of them leading anywhere. Rather they
form a concentric pattern, each reproducing on a larger scale
Arturo's first and fundamental experience. The death of his dog
Immacolatella, the intrusion of Nunziata, the birth of his half-
brother Carmine Arturo, Nunziata's rejection of his sexual
advances, the unmasking of Wilhelm and Arturo's final expulsion
from the island are each a repetition and an expansion of Arturo's
primal exclusion from the mother who died when he was born and
denied herself to him.

   If this interpretation is correct, Morante's most recent novel,
Aracoeli, engages upon a striking return to the theme of separation
from the mother twenty-five years after the publication of *Isola*.
Only, in the new novel, the pattern of repeated exclusions is more
directly and centrally organized around the relation of mother and
son, which as in 'Lo scialle andaluso', is the explicit theme of the
book. *Aracoeli*, set in 1975, is organized around the memories of the
protagonist-narrator, which are sparked off by his sudden
decision, at the age of 43 (conspicuously the oldest of all Morante's
heroes), to visit for the first time his mother's birthplace in
Andalusia. Emanuele, the narrator, was six when his mother – who
bears the liturgical name of Aracoeli (Altar of Heaven) – died. More
than half the novel, in fragmentary episodes interspersed with
more recent occurrences and the narrator's present journey as well
as in longer narrative passages, is given over to the re-evocation of
their life togther, first in the 'exclusive intimacy' of a semi-
clandestine life in the Monte Sacro district of Rome (she is a
Spanish peasant girl, Emanuele's father is a serving officer in the
Royal Italian Navy: for a number of years they are unable to
marry), then in the more public environment of a middle-class
apartment block in the Quartieri Alti. In particular, it is the last
year of Aracoeli's life which dominates the recollections of her son,
the period during which, crazed by the loss of her second child, a

girl, she rejects both the bourgeois decencies of the Quartieri Alti and the awkward attempts of Emanuele to restore the bliss of Monte Sacro. One emblematic scene – regrettably too long to quote here – initiates the story of Aracoeli's decline and Emanuele's rejection. It is one morning shortly after baby Carina has died. Emanuele comes home early from school and finds his mother asleep. Her nightdress is unbuttoned and unhesitatingly, though deeply agitated, the boy climbs into bed beside her and begins to suckle: he has replaced his baby sister and is rewarded by what taste to him like drops of milk. His joy is boundless. Suddenly, Aracoeli is awake and staring at him in horror, yelling at him to get out as he scurries to the door, 'verso un pozzo di luce meridiana terribile e accecante' ('towards a pool of noonday light, fearful and blinding', 209).

Such a scene seems to me to illustrate the best and the worst in Morante's writing. It is a wonderful evocation of the unhappiness of childhood, of the anxiety of a child who senses, without being able to identify the source of his fear, without even knowing quite what would be the consequences were his fear to be realized, that he is in some way being left out, uncherished. The very exaggeration of his actions represent accurately the panic lack of measure of those early years, years of darkness and terror. But at the same time the whole episode, in as much as it symbolizes very crudely, from the adult's point of view, a radical separation between mother and child – the definite dismissal from the garden – is an important underpinning to an ideological structure which it is hard for the reader to assent to with quite the enthusiasm that the author shows. Emanuele's unsuccessful relation with his mother, who shortly turns to sexual promiscuity and prostitution, is taken in fact as the basis for the formation of a neurotic, unable to relate to other people whether as individuals or collectively except masochistically, barely capable of functioning in a physical and material sense, excluded on all sides and – what seems to be taken in the novel as a mark of particular deviance – homosexual. But his neurosis is only a question of degree: every living creature, animal as well as human, is condemned to search for love; all of us are 'orfani e mai svezzati' ('orphans and never weaned', 108), all of us like the stray dogs who keep crossing Emanuele's path. And universal exclusion leads to universal humiliation. Not by accident, Emanuele's search for his mother ends with him finding the memory of his last meeting with his father, in 1945. The ex-naval officer is reduced to an alcoholic wreck, but it is not *his*

humiliation that we are concerned with. The twelve-year-old
Emanule is embarrassed and confused and simply wants to escape;
only thirty years later does he realize that the obscure sensation he
felt on leaving his father was the desire – impossible to realize – to
make a declaration of love to him. Is the father here simply a
substitute for the departed Aracoeli? Or is he in some sense the
'real' object of Emanuele's masochistic urge to submit to a loved
one? It is an enigmatic presence at the end of the novel, but one
which confirms the ideological lesson: we are all excluded.

Although, as I have suggested, *Aracoeli* returns to certain themes of
the 1950s, the way in which the novel brings its ideological
assumptions out into the open is much more in keeping with the
trend of Morante's writing since *L'isola di Arturo*. This
forthrightness has coincided with the writer's growing conviction
that the fate of exclusion is common to us all, but is reinforced by
society as it is at present organized for the oppression of the weak
and particularly by modern industrialized and technological
cultures: our collective condition is one of 'alienation' or
'unreality'. A few elect spirits escape this fate and attain, or rather
retain, for most of them are children, the existential goal of
wholeness (*integrità*). The artist is entrusted with a social mission,
to bear witness to the truth and alleviate the sufferings of the
audience. The artist, Morante wrote in 1959, (two years after the
publication of *Isola*), is 'the sun-figure (*il protagonista solare*) who
in myth confronts the dragon of the night, to liberate the
frightened city' (1959, 33; she uses virtually the same expressions
twice more in the following decade – 1965, 36 and 1968, v). It should
be noted that the evangelical fervour of this sense of mission owes
as little to Marx as her psychology (in which the moment of
'corruption' seems to coincide with the child's actually becoming
aware of his exclusion) does to Freud. Morante sees herself as an
anarchist, her declared political goal is Utopia; if she tries to 'speak
for' others it is as a 'blessed propagandist' like Fra Angelico on
behalf of beauty and unalienated reality, not as the accredited
representative of a political party or ideology exercising or in
pursuit of power (1970). Her commitment is precisely that of the
artist I described at the beginning of this essay, who risks all on the
imagination.

Both of the books which follow *Isola*, *Il mondo salvato dai
ragazzini* (*The World Saved by Little Children*, 1968) and *La*

Storia (*History*, 1974), reflect these concerns and this commitment. *Mondo* is a collection of poems (most of them narrative or dramatic rather than strictly lyrical) in which, after a period of personal upheaval and wide travel, Morante draws on a new language, to some extent influenced by American models (Beat poetry, the blues) to specify issues that had previously been left vague, in terms that correspond exactly to the dominant themes of mid-to-late 1960s youth culture or counter-culture: the denunciation of military violence (especially in Vietnam) and of Fascism (the colonels' Greece being the topical case); the exaltation of certain values – love, happiness, carefreeness, youth itself – believed to be in dangerous conflict with the productivist mentality of neo-capitalism; the conviction (following R.D. Laing) that madness (neurosis, schizophrenia) is a social, not an individual, condition; an infinite suspicion of the mass-media and their power; the celebration of the imagination against the alienating effects of an imposed social order.

What immediately strikes the reader of the poems published in 1968 is a sense of urgency quite absent from the measured stateliness of Morante's earlier work. The poet howls a protest, desperately seeking to awaken her contemporaries to the violent and dangerous 'unreality' of their world. In this task, she can count at best on the understanding and support of the 'Felici Pochi', the Happy Few, who within themselves, whether the 'world' sees it or not, are beautiful and happy. The poems of *Il mondo salvato dai ragazzini* are like a gallery of these anarchistic free spirits: the young American painter Bill Morrow, loved and mourned by Morante (*Addio, Farewell*), a visionary Oedipus (*La serata a Colono, Evening at Colonus*), and above all the Pazzariello, bastard, orphan, stateless, homeless, jobless, illiterate and resistant to all known forms of social discipline (*La canzone clandestina della Grande Opera, The Secret Song of the Great Opera*). It is also a record of the constant attempts of Morante's Unhappy Many to suppress them – a conflict that will form the backbone of Morante's third novel.

Within a year of publication, aided by astute publicity, *La Storia* sold nearly a million copies: Morante was suddenly a best-seller. The best-seller is a different phenomenon from the merely successful novel, and certainly from the 'popular' novel, though it may well incorporate certain devices of popular fiction. It implies a highly organized publishing industry and the ability on the part of the readership to perceive the book as a product with features readily distinguishable from those of its competitors. The 'strangeness' of Morante's case, the infrequency of her literary production and its rare artistic quality, her refusal to be drawn into literary and political debate except in her works, and at the same time her idiosyncratic association with the youth movements of the 1960s all enabled the publisher to create an unusual air of expectation around the new novel, while the direct publication in paperback and the selling price of 2,000 lire helped create the impression that this was something unique, that had to be read (cf. Chapter 1, p. 18). It may seem strange to find Morante collaborating, consciously or not, with the advanced capitalism she despises and denounces in her writing, but *La Storia* seems both to have met a certain political demand (although very far from the positions of the PCI, the novel does echo a certain nostalgia for the 1940s, the years of anti-Fascist resistance and firmness of democratic purpose which in 1974-76 the left were insistently evoking in the name of national unity) and, more fundamentally, to have stimulated a process of sado-masochistic identification among its readers.

The story is centred on the brief existence of Useppe Ramundo, between January 1941 and the summer of 1947, in and around Rome. These are years of war and post-war deprivation. Useppe is conceived of a rape; with his widowed mother Ida he suffers bombing, homelessness, evacuation, hunger and illness; from his mother he inherits the propensity to epilepsy which will kill him. They are years of fear, and Ida's fear is such that she can barely function as an adult human being. They are years too of bitter civil strife, the slaughter of innocents, and genocide (not essentially different from the rest of history, in Morante's view), and Useppe will bear witness to these things and to the human wreckage that results. Yet Useppe is also a celebration in the novel, a 'festa', the focus of all those forces which exalt life over death, beauty over ugliness, reality (in Morante's terms) over the cruelty and repression of modern civilization.

What relation do these individual lives, Useppe, Ida, her other, teenage son Nino, the anarchist Davide Segre and all the rest, bear to the History (always with a capital letter) which gives the novel its title and to which the reader's attention is forcefully drawn before he even opens the book by the strong double qualification of the title (*La Storia* is both 'A novel' and 'A scandal which has lasted ten thousand years')? The immediate answer is that from the point of view of the characters History is remote and foreign, something that conditions individual lives and at the same time is quite alien from them. But this withdrawal from History does not stop at mere ignorance or indifference, it goes beyond the mindlessness of the Unhappy Many so often denounced by Morante, in order to reach a reality, and an awareness of reality, that seems to be posited not only as different from History but as an alternative to it.

The process is clear in the opening pages of the novel. It opens with what will be a structural feature of all the chapters (which correspond to single years, with the exception of the first and the last which are dated 19**): a run-through, in the style of a school-manual but with clear authorial underlinings and comments, of the main historical events of the 'secolo atomico' ('atomic century', 7), up to the winter of 1940. The chronology, all in small type, is followed by a rhythmic passage, almost a voice-over or caption, which bridges the gap between historical and fictional narration:

> Un giorno di gennaio dell'anno
> 1941
> un soldato tedesco camminava
> nel quartiere di San Lorenzo a Roma.
> Sapeva 4 parole in tutto d'italiàno
> e del mondo sapeva poco o niente.
> Di nome si chiamava Gunther.
> Il cognome rimane sconosciuto.
>
> (*Storia*, 13)

> (One January day in the year
> 1941
> a German solider was walking
> in the San Lorenzo district of Rome.
> He knew altogether 4 words of Italian
> and of the world next to nothing.
> His Christian name was Gunther.
> His surname is unknown.)

These words are repeated and developed in the first couple of pages of the prose description that follows: the reader is now within the private· world of the boy-soldier, and within that world an analogous distancing from History takes place. The youth comes from Dachau: the underlining of the *historical* significance of the place only serves to establish its *lack* of any significance for the characters in the story, starting with Gunther himself. And his other 'place', Rome, the city where he now finds himself on his way to the North African front, suffers a similar fate: the few bits of culture he's picked up at school are quickly forgotten under the pressure of more instinctual needs:

> A quest'ora, per lui Campidogli e Colossei erano mucchi d'immondezza. La Storia era una maledizione. E anche la geografia. Per dire il vero, l'unica cosa che in quel momento lui andasse cercando, d'istinto, per le vie di Roma, era un bordello.
>
> (*Storia*, 18)

> (At this hour, Capitols and Colosseums were heaps of rubbish. History was a malediction. And geography. To tell the truth, the only thing he was looking for at the moment, by instinct, in the streets of Rome, was a brothel).

Wandering through the deserted working-class district on this warm afternoon, the wine he's drunk goes to his head, he wants to snuggle down and sleep like a child; homesick and just sick, he would be comforted by any female creature, not just 'una comune ragazza o puttanella di quartiere, ma qualsiasi animale femmina: una cavalla, una mucca, un'asina' (20: 'not just a common-or-garden girl or neighbourhood whore, but any female animal: a mare, a cow, a she-ass') In a few lines Gunther has been transformed from soldier of the Reich to child, to small creature, an animal.

In a bizarre way, he meets his perfect match, for the female creature to whom it falls to mother Gunther (and the son Useppe that she bears him), Ida, is at once presented as a combination of all these features: terrified by History (its specific manifestation in her case is the race-laws: Ida is half-Jewish and living in the constant anxiety that the authorities will find out), she has been left by her fear of the world in a state of permanent childishness, signalled by the 'dolcezza passiva' ('passive sweetness') of her eyes whose strangeness 'ricordava l'idiozia misteriosa degli animali, i quali non con la mente, ma con un senso dei loro corpi vulnerabili, 'sanno' il passato e il futuro di ogni destino' (21: 'recalled the mysterious idiocy of animals, who not with their minds but with a sense of their vulnerable bodies, 'know' the past and the future of all destinies'). And when these two child-animals are finally brought together by the narrator in what it is difficult to remember is a violent rape, the violation itself is experienced by Ida in terms of something from her childhood (in fact a recurrence of her fainting fits), while it begins with another evocation of the name of Dachau and a strange transformation of Gunther's eyes (68ff.); the eyes, like Ida's, are mentioned again at the end (73) with their 'sguardo straziato, di una ignoranza infinita e di una consapevolezza totale' ('tortured look, infinitely ignorant and totally aware').

This look, and the visionary state of consciousness to which it corresponds, crops up repeatedly in the novel, especially in Ida and, even more, in Useppe (his half-brother Nino, though he too is firmly on the side of life in the novel, does not have this insight: he is all movement and surface). It is in fact the privileged counterpoint to the historical discourse, the monotonous recounting of one outrage after another. It is the means by which History is seen through, and judged, but also suffered, by the most sensitive of its victims, those who are in some sense saved. It is used particularly to comment on the fate of the Jews of the Roman ghetto whose existence and destruction forms one of the leitmotifs of the novel. Ida and her two-year-old child chance to witness the embarcation of hundreds of Jews for deportation at the Tiburtina Station: it is October 1943. Neither has any precise idea of what is going on. For Ida the sound is translated into a kind of memory that is akin to death:

> E Ida riconosceva questo coro confuso. Non meno che le strida quasi indecenti della signora, e che gli accenti sentenziosi del vecchio Di Segni, tutto questo misero vocio dei carri la adescava con una dolcezza struggente, per una memoria continua che non le tornava dai tempi, ma da un altro canale: di là stesso dove la ninnavano le canzoncine calabresi di suo padre, o la poesia anonima della notte avanti, o i bacetti che le bisbigliavano carina carina. Era un punto di riposo che la tirava in basso, nella tana promiscua di un'unica famiglia sterminata.
>
> (*Storia*, 245)

> (And Ida recognized this confused chorus. No less than the almost indecent cries of the woman and old Di Segni's pompous tones, all this wretched murmuring from the wagons drew her in with painful sweetness, by virtue of a constant memory that came to her not from past times but from another channel: from the same place as her father's Calabrian songs which used to lull her off to sleep, or the

anonymous poem of the night before, or the little kisses whispering darling, darling, It was a point of repose that pulled her down into the swarming den of a single, unbounded family.)

Later, drawn back to the now deserted ghetto (itself a kind of 'tana' or den), she will similarly 'hear' the voices of its inhabitants and suddenly realize they are all dead (*Storia*, 340). Likewise, Useppe's perception of the deportation merges into previous and subsequent experiences; in particular it sparks an unconscious recollection of his one previous visit to the Tiburtina, with Nino, when the only visible traveller was a calf with a ticket round its neck, in whose 'occhi larghi e bagnati si indovinava una prescienza oscura' ('big damp eyes you guessed at some obscure foreknowledge'); Nino's dog Blitz (but not Nino) seems to understand, and so does the baby Useppe: 'Una specie di tristezza o di sospetto lo attraversò, come se una tenda buia gli calasse davanti' (12: 'A kind of sadness or suspicion passed across his face, as if a dark curtain had been lowered before him').

La Storia is the only one of Morante's full-length novels to date to use a third-person narrator. While this device reinforces the illusion that the narrator has a broad and superior knowledge of the events to be related and is, therefore, specially qualified to do so, it also leads to problems. The textbook historical summaries at the beginning of each chapter and the moments of intuitive pre-logical insight I have just been describing are two extremes of a narration which for a great many of the novel's 700 pages does no more than register flatly the events of passing time: it is a kind of skindeep narration which refuses the explanatory potential of historicist writing and can only allude to the knowledge of the unconscious and the preconscious which was in a sense the touchstone of *Menzogna e sortilegio*. At this point we come back finally to Morante's next and most recent novel, for in *Aracoeli* she returns to the use of a first person and the dimension of memory. By doing so, she has given herself more space to do what she is really good at: to take what she calls 'il seme di quel mio pianto' ('the seed of my tears', 327) and explore its every component through the jungle of the imagination: the stifling heat of that jungle, if I may pursue the metaphor, suits her better than the airy plain she found herself on in *La Storia*. Not that this congeniality of technique makes her view of human destiny any less despairing. If anything, the internalization of the first-person narration reinvests her writing with an emotional force which tended to be dissipated in *La Storia*. But there is also in her new book an added note of what seems like renunciation. Whereas the 1974 novel recounts the slaughter of innocents, *Aracoeli* maps the self-destruction wrought by experience. Morante seems to take her distance equally from History, and from those who at one time seemed as though they might be the bearers of an alternative history. At any rate, she has chosen a middle-aged protagonist who admits: 'La mia natura è negata alla politica e alla storia: miseri e vani i miei tentativi di smentirlo' (142: 'I am by nature quite unsuited to history and politics: my attempts to deny it are foolish and vain'), who perceives demonstrating youngsters as mindless slogan-shouters and in whose experience the revolutionaries of 1968 have become exponents of what the novel satirizes as the 'Moderate Half-Right'. At the same time, however, Emanuele has lost the visionary confidence of his younger predecessors Elisa and Arturo: he is short-sighted and takes off his glasses when he does not want or cannot bear to see; he acknowledges repeatedly the fallibility of memory, he knows that his search is vain and that at the end of his journey he will find nothing: a private futility that is matched at the public level by General Franco's unconscionable time a-dying (we are at the beginning of November 1975). *Aracoeli* is not simply a throwback to the 1950s or a continuation of the ideological explicitness of *Mondo* and *Storia*, but introduces, it seems to me, a note of scepticism more pronounced than any we have heard in Morante before.

BIOGRAPHICAL NOTE

Elsa Morante was born in 1918 in Rome, where she still lives. Though for nearly four decades she has been at the centre of the tangle of alliances, friendships and quarrels that make up the Roman literary scene, she is extremely jealous of her private life and reticent about her early years (her date of birth has also been given as 1912 or 1916). She left her lower-middle-class home when she was eighteen and her first short stories were published in magazines in the late 1930s. In 1941 she married the novelist Alberto Moravia from whom she separated in 1962. Although her first novel, *Menzogna e sortilegio* (Viareggio Prize 1948) was hailed by Gyorgy Lukács as 'the greatest modern Italian novel', it was the international success of *L'isola di Arturo* (Strega Prize 1957) which provided her with the means to live independently and travel widely. Except for a brief period between 1957 and 1965, she has steadfastly refused to give interviews or to engage in public discussion or debate, insisting instead that everything that needs to be known about her is to be found in her books.

BIBLIOGRAPHY

PRINCIPAL WORKS

Il gioco segreto (stories), Einaudi, Turin, 1941
Menzogna e sortilegio, Einaudi, Turin, 1948; ed. cited Mondadori, Milan, 1966; (trans. A. Foulke) *House of liars*, Harcourt, Brace, New York, 1951
L'isola di Arturo, Einaudi, Turin, 1957; ed. cited Mondadori, Milan, 1969; (trans. I. Quigly) *Arturo's island*, Collins, London, 1959
Alibi (poems), Longanesi, Milan, 1958
Lo scialle andaluso (stories), Einaudi, Turin, 1963
Il mondo salvato dai ragazzini, Einaudi, Turin, 1968; ed. cited paperback edition 1968
La Storia, Einaudi, Turin, 1974; (trans. W. Weaver) *History: a novel*, Knopf, New York, 1977; Penguin, Harmondsworth, 1980
Aracoeli, Einaudi, Turin, 1982

WORKS CITED

Bontempelli, M., *L'avventura novecentista*, ed. R. Jacobbi, Vallecchi, Florence, 1974
Calvino, I. Reply to 'Nove domande sul romanzo', *Nuovi argomenti* 38–39 (May–Aug. 1959), 6–12
Morante, E. Reply to 'Nove domande sul romanzo', *Nuovi argomenti* 38–39 (May–Aug. 1959), 17–38
—, 'Pro o contro la bomba atomica', *L'Europa letteraria* 6, 1965, 31–42
—, Nota introduttiva, *Il mondo salvato dai ragazzini*, paperback ed., Einaudi, Turin, 1968
—,'Cenni sulla vita e sulle opere', *L'isola di Arturo*, Mondadori, Milan, 1969
—, 'Il beato propagandista del Paradiso', *L'opera completa dell'Angelico*, Rizzoli, Milan, 1970, 5–10

FURTHER READING

Cases, C. 'La Morante pro e contro la menzogna' [1974], in *Sociologia della letteratura*, ed. F. Ferrara et al, Bulzoni, Rome, 1978, 268–278
Debenedetti, G. 'L'isola di Arturo', *Nuovi argomenti* 26 (May–June 1957), 43–61
Ferrone, S. 'Davanti a un plotone d'esecuzione', *Il Ponte* 30 (1974), 10, 1151–1163
Ferrucci, F. 'Elsa Morante's Limbo without Elysium', *Italian Quarterly* 7 (1963), 27/28, 28–52
Pupino, A.R. *Struttura e stile della narrativa di Elsa Morante*, Longo, Ravenna, 1968
Ravanello, D. *Scrittura e follia nella narrativa di Elsa Morante*, Marsilio, Venice, 1980

Ricci, G. 'Tra Eros e Thanatos: storia di un mito mancato. Analisi tematico-narrativa de "L'isola di Arturo",' *Strumenti critici* 38 (Feb. 1979), 126–168

Sgorlon, C. *Invito alla lettura di Elsa Morante*, Mursia, Milan, 1972

*Venturi, G. *Morante*, La Nuova Italia (Il Castoro), Florence, 1977

Verina R. Jones

10 Leonardo Sciascia

Most of Sciascia's narrative works begin with an epigraph. Two of these can be taken as statements of the author's views of the status of writing:

> The sulphur-miners from my town call fire-damp *antimonio*. Sulphur-miners believe that this name derives from anti-monk, since in the old days it was used by monks, and, when carelessly handled, it killed them. Also, antimony is used in the making of both gun-powder and type-metal, and was a component of cosmetics in the past. It is for all these reasons that I have given this story the title 'L'antimonio'.
>
> ('L'antimonio', 'Fire-damp', 1961)

> Let it not be supposed that I am detailing any mystery, or penning any romance. Poe, *The Murders in the Rue Morgue*.
>
> (*A ciascuno il suo, To Each His Own*, 1966)

The quotation from Poe warns the reader that the text which follows is not, or not merely, a good yarn to be read as a source of pleasure. The novel, then, is justified by the fact of being something other, or something more, than literature: writing is, or should be, a tool for the understanding of a reality other than itself. The epigraph to 'L'antimonio' establishes a parallel between the fire-damp which haunts the sulphur-miners, death, gun-powder, the printed word, and the making of cosmetics. Here Sciascia appears to be suggesting that writing is not a neutral, harmless tool: it can be destructive, or it can mask reality, but on the other hand it can be a valid weapon with which to fight. The narrator-protagonist of the story has to be catapulted by the fire-damp explosion in the Sicilian mine 'nel fuoco della Spagna' ('into the burning hell of Spain') before he can 'parlare e parlare' ('talk and talk'), understand himself and reality, and write about it.

Sciascia's view of writing, at least until 1970, is situated consistently between these two poles: writing as mystification of reality, or writing as revelation of reality. This approach would seem to define Sciascia as a perfect example of the 'committed writer' demanded by Neo-realist programmes of literature. His first important book (*Le parrocchie di Regalpetra, The Parishes of Regalpetra*) appeared in fact in 1956, at a time when Neo-realism was entering its crisis. In some important ways this book represents precisely Sciascia's attempt to come to terms with the Neo-realist tradition, to measure his distance from it, and to define his own space within the Italian literary scene.

Le parrocchie di Regalpetra is a collection of nine documentary essays on the life of a poor Sicilian town, Sciascia's own town. The author's investigation encompasses the working conditions of the local salt-miners and sulphur-miners, the sub-standard housing and the under-nourishment to which the poor are subjected, the curse of emigration, the deficiencies of the school system, and also the local folklore, the political intrigues and electoral vicissitudes of the recent past, the role of the clergy, the intellectual and sexual outlook of the middle class who frequent the local *circolo* (gentlemen's club). Although the main emphasis is on the contemporary life of the town, all the essays contain frequent references to the past, and one of them, 'La storia di Regalpetra' ('The History (or Story) of Regalpetra'), is focused specifically on its past history. This historical dimension, which persists in Sciascia's later writings, is a fundamental aspect of his approach to social reality. The ills of present-day Regalpetra are not to be seen merely as something to be observed and denounced, but as problems to be overcome; if they are to be overcome, they must be understood, and an analysis of the past will provide at least an explanation of the present condition. 'La storia di Regalpetra' undoubtedly presents the picture of an almost unbroken line of inept and rapacious rulers, of violence and class oppression. But the denunciation is accompanied by a constant attempt to make sense of this bleak reality, and to provide a key to its apparent paradoxes, and therefore a key to the apparent inevitability of the ills of Regalpetra. There is no sentimental populism in *Le parrocchie*, no notion that the poor and oppressed are the carriers of the correct approach to things; there is no identification between the oppressed of Regalpetra and the intellectual who writes about them. At the time of writing *Le parrocchie* Sciascia was a teacher in the local primary school, a job which he was to leave soon after. He does not claim to be anything other than the middle-class teacher whose life 'si svolge tra la scuola e il circolo' ('is played out between the school and the club'). The school and the *circolo* are the two principal literary spaces of the book; they are the only spaces which are described from within, while all other environments, the places where the poor live and work, are observed from outside. Sciascia's denunciation of the appalling injustices to which the poor are subjected is filtered entirely through his own rationalistic analysis.

Although Sciascia's analysis of social reality in *Le parrocchie* is inspired by a broadly left-wing perspective, he rejects the orthodoxies of the left. Both the Socialist Party and the Communist Party are presented in a critical light; the trade unions are shown as incapable, or unwilling, to organize the salt-mine workers; the myth of the *Garibaldini*, dear to the imagination of the left, is pointedly debunked. When Garibaldi's troops come through Regalpetra, they shoot a petty thief, a poor man; the officer who executes him is 'biondo come un tedesco' ('blonde like a German'), just another invader. It is in fact the Bourbons, the rulers who were unseated by Garibaldi's invasion, whom Sciascia singles out as marginally better, more honest, less corrupt, than other rulers of Sicily.

Sciascia in fact, in his own preface to the first edition of *Le parrocchie*, presents himself self-consciously as a writer who will toe no party line:

> Con queste pagine non metto una bandiera rossa al pianterreno: non saprei goderne l'effetto dalla terrazza; né, restando al pianterreno, potrei salutarla con fede. Credo nella ragione umana, e nella libertà e nella giustizia che dalla ragione scaturiscono; ma pare che in Italia basta ci si affacci a parlare il linguaggio della ragione per essere accusati di mettere la bandiera rossa alla finestra.
>
> (*Le parrocchie*, 11)

> (With this book I do not intend to put a red flag out from the ground-floor: I could neither enjoy looking at it from upstairs nor salute it with faith if I remained downstairs. I believe in human reason, and in the freedom and justice which arise from reason; but in Italy anyone who speaks the language of reason is accused of hoisting the red flag.)

While rejecting any specific political involvement, Sciascia bases his writing on a belief in the crucial role of reason. Reason is for him the essential tool for approaching reality. A rational approach to reality will produce positive results, the bringing about of freedom and justice, and writing has the function of enlarging the area of rationality. But the link between writing and reality begins to loosen very soon after *Le parrocchie*. The whole of Sciascia's subsequent career as a writer is marked by a tension between a view of writing as an active intervention in reality and writing as an alternative to reality.

The type of language used in *Le parrocchie* is consistent with Sciascia's view of writing as rational organization of reality. He does not disdain to use the modes of the popular spoken language, with its attendant regionalisms, but does not give them a privileged status. He uses a variety of registers and narrative styles. There is free indirect speech, although not used in a systematic fashion, and not with the function of organizing the narration; it is in fact often manipulated for ironic purposes. There is specialized technical language, as in the description of the salt-mine and the professional diseases of salt-miners, straight reporting language, Sicilian dialect, which is nevertheless consistently presented in italics and therefore distanced from the rest of the text, popular everyday language, highly literary language studded with elaborate lyrical imagery, short isolated one-clause sentences, as well as elaborate sentences with a wealth of subordinate clauses. Sciascia will continue using this type of linguistic *montage*, albeit with the refinements that one would expect from greater experience, in his later works.

Le parrocchie would appear to lay a claim to literal truth. But the real name of Sciascia's home town is Racalmuto; Regalpetra is a fictional name:

> Esistono in Sicilia tanti paesi che a Regalpetra somigliano; ma Regalpetra non esiste. Esistono a Racalmuto, un paese che nella mia immaginazione confina con Regalpetra, i salinari . . . La Sicilia è ancora una terra amara.
>
> (*Le parrocchie*, 12)

> (In Sicily there are many towns like Regalpetra, but Regalpetra itself does not exist. In Racalmuto, a town which in my imagination adjoins Regalpetra, there exist the salt-miners . . . Sicily still is a bitter land.)

The whole book contains only one other mention of Racalmuto, in the essay 'I salinari' ('The Salt-miners'), and in the context of a straight technical discussion of the professional diseases of salt-miners: it is a 'paese il cui territorio confina con quello di Regalpetra, e altrettanto ricco di saline' ('a town whose lands adjoin those of Regalpetra, and which is equally rich in salt-mines'). Here the author might be recognizing implicitly that, apart from the description of salt-mining, his documentary essays do not necessarily relate facts which have really happened, that the Regalpetra of the text is meant to present a synthesis, his synthesis, of Sicilian small-town life, that his essay-writing is beginning to flow into narrative.

Gli zii di Sicilia (*Sicilian Uncles*, 1958) is a work of out-and-out narrative. But it is interesting to note that in Sciascia's subjective judgement the difference between essay-writing and narrative in his own work is marginal; as late as 1970 he declared in an interview with Walter Mauro: 'My subject matter . . . is that of the essayist, which then assumes the "modes" of narrative . . .' (Mauro 1970, 2). *Le parrocchie* will remain in any case the storehouse for themes, characters, situations, images, turns of phrase which can be traced in his later writings. *Gli zii di Sicilia* especially can be read in some important senses as a continuation of what was said in *Le parrocchie*, in particular as a continuation of 'Breve cronaca del regime' ('Short Chronicle of the Regime'), which more than the other essays assumes the narrative mode. 'Breve cronaca' is a short autobiographical piece; it consists of Sciascia's own recollections of Fascism from the age of three, at the time of the assassination of Matteotti, to the American landing in 1943. It is essentially the story of an acquisition of consciousness, a voyage from ignorance to a rational understanding of the reality of Fascism.

Gli zii di Sicilia consisted initially of three rather long stories. 'La zia d'America ('The American Aunt') investigates the reactions of a Sicilian boy to the events at the end of the war, from the landing of the American troops in Sicily in July 1943 to the first general election with its landslide for the Christian Democrats in April 1948, and the ensuing visit from the American relatives. 'La morte di Stalin' ('The Death of Stalin') is the story of a Communist Sicilian cobbler's attempts to cope with the successive waves of puzzlement and disillusion engendered by Soviet policies and events, from the Ribbentrop-Molotov pact in 1939 to the publication of Khruschev's report on Stalin's crimes in 1956. 'Il quarantotto' ('1848') looks at the repercussions, and the failed expectations, of the Italian Risorgimento on a small Sicilian coastal town in the period 1848–1862, seen through the eyes of a local workman's son. In 1961, the year of the publication of Sciascia's first full-length novel, *Gli zii di Sicilia* was re-issued with the addition of a fourth story, 'L'antimonio'. It narrates the experiences of a Sicilian sulphur-miner who, following a fire-damp explosion in his mine, enrols with the Italian troops fighting in Spain on Franco's side, and learns some fundamental lessons from the Spanish civil war.

Each one of these tales is the story of a voyage towards understanding undertaken, consciously or unconsciously, by the central character. The objects of the quest are invariably certain historical periods and problems which are seen as crucial for the reality of Sicily, and, to a certain extent, Italy: Fascism, the transition from Fascism to democracy, the Risorgimento, the myth of the Soviet Union.

In three of the four stories Sciascia uses the techniques of first-person narration. The central characters of all four tales are presented in a sympathetic light, but it is significant that the one who does not act as first-person narrator, and therefore the one with whom the author identifies the least, is Calogero Schirò, the hero of 'La morte di Stalin', the Communist cobbler who goes in search not so much of rational understanding, but of authoritative explanations that will allow him to keep intact his faith in Stalin, 'l'uomo che aveva fatto della Russia la patria della speranza umana' ('the man who had turned Russia into the fatherland of hope'). Calogero Schirò is constantly reasoning, but his 'ragionare' (a word which recurs with great frequency in this story) comes to acquire the opposite meaning: Sciascia guides Calogero's 'reasoning' through a series of stages each of which is an increasingly uneasy state of faith. Calogero is only allowed to catch glimpses of a possible road to real reason, real understanding, when he allows himself to give way to his own feelings, which may go against Communist orthodoxies:

> Intanto Hitler si mangiava la Polonia, il suo esercito si muoveva come uno schiaccianoci, la Polonia di colpo frantumata; la Polonia marcia di latifondismo, pensava Calogero, l'eroico popolo polacco, quei marci latifondisti che guidavano cariche di cavalleria contro i carri armati di Hitler, tutta la Polonia con un solo grande cuore, viva la Polonia eroica e sventurata.
>
> (*Gli zii di Sicilia*, 66)

(In the meantime Hitler was swallowing Poland, his army moving like a nutcracker, Poland shattered with one blow; Poland rotten with feudalism, thought Calogero, the heroic people of Poland, rotten feudal land-owners leading cavalry charges against Hitler's tanks, the whole of Poland together with one big heart, hurrah for Poland heroic and stricken.)

Calogero's constant attempts at 'reasoning' are presented in a way which is all the more ironical because of the overt faith which permeates his attitude towards Stalin and Communist dogma. Sciascia plays endlessly with Calogero's basically religious attitude towards Stalin. But Calogero is a Sicilian Communist, so Stalin takes on in the mind of Calogero Schirò the connotations of a benevolent mafia chief, as well as those of an almost omnipotent saint: 'Il compagno Stalin, il maresciallo Stalin: lu zi'Peppi, lo zio di tutti, il protettore dei poveri e dei deboli' (79: 'Comrade Stalin, Marshal Stalin; good old uncle Joe, everybody's uncle, the protector of the poor and weak'). When the priest offers to give him a picture of St Joseph to display in his shop instead of Stalin's picture, Calogero replies: 'lei mi da il San Guiseppe e io lo metto a lato a Stalin, che è un santo lavoratore e non ci sfigura' (77: 'you give me St Joseph and I'll put it up next to Stalin, St Joseph is a worker saint so he won't look out of place'); a passage which in its transparent irony builds up nothing less than a St Joseph Stalin.

The stories which most clearly develop from 'Breve cronaca del regime' are 'La zia d'America' and 'L'antimonio'. Both pursue further the search for understanding with regard to events and ideals which were crucial to Sciascia's generation. The first-person narrator of 'La zia d'America' recollects historical events almost exactly from the point where 'Breve cronaca' ended: the landing of American troops in Sicily. While 'Breve cronaca' is meant to be autobiographical, 'La zia' is not; but the two pieces are placed along a historical continuum, which is manifested even in the use of repetition. On the very last page of 'Breve cronaca' we find 'Qualche giorno dopo il proclama di Roatta scomparve sotto un proclama bilingue di eguali dimensioni – *I, Harold Alexander . . .*' (*Le parrocchie*, 50: 'A few days later General Roatta's proclamation disappeared beneath a bi-lingual proclamation of the same size – *I, Harold Alexander . . .*'). 'Attaccarono in piazza manifesti. Uno cominciava – *I, Harold Alexander . . .*' (*Gli zii di Sicilia*, 20: 'They stuck up posters in the square. One started – *I, Harold Alexander . . .*') expresses one of the first recollections of the narrator of 'La zia'. The same recollection is described in the two instances with different linguistic registers. The 'I' of 'Breve cronaca' is a twenty-two-year-old at this stage, who has already reached awareness, while the 'I' of 'La zia' is an eight-year-old at the start of his journey towards discovery. 'Breve cronaca' follows a longer time-span than 'La zia' (nineteen as opposed to five years); it can therefore continue the recollections beyond the point where they can only be registered in terms of what a child would see and/or hear. The rational understanding for the narrator of 'breve cronaca' coincides with the discovery of American literature (Dos Passos) and the Spanish civil war when he was fifteen. The 'I' of 'La zia' is on the point of reaching understanding, at the age of thirteen, when the narration ends. There are some interesting similarities, and equally interesting differences, between the characterizations of the two narrators. Both belong to families which profess no anti-Fascist sentiments. Both families have glimmers of the crimes of Fascism, in both cases the assassination of Matteotti. Both narrators first hear of Socialism through local artisans, the builder and saddle-maker, and to a certain extent the tailor uncle, in 'Breve cronaca', who merge into the character of the overtly Socialist carpenter of 'La zia'. On the other hand, the narrator of 'La zia', characterized as he is as a little rascal, can be the vehicle for far wider experiences than the presumably well-behaved, protected child of 'Breve cronaca', and, therefore, for an accumulation of greater potential for knowledge.

At one important level 'La zia' not only continues the quest where 'Breve cronaca' left off, but puts paid to one crucial stage of Sciascia's own formation as a writer, indeed to one crucial myth of the Neo-realist generation. The 'I' of 'Breve cronaca', in common with other closet anti-Fascists under the regime, reads American literature. The 'I' of 'La zia' begins his voyage with a strong myth of America as the land of liberty, wealth and all the good things of life. When the American relatives arrive, they bring with them nothing but disillusions. Sciascia dwells insistently of the nasty aftertaste of American goodies: 'biscotti che sapevano di menta e spaghetti in scatola ... e vestiti camicie cravatte a fuoco d'artificio...' *(Gli zii di Sicilia*, 40: 'biscuits with a taste of peppermint and spaghetti in tins ... and dresses shirts ties as jazzy as fireworks...'); 'gli americani avevano pomodori tagliati a metà e ripieni di una pasta scura, un pezzo di pesce bianco e gelatinoso . . .' (47: 'the Americans were eating tomatoes cut in half and filled with a dark paste, and a piece of pale slimy fish . . .').

The narrator in fact begins to move towards a real understanding after he has rejected Saroyan's book (*The Human Comedy*) 'che avevano portato i soldati americani per educarci all' America' ('which the American soliders had brought with them so we would learn about America'). Only then does he begin the search, albeit unconscious, for understanding; a search which, significantly, cannot continue in the presence of the American cousin: 'Ma quando veniva mia cugina smettevo di cercare o di leggere, lei sedeva su una cassa e mi raccontava cose dell' America' (56-7: 'But when my cousin came along I would stop searching or reading, she would sit on a crate and tell me about America').

The beginning of rational understanding in 'Breve cronaca' coincided with the discovery not only of American writers, but also of the true face of the Spanish civil war and of the implications of the regime's involvement in it. 'L'antimonio' attempts to present the voyage towards this same discovery within the mind of a proletarian protagonist. The narrator of 'Breve cronaca' had understood that the 'contadini e artigiani del mio paese' ('peasants and craftsmen from my town') went to die for Fascism because there was no work at home; they were then recompensed, if they returned alive, with 'un posticino di bidello o di usciere' ('a miserable job as caretaker in some school or public building'). In 'L'antimonio' the peasants and craftsmen of 'Breve cronaca' are transformed into the sulphur-miner who is the narrator of the story, and the perspective is shifted from that of the young intellectual in 'Breve cronaca' to that of a young proletarian. He enlists for the Spanish war in order to escape the horror of his work. Except that for him, a poor man and an uneducated man, the Spanish war is a catalyst for the acquisition of understanding, and of the ability to articulate this understanding and to continue the search. When on his return home he is offered a job as school-caretaker, he asks to be sent to a school in a big city, away from Sicily, because he wants to 'vedere cose nuove' ('see new things'). 'L'antimonio' is the only one among Sciascia's works where the point of observation is exclusively that of a protagonist who is clearly characterized as a proletarian throughout.

'Il quarantotto' delves into one of the many missed opportunities of Sicilian history. The 1848 'revolution' is appropriated by the barons and bishops; after a 'triste inverno di fame' ('wretched winter of hunger') comes a 'gracile primavera' ('fragile spring'); the ephemeral *printemps des peuples* of the Sicilians ends in the renewed blossoming of the Bourbon lily:

'gigli rifiorirono sulle porte dei pubblici edifici' ('lilies bloomed again on the doors of public buildings'). 'Il quarantotto' also advances, for the first time in Sciascia's writings, the claim of a special status for writing as an alternative to reality, as a carrier of truth *per se*, albeit a nebulous, ill-defined notion of truth. The narrator refers at one point to events beyond the time range of the story, events which signal further struggles and further historical disillusionments; his drawing aside from active involvement coincides with his decision to crystallize his recollections on the written page:

> carabinieri e soldati del Regno d'Italia arrestano . . . gli
> uomini che lottano per l'umano avvenire. Sento rimorso per
> essermi sottratto all'arresto: ma la galera mi fa paura . . . E
> scrivere mi pare un modo di trovare consolazione e riposo; un
> modo di ritrovarmi, al di fuori delle contraddizioni della vita,
> finalmente in un destino di verità.
>
> (*Gli zii di Sicilia*, 110)
>
> (*carabinieri* and soldiers of the Kingdom of Italy are
> rounding up . . . the men who fight for the future of mankind.
> I feel guilty for escaping arrest: but prison frightens me . . .
> And writing seems like a way of finding solace and rest; a way
> of reaching at last beyond the contradictions of life into a
> destiny of truth.)

In 1961 Sciascia's first full-length novel appeared. This was *Il giorno della civetta* (*The Owl by Day*), and it was a detective story. Sciascia was to write three more detective novels, *A ciascuno il suo* (1966), *Il contesto* (*The Contest* or *The Context*, 1971), and *Todo modo* (*In Every Way*, 1974), with the interlude of the historical novel *Il consiglio d'Egitto* (*The Council of Egypt*, 1963).

Why the detective story? Sciascia's own answer to this question is very simple. He has something important to say and wants to make sure that it is going to be read:

> My subject matter . . . is that of the essayist, which . . . then
> becomes narration. . . . I pay especial attention to narrative
> technique. In fact I often use the most unfair of narrative
> techniques, which makes it impossible for the reader to put
> the book down; I am referring to the technique of the
> detective story.
>
> (*Mauro* 1970, 2)

Sciascia's detective novels, then, as one would expect, are detective novels with a difference. Once readers have finished reading these compelling stories, they are supposed to have also absorbed a lesson.

Il giorno della civetta tells the story of a mafia murder in an unspecified Sicilian town. Salvatore Colasberna, a local builder who refuses mafia protection, is killed. The *carabinieri* captain in charge of the investigation, Bellodi, doggedly follows the right track, which leads him to arrest the local mafia chief, Don Mariano Arena. But Arena has powerful political connections reaching up to the highest level; so Bellodi eventually fails, and the police investigation is directed along the usual safe lines of the *crime passionnel*. In *A ciascuno il suo* the *crime passionnel* is compounded with an equally powerful political motive. Doctor Roscio is murdered (along with the pharmacist Manno, who receives an anonymous letter warning him of his impending death, the letter having the function of diverting the police investigations onto a false scent) by a killer hired by his wife's cousin and lover, Rosello, a local Christian Democrat notable. Roscio had already discovered the adulterous affair, and also Rosello's murky political and financial intrigues, and had threatened to reveal all if the affair did not stop. While the police soon reach a dead end following up the possible motives for Manno's killing, Paolo Laurana, a school-teacher, stumbles on a series of right clues, and is silenced with death.

With *Il giorno della civetta* Sciascia specifically addresses the Northern Italian reader for the first time. Captain Bellodi, 'emiliano di Parma' ('an Emilian from Parma'), tall, fair-haired, ex-Resistance fighter, incorruptible in his respect for the law, does not signal a belief on Sciascia's part that the solution to Sicily's ills will come from the North. In fact, although Bellodi is to a certain extent a positive hero, the author carefully distances himself from his reflections. Bellodi's 'foreignness', rather, is a vehicle for explanations regarding Sicilian speech and customs, which would be totally unmotivated if the hero of the book were to be a Sicilian.

These two novels undoubtedly confront a series of problems, both political and psychological, and attempt to go below the surface, and to offer an explanation for them. The most obvious theme of *Il giorno della civetta* is the mafia, but the book is not simply an attack on the mafia; it attempts to do something more complicated, to reveal what the mafia really is (far worse, far more ominous than it is, or was, generally imagined to be), and also to explain what it is that makes a *mafioso*. Sciascia tries to show that the Sicilian mafia is not merely a more or less colourful protection racket, involved in the acquisition of building contracts and such like; it is also an electoral machine, if not *the* electoral machine, in Sicily, and is in fact an inseparable aspect of the political game at the national level. But he also tries to explain the kind of mentality that makes it possible for the mafia to flourish: the *omertà*, the conspiracy of silence which surrounds its activities; the curious mixture of contempt and wonder at the civilized ways of the Northerners; the lack of faith in law and reason; the historical causes of this lack of faith. Significantly, the local *mafiosi* themselves are treated as interesting characters. Marchica, the mafia's hired killer, is accorded the privilege of the interior monologue. Don Mariano Arena himself, the local mafia boss, is allowed to be Bellodi's own equal in a long face-to-face conversation.

The book also shows a preoccupation with the historical paradox presented by the 'anti-Fascism' of the *mafiosi*. There are insistent references to the anti-mafia campaign initiated in 1926 by the Fascist prefect Mori, to the fact that for ordinary peace-loving Sicilians the Fascist regime had represented freedom from the fear of the mafia. In this light Bellodi, the ex-partisan and scrupulously law-abiding *carabiniere*, represents the alternative way of fighting the mafia, not with force against force, but by pitting reason and the law against irrationality and iniquity.

Bellodi fails. In fact at the end of the novel he withdraws, rather inexplicably, from the investigation. But the message retains a margin of hope. Bellodi was in fact not entirely alone in his pursuit of justice: the local *carabinieri* officers, after an initial live-and-let-live attitude, become enthused by his plan, and the *procuratore della repubblica* (state prosecutor) supports him. Also, Bellodi exits from the text, after his ritual journey through the sweet temptations of liberated, snow-bound Parma, with a lucid awareness of his love for Sicily, and of his determination to return. The very last words in the book belong to him: ' –Mi ci romperò la testa – disse a voce alta.' But his words are ambiguous: they mean either: 'I am going back if it kills me' or: 'It will kill me', and look forward to the death of Paolo Laurana, the detective of *A ciascuno il suo*.

In the tension between hope and despair which characterizes Sciascia's writings, *A ciascuno il suo* gravitates towards despair. The detective himself is not particularly far-sighted, nor is his investigation motivated by an ideal of justice: it is mere intellectual curiosity. The whole social fabric of the town is shown as impregnated with hyprocrisy and double-talk. Virtually all the characters, even those who do not stand for evil as such, are imbued with political opportunism. Doctor Roscio's decision to expose the malpractices of his wife's lover is spurred by jealousy rather than political idealism. This bleak outlook extends beyond the political dimension: the book also dwells at length on the immature prurient attitude to sex of the men, and the misguided contamination between sex and concern for property of the women. The only characters who have a lucid view of things are the old, blind eye-specialist, the 'mad' Don Benito, and the parish priest of St Anna's, three individuals who are consistently presented as outside their society in various ways.

A ciascuno il suo also opens the examination of the omnivorous all-encompassing nature of power which dominates Sciascia's later writing. The novel is set at the beginning of the centre-left experiment in Italy, and Rosello is presented very much as the power-seeking politician who will embrace and transform any political ideology to his own ends. But Sciascia also contemptuously begins to dissect the forces of the left, though, curiously, not the Socialist Party who were the Christian Democrats' partners in the centre-left government, but the Communist Party. The Communist member of Parliament is made to scorn the notion of moral principles as the inspiration for political action, and one of the three outsiders who understand what is going on, the old eye-specialist, refers to the Communists as being 'anch' essi, in certo modo, al potere' ('also in power, in a sense').

In his own preface to the 1967 edition of *Le parrocchie di Regalpetra* Sciascia associated his interest in the detective story with a search for a good narrative technique. Since his aim is 'documenting and narrating with a good technique', he is more interested in following 'the development of the detective story than the evolution of aesthetic theories'. Fourteen years earlier he had published a short article (1953), which shows him to be a keen follower of this aspect of the 'sottobosco letterario' ('literary undergrowth') and related critical writings. At this stage he expressed the conviction that good detective stories have helped the development of main-stream fiction, in that they have conveyed a lesson of taut, stream-lined narration. In particular he admired the lucid, rigorous pursuit of a solution to the puzzle; conversely he deplored what he considered to be the recent intrusion of the macabre and the erotic into the detective story. In the following year he returned to the question of the detective story with two articles. One suggested the categorization of the modes of investigation of literary detectives into three basic types: Sherlock Holmes, Poirot, and Maigret (1954a). The other attempted to come to terms with the apparently anomalous contamination between detective literature and 'Gothic' literature by putting forward a Freudian interpretation of the detective story: below the overt rational surface lies a submerged level, which the logic of the reconstruction of the puzzle attempts to exorcise (1954b).

When Sciascia comes to trying his hand at using the techniques of the detective story, then, he has at his disposal not only a pretty thorough knowledge of the tricks of the trade, but also certain critical insights into the subterranean workings of the genre. It is interesting to see how his own detective stories make use of these tricks, in a way which amounts to a comment on the whole genre and its common assumptions. What is more, in the light of his insistence on rational understanding, his exploration of a genre which presupposes the essentially rational comprehensibility of apparently inexplicable mysteries becomes a fundamental factor in what he has to say.

Contrary to the expectations of conventional detective stories, where the detective always triumphs at the end, both Bellodi and Laurana fail; Laurana indeed is eliminated. In both cases even their limited successes are made possible by the intervention of elements beyond their control. Bellodi does start on the right track (the building contracts business): he is intelligent, well-informed, and honest. But the actual solution of *this* puzzle (who has committed the murders and who is behind them), has nothing to do with Bellodi's ability. The revelation of two of the crucial names comes from Parrinieddu the police informer, and here Bellodi retains something of the characteristic of the conventional detective. It is his personality which acts as a catalyst on poor frightened Parrinieddu, who on two occasions gives the right information, disclosures which will lead to his death. When it comes to discovering the name of the killer, it is the menacing look of his subordinate which succeeds where Bellodi's polite, subtle interrogation had failed.

In *A ciascuno il suo* Laurana has none of Bellodi's understanding of the general situation, a lack of understanding which will lead him to walk straight into the trap laid for him at the end. The working of his 'little grey cells' is limited to the attempt to discover the origin of the newspaper from which the anonymous letter had been cut out, a vital clue which he had stumbled on by chance. He can only go beyond this point through the workings of chance events: first the encounter with the Communist member of Parliament who reveals that doctor Roscio intended to expose a Christian Democrat notable from his town, and then the encounter with Rosello accompanied by the man smoking the unusual brand of cigar which had been found by the police on the scene of the murder.

If chance, grassing, anonymous revelations play a vital part in the solution of both puzzles, *A ciascuno il suo* goes further than *Il giorno della civetta* in laying bare the devices of the genre. Chapter 7 opens in fact with a comment on the conventional detective story, where Sciascia clearly also measures his own distance from it:

> Che un delitto si offra agli inquirenti come un quadro i cui elementi materiali . . . consentano, se sottilmente reperiti e analizzati, una sicura attribuzione, è corollario di tutti quei romanzi polizieschi cui buona parte dell'umanità si abbevera. Nella realtà le cose stanno però diversamente: e i coefficienti dell'impunità e dell'errore sono alti non perché (o non soltanto, o non sempre) è basso l'intelletto degli inquirenti, ma perché gli elementi che un delitto offre sono di solito assolutamente insufficienti . . . Gli elementi che portano a risolvere i delitti che si presentano con carattere di mistero o di gratuità sono la *confidenza* diciamo professionale, la delazione anonima, il caso. E un po', soltanto un po', l'acutezza degli inquirenti.
>
> (*A ciascuno il suo*, 53)

(A corollary of all those detective novels which are lapped up by a large number of people is the notion that a crime is like a painting, where . . . intelligent investigation and analysis of its constituent elements will lead to a correct identification of the author. But the real world is different: a large number of crimes are never solved or are wrongfully attributed not (or not only, or not always) because the investigators are unintelligent, but because a crime does not usually provide sufficient elements for analysis . . . The solution of crimes which appear mysterious or gratuitous is due to what we might call professional informers, anonymous denunciation, or mere chance. The acumen of the investigators only plays a very small part.)

Sciascia is not altogether right in saying that in conventional detective stories chance elements play no part; they often do, but in ways which tend to conceal them as such and to emphasize instead the power of the detective in putting together the disconnected pieces of the puzzle. Sciascia does the opposite: he draws attention to chance elements exactly for what they are, and also therefore to the spurious rationality of the detective story.

Another two constant features of the conventional detective story are the suspense regarding the correct solution of the puzzle, and the linear summing-up by the detective himself at the end. The conventional story will contain a number of false clues which have the function of sending the reader up blind alleys, with the expectation that everything will be put right at the end by the infallible detective. In both Sciascia's novels the suspense element is shifted very early from the solution of the initial puzzle (the murders) to the question of whether or not the detective will succeed and/or survive.

In *Il giorno della civetta* the reader learns who has committed the murders and who is responsible for them a third of the way through the novel. At this point the reader is given heavier and heavier indications of the plot woven by the political authorities to destroy Bellodi's reconstruction. It is this knowledge, a knowledge, moreover, which Bellodi does not share, which generates the suspense. In *A ciascuno il suo* the author gives the reader an increasing number of clues to the solution of the puzzle long before Laurana stumbles on the vital information, but also clues pointing to the danger that poor, naive, obtuse Laurana is incurring. The element of surprise at the end consists in the fact that the solution of the puzzle was common knowledge in the town right from the beginning. The revelation, which comes from three members of the local *circolo*, also provides, in a subverted form, the linear summing up which one would expect from a detective story. This type of ending points to the uselessness not only of Laurana's death, but of the whole process of reconstruction of the puzzle. There was no puzzle at all, simply a universal consensus to keep the truth hidden beneath the surface.

With *A ciascuno il suo* Sciascia points to the total collapse of reason, and he will return to this theme in *Il contesto* and *Todo modo*. But three years before the publication of *A ciascuno il suo* he had published *Il consiglio d'Egitto*, a historical novel which can be read as an attempt to confront the question of reason in its own historical *locus*, the Enlightenment. *Il consiglio d'Egitto* is set in

Palermo in the period 1782-1795. It follows emblematically the descending parable of reason in the *siècle des lumières*, from the enlightened reforms of Viceroy Caracciolo to the turn of the screw against the reformers-turned-Jacobins after the rumbles from Paris have made the ruling classes close ranks. This novel still has a positive hero, Francesco Paolo Di Blasi: he stands, and speaks, for human equality, freedom, justice, and reason throughout. The book closes with his execution for his part in the Jacobin conspiracy. The council of Egypt of the title refers to a newly found Arabic manuscript which deals a mortal blow to the historical justification for the power of the feudal barons vis-à-vis the crown. However, the council of Egypt is a fake. It is the fabrication of Giuseppe Vella, a poor Maltese priest who hopes to gain glory and wealth as a result. The fortunes of Vella rise and fall with the political vicissitudes of the kingdom. When the struggle against the baron ceases to be the objective of the crown, the mounting suspicions regarding the authenticity of the manuscript gather momentum, and Vella is arrested.

Di Blasi is an aristocrat, and speaks the language of reason; Vella is a man of humble origins who is after personal gain through deceit, or so it would appear at first. But an important theme in the course of the novel is the journey of Vella from selfishness towards enlightenment, a journey in which Di Blasi's personality acts as the catalyst. At the point where Vella reaches enlightenment, the light is about to be extinguished over the brief honeymoon between Sicily and reason, and over Di Blasi's life. Di Blasi speaks the language of reason to the very end. Under torture, his thoughts are of a future world 'illuminato dalla ragione' ('illumined by reason') where torture will be unthinkable. At this point Sciascia intervenes with a direct comment which corrects Di Blasi's historical optimism with a reference to the Nazi genocide and the French authorities' practice of torture in Algeria.

(E la disperazione avrebbe accompagnato le sue ultime ore di vita se soltanto avesse avuto il presentimento che in quell'avvenire che vedeva luminoso popoli interi si sarebbero votati a torturarne altri; che uomini pieni di cultura e di musica, esemplari nell'amore familiare e rispettosi degli animali, avrebbero distrutto milioni di altri esseri umani: con implacabile metodo, con efferata scienza della tortura; e che persino i più diretti eredi della ragione avrebbero riportato la *questione* nel mondo: e non più come

elemento del diritto, quale almeno era nel momento in cui
lui la subiva, ma addirittura come elemento dell'esistenza).
                                    (*Il consiglio d'Egitto*, 177-8)

((He would have spent the last few hours of his life in despair
if he had only suspected that in the future which he saw
radiant with light whole nations would torture other
nations; that men full of culture and music, exemplary
family men, kind to animals, would destroy millions of other
human beings, and would do so in an implacably methodical
way and with savagely scientific refinement; that even the
most direct heirs of reason would bring the question of
torture back into the world, no longer as an element of law,
such as it was while he was a victim to it, but as an aspect of
life itself.))

Di Blasi's vision of the world's linear progress towards a better
future is patently wrong, and yet the message of this book is not one
of despair. The rational, principled approach of Di Blasi,
inadequate at this stage as a tool for sweeping changes, has sown a
seed in the mind of Vella, and even affects, at a subliminal level, the
brutalized personality of the executioner.

The story of the forged historical manuscript allows Sciascia to
delve further into the relationship between writing and reality.
The text of this novel is dotted with references to writing: writing
as fraud, writing as truth, even writing as fetish, in the insistent
allusions to the tools of writing. What status does Vella's historical
fraud have in relation to historical truth? Is it any more fraudulent
than the skilful weaving of the feudal legal tradition which Vella's
manuscript is now attempting to subvert? Is it not in fact simply
the reversed mirror image of the fraud of history? Does history
contain any truth at all when it has been the history of 'i re, i vicerè,
i papi, i capitani' ('kings, viceroys, popes, generals'), when it has
ignored the lives of those who have been unable to write their own
history? To these questions, raised sometimes through Vella's own
interior monologue, sometimes through direct intervention,
Sciascia does not offer clear-cut answers.

Vella exits from the text with the disturbing thought that 'il
mondo della verità fosse questo: degli uomini vivi, della storia, dei
libri' ('this might be the world of truth: the world of living men,
the world of history, the world of books.'), a thought which,
significantly, is shared at that very moment by Di Blasi who is
about to die. Truth, life, history, writing, form an equation which

will no longer be possible without a belief in the rational comprehensibility of reality.

Since *A ciascuno il suo* Sciascia has written two more detective novels, *Il contesto* (1971), and *Todo modo* (1974), and a philosophical fable modelled on Voltaire's *Candide* (*Candido*, 1977).

In *Il contesto* several judges are killed. While the police authorities pursue at first the hypothesis of a mentally deranged killer, and of political murders perpetrated by an extreme left group, inspector Rogas follows up the line of revenge murders by a man who had been unjustly sentenced. But at the point when he has caught up with his quarry, Rogas begins to identify with him, and does nothing to stop him killing another judge. Rogas is found dead, together with the dead body of Amar, the leader of the main opposition party, the Partito Rivoluzionario Internazionale. The revolutionary party does not want the truth about these killings to come out for fear of provoking a revolution.

The novel uses the clichés and devices of the detective story in a paradoxical, parodistical fashion, as Sciascia himself points out in the note appended at the end of the book. The novel ends without a clear explanation of the killings of Rogas and Amar. This open ending postulates a chaotic, elusive reality which reason is no longer able to comprehend, which writing can no longer organize.

Il contesto, unlike Sciascia's previous work, is no longer set in Sicily, nor in Italy. The place is an unspecified country: some features suggest Sicily, some Italy, some a South American environment. This lack of geographic determination would seem to imply, metaphorically, that the total collapse of political opposition, the total collusion of power, is not a peculiarly Sicilian, or Italian, situation, but a universal one.

If *Il contesto* ends without a clear solution to the mystery, *Todo modo* offers no solution at all, it just ends, in the middle of dialogue. *Todo modo* is set in Sicily, but does not carry specifically Sicilian connotations; the bishops, cardinals, industrialists, high-ranking politicians who withdraw to the Sicilian hermitage for a highly suspect session of 'spiritual exercises' come from all over Italy.

The protagonist of *Candido*, Candido Munafo, moves from his native Sicily to Turin in the North, and eventually to Paris. In Sicily Candido suffers a series of disillusionments, personal and political, and his journeys elsewhere only confirm these disappointments but in Paris he escapes into happiness and freedom, away from all authorities, even that of Voltaire. In Candido's experiences Sciascia telescopes his own journey as a writer. Candido is born in July 1943, during the American landings in Sicily, the historical crux of 'Breve cronaca del regime' and 'La zia d'America'. His mother Maria Grazia marries an American officer, and he never sees her again until he bumps into her in Paris, in the last chapter of the book. Maria Grazia has become Grace, as had one of the American cousins in 'La zia d'America'. In the Parisian café where he meets Maria Grazia-Grace, Candido is talking with his old mentor don Antonio, newly arrived from Sicily,

> di Hemingway e di Fitzgerald, ... degli scrittori americani da don Antonio letti negli anni del fascismo, e gli parevano allora grandissimi tutti, e da Candido . . . . letti poi distrattamente e persino con insofferenza.
>
> (*Candido*, 130)

> (of Hemingway and Fitzgerald, . . . of the American writers which don Antonio had read during the Fascist regime, and which he had considered great without exception, and which Candido . . . had later found uninteresting and even irritating.)

The myth of American literature, which the protagonist of 'La zia d'America' had to overcome before he could begin to understand, is here reduced to nothing. The book ends with Candido free of Maria Grazia-Grace, who will return to America without him, and free also of the myth of the Enlightenment, which don Antonio is trying to cling to:

> Davanti alla statua di Voltaire don Antonio si fermò, si afferrò al palo della segnaletica, chinò la testa. Pareva si fosse messo a pregare. – Questo è il nostro padre – gridò poi – questo è il nostro vero padre.
> Dolcemente ma con forza Candido lo staccò dal palo, lo sorresse, lo trascinò. – Non ricominciamo coi padri – disse. Si sentiva figlio della fortuna; e felice.
>
> (*Candido*, 134-5)

> (Don Antonio stood still in front of Voltaire's statue, grabbed hold of the sign-post, and bowed his head. He looked as if he was praying. Then he shouted: "This is our father, this is our true father."
> Gently but firmly Candido detached his arm from the post,

held him up, and dragged him away. "Let's not start all over again with fathers." he said. He felt himself to be a son of fortune; and happy.)

Since *Candido* Sciascia has not published any works of narrative. On the other hand, his name has not by any means ceased to appear in print, with essays, newspaper articles, and numerous interviews. Sciascia began writing essays in the early 1950s, and always pursued this activity vigorously, side by side with his narrative works. Sciascia's essays and narrative works are not unconnected: in fact many of his essays can be read as the historical and ideological workshops for his short stories and novels. They fall broadly into two types. The earlier ones consist of analyses and critiques, often extremely well researched, of Sicilian history and literature, such as the collection *Pirandello e la Sicilia* (*Pirandello and Sicily*, 1961), and *Morte dell'inquisitore* (*Death of the Inquisitor*, 1964). Most of the essays published from the 1970s onwards are investigations and reconstructions of real-life mysteries, often based on the examination of historical or judicial documents. The most significant in this latter group are *Atti relativi alla morte di Raymond Roussel* (*Official Records on the Death of Raymond Roussel*, 1971), *La scomparsa di Majorana* (*The Disappearance of Majorana*, 1975), *I pugnalatori* (*The Knifemen*, 1976), *L'affaire Moro* (*The Moro affair*, 1978), *Dalle parti degli infedeli* (*From the World of the Infidels*, 1979), *Il teatro della memoria* (*The Theatre of Memory*, 1981). But in recent years Sciascia has acquired increasingly the position of a public figure whose opinion is much sought, and this reader at least cannot help wondering whether his frequent pronouncements have added anything of value either to Sciascia's writings or to the understanding of the public at large.

Sciascia as a narrator appears to have reached a point beyond which lies uncharted ground. While his earlier works described a series of defeats of reason, they were based on the notion that reality can be understood, even though with difficulty. With the transition to the view of a chaotic reality, where power *per se* is the only certainty, the parameters of reason have ceased to be valid tools for organizing this reality, and the writer is pushed into a position of global critique, often of a nihilist type. This would require the use of completely new narrative tools, which Sciascia appears not to have discovered, or not yet.

BIOGRAPHICAL NOTE

Leonardo Sciascia was born in Racalmuto, near Agrigento in Sicily, in 1921. He trained as a primary school teacher at the Istituto Magistrale in nearby Caltanissetta. He lived in Racalmuto until 1956, working first as a local civil servant, and then as a teacher. He was employed as an educational administrator in Caltanissetta from 1956 to 1958, when he moved to Rome, to an administrative post in the Ministry of Education. In 1968 he went to live in Palermo; two years later he took early retirement. Since then he has resided partly in Racalmuto, partly in Palermo, and, more recently, in Paris. His first published book, *Le favole della dittatura* (*Fables of the Dictatorship*, 1950), satirized the Fascist regime. Two years later he published a collection of poems, *La Sicilia, il suo cuore* (*Sicily, its Heart*). He began publishing articles in newspapers and journals in the 1940s, and has pursued his activity as a journalist to this day. In the 1975 local election he stood for the Palermo city council as an independent candidate on the Communist Party list, and was elected. Two years later he resigned. He has since joined the Radical Party, and has been a member of both the Italian Parliament and the European Parliament. He has been awarded a number of literary prizes for his work as a narrator and essayist.

BIBLIOGRAPHY

PRINCIPAL WORKS

Le parrocchie di Regalpetra, Laterza, Bari, 1956; ed. cited Laterza, Bari, 1975; (trans. J. Green) *Salt in the Wound*, Orion Press, New York, 1969 (also contains *The Death of the Inquisitor*)

Gli zii di Sicilia, Einaudi, Turin, 1958; Einaudi, Turin, 1961 (includes 'L'antimonio'); ed. cited Einaudi, Turin, 1972

Pirandello e la Sicilia, Sciascia, Caltanissetta, 1961

Il giorno della civetta, Einaudi, Turin, 1961; (trans. A. Colquhoun, A. Oliver) *Mafia Vendetta*, Jonathan Cape, London, 1963

Il consiglio d'Egitto, Einaudi, Turin, 1963: ed. cited Einaudi, Turin, 1976; (trans. A. Foulke) *The Council of Egypt*, Knopf, New York, 1966; Jonathan Cape. London, 1966

Morte dell'inquisitore, Laterza, Bari, 1964; (trans. J. Green) *The Death of the Inquisitor*, Orion Press, New York, 1969 (also contains *Salt in the Wound*)

A ciascuno il suo, Einaudi, Turin, 1966; ed. cited Einaudi, Turin, 1973; (trans. A. Foulke) *A Man's Blessing*, Harper & Row, New York, 1968; Jonathan Cape, London, 1969

Atti relativi alla morte di Raymond Roussel, Edizioni Esse, Palermo, 1971

Il contesto, Einaudi, Turin, 1971; (trans. A. Foulke) *Equal Danger*,
 Harper & Row, New York, 1973; Jonathan Cape, London, 1974
Todo modo, Einaudi, Turin, 1974; (trans. A. Foulke) *One Way or
 Another*, Harper & Row, New York, 1977
La scomparsa di Majorana, Einaudi, Turin, 1975
I Pugnalatori, Einaudi, Turin, 1976
Candido ovvero un sogno fatto in Sicilia, Einaudi, Turin, 1977; (trans.
 A. Foulke) *Candido or A Dream Dreamed in Sicily*, Harcourt Brace
 Jovanovich, New York 1979; Carcanet New Press, Manchester, 1982
L'affaire Moro, Sellerio, Palermo, 1978
Dalle parti degli infedeli, Sellerio, Palermo, 1979
Il teatro della memoria, Einaudi, Turin, 1981

WORKS CITED

Mauro, W. *Sciascia*, La Nuova Italia (Il Castoro), Florence, 1970
Sciascia, L. 'Letteratura del giallo', *Letteratura* 3, 1953, 65–67
—, 'La carriera di Maigret', *Letteratura* 10, 1954, 73–75 (cited as 1954a)
—, 'Appunti sul giallo', *Nuova corrente* 1, 1954, 23–34 (cited as 1954b)

FURTHER READING

Ambroise, C. *Invito alla lettura di Sciascia*, Mursia, Milan, 1974
Ghetti Abruzzi, G. *Sciascia e la Sicilia*, Bulzoni, Rome, 1974
Macchioni Jodi, R. Leonardo Sciascia, *Letteratura italiana. Novecento*,
 VIII, 7145–7180, Marzorati, Milan, 1980
Renard, P. 'Les lunettes de Sciascia', *Italianistica*, 2 (1977), 390–397
Ricorda, R. 'Sciascia ovvero la retorica della citazione', *Studi
 Novecenteschi*, 16 (1977), 59–93

Richard Andrews

11 Italo Calvino

'Up to now my chief concern has always been to
disprove the definitions of me offered by critics.'
(Calvino, 1960)

Like a number of other authors discussed in this book, Italo
Calvino is capable of deciding that words are a distortion and a
trap (and, by that logic, a critic's words about his words must have
an even more dubious status). He also knows, however, that words
are unavoidable – they are the signs which humans habitually use
to give meaning to the world (and to other people's words). His
response to the arguments about the precarious nature of literature
and of language is to continue writing in spite of them, and indeed
to use the negative arguments as raw materials for a positive
achievement. A number of critics have seen such issues reflected in
Calvino's books, and to describe them again would be merely
repetitive if it were not for two points of contention. In the first
place, because objections to literature are so clearly formulated
by Calvino, commentators have often been led into seeing his
position as one of near surrender (e.g. Calligaris 1972, 57–8 and
72–77; Cannon 1981, chs. II–III) – a view against which this essay
will attempt to react. Secondly, although Calvino does write about
writing, and about coming to grips with the world via words and
concepts, it needs to be stressed that for him writing is
representative of a range of other activities, through which a
positive impact is made upon the world.

To speak of 'making an impact' implies bringing something to
bear on life as we find it, attacking it from 'outside', usually with
the premise that some of it ought if possible to be changed. The one
constant of Calvino's fiction, which in most respects has been
exhilaratingly variable and inconstant, is that he has never been

trapped (as he would see it) into a mere photographic representation of the world in which he lives. If absolute realism were possible, he would avoid it on principle. When he has chosen to write about contemporary Italy in his fiction, he has always brought to bear on it either a selective slant based on style and imagery, or else a single filtering viewpoint of which the reader is constantly aware. In either case, we are made conscious that we are reading an artefact, listening to one voice among many, and we cannot be tempted into a facile suspension of disbelief. Just as often, however, Calvino does not set his stories in the contemporary world at all, but in a world of which he is entirely in control – a world which may offer a patina of apparently precise history or cosmology, but which is really open fantasy. Fantasy approaches the world from 'outside': it offers parallels or metaphors for real life, which allow the reader to view it from new angles; and at the same time it acts as a kind of mental gymnastics, accustoming the imagination of writer and reader to the notion that things could be other than what they are.

Calvino's first work of fiction, the novel *Il sentiero dei nidi di ragno* (*The Path to the Spiders' Nests*, 1947), is in its narrative content rooted in personal and national history. It deals with the partisan Resistance to the Nazis and Fascists between 1943 and 1945, which was the formative experience of a generation and the first adult activity of the author's own life. He chose to present the partisans indirectly, through the uncomprehending eyes of Pin, a small boy from the slums, who tries to 'read' this adult world in upheaval, but is not old enough to grasp all its vocabulary. The reader of the novel thus has to re-interpret those signals which Pin does not understand, by first of all reading Pin's mis-reading, and then making his own corrections. This first attempt by Calvino at filtering experience in order to criticize it brings equivocal results, because Pin as a character is inarticulate and incapable of development. The difficulty is reflected in the ninth chapter, where Calvino feels obliged to bring in a more sophisticated viewpoint in order to fill certain ideological gaps. Pin never comes to understand what he has been through, and his comrades are a motley gang of semi-reject partisans who, in different ways, are as immature as he is. So it is left to the educated political commissar, with the Kiplingesque nom-de-guerre of Kim, to explain how the confused and unreliable motivation of these vagabonds can be part of a mass movement of genuine national liberation. Whether they know it or not, says Kim, these desperate inadequates are firmly on the side of a Marxist conception of history.

Already in this book Calvino has taken up a number of themes which he has never since abandoned: the struggle of a single mind to interpret and respond to the world around it; notions of growth, change, and maturity; and the perplexing relationship between a single phenomenon and the composite entity of which it seems, implausibly, to form a part.

Even much later Calvino was content to accept categorization of his first novel as part of the Neo-realist current of its time. Whatever reservations one may now have about the meaningfulness of this term, the book did at least make reference to events which its readers knew either did happen or could have happened at a moment in recent history. By 1959, however, no one would have said that 'realism' of any sort was the principal strand in Calvino's writing. In his short stories he had increasingly chosen to view contemporary life through the distorting lens of ironic humour, his grotesqueries sometimes reminiscent of a verbal cartoon (either strip or animated). The Marcovaldo stories in particular recount the misadventures of a bewildered innocent in a modern industrial city. They would read like written post-war versions of silent film comedy, were it not for the sustained and coherent distaste which they express towards the indignities inflicted by an impersonal, mechanized society. In writing like this, realism is replaced by satire, and a left-wing intellectual in search of a rigorously 'committed' literature could still accept what Calvino was doing. But what about his novels? From the point of view of socialist realism, which was still taken seriously in official left-wing circles, the trilogy *I nostri antenati* (*Our Ancestors*) left a great deal to be desired. In·*Il visconte dimezzato* (*The Cloven Viscount*, 1952) a seventeenth-century aristocrat returns from the Turkish wars in two halves, split down the middle by a cannon-ball. His Good Half and his Bad Half wreak rival havoc in the home community with their inhumanly one-sided caricatures of virtue and malice, until they fight a duel with each other over a girl, open the old wound, and are sewn together again. In *Il barone rampante* (*The Baron in the Trees*, 1957) an eighteenth-century aristocrat vows never to set foot on the ground, and lives through the Enlightenment, the Revolution, and the Napoleonic aftermath, as a sociable but inflexible arboreal eccentric. In *Il cavaliere inesistente* (*The Non-existent Knight*, 1959) one of Charlemagne's paladins in the legendary middle ages turns out to be a suit of armour without a body inside, held together only by a rigid, methodical force of will.

All three contain a vein of comedy which is elegantly expressed but often vulgar in content; and the trilogy as a whole, as it progresses, becomes increasingly self-conscious about its own exuberant virtuosity.

Calvino had left the Italian Communist Party in 1957, at the time when *Il barone* was first published, but he was still concerned about commitment in literature and the force which intellectuals should exert in favour of social change. He was also naturally influenced by the long-standing Italian assumption that a writer has to be theoretically aware of what he is doing. Between 1955 and 1962 he published three major essays (the last two in a new periodical, *Il Menabò*, which he founded together with Elio Vittorini), in which he explores the function of literature in society, and speculates on what type of writing can best fulfil that function. His premises are firmly left-wing, though not subordinated to party orthodoxy, and in the first essay in particular, 'Il midollo del leone' ('The Lion's Marrow', 1955), he seems very conscious of his divergence from the demands of Soviet-style socialist realism. In the later two, entitled 'Il mare del-'oggettività' ('The Sea of Objectivity', 1960) and 'La sfida al labirinto' ('Defying the Labyrinth', 1962), he goes some way to explaining his fantasy novels, without referring to them directly. A meticulous realism, he suggests, involves, or at least risks, accepting the world as it is, whereas a writer should be promoting the autonomy of the rational critical mind from the systems which surround it. New formulations, even perverse formulations, it is implied, serve to break up habitual conceptual moulds and open the way to change. Writers and intellectuals should be defying the labyrinth of modern industrial society, rather than attempting to draw a plan of it. It is clear, however, from the introduction which he later wrote for *I nostri antenati* and from an interview given in 1959, that the demands of his own personal style were at least as important a factor as ideology. By remaining a Neo-realist he would have destroyed this style, and thus made himself incapable of making an individual contribution. The important thing to salvage from his earliest writings was not realism as such, but the attitude which young revolutionaries brought to bear on reality:

> From that early narrative of ours we could choose to remain faithful either to historical reality, by flopping into it, or to the attack (*piglio*), the drive, the energy which we had then. With my fantasy novels I have tried precisely to keep alive the

attack, the energy, the spirit – in other words, as I see it, the most important part.

(Interview, *Il Giorno*, 18 August 1959; quoted Calligaris 1973, 33)

Behind this lies the assumption that, after the victory of the Resistance over Fascism, a chance had been lost and Italy had taken the wrong turning, so that historical reality had become rather dismal. It was at this time that Calvino associated himself with the Gramscian formula: 'Pessimism of the intellect, optimism of the will.'

Both characteristics are demonstrated, in their way, in the trilogy itself. None of the three novels ends on a note of optimistic achievement, as far as the story is concerned. When the two halves of the cloven Viscount Medardo are sewn together, all that is achieved is a restoration of normality, plus some undramatic steps towards maturity on the part of some characters. Medardo may have gained from the experience of being incomplete, but the world is not radically changed as a result. Baron Cosimo di Rondò lives his life in the trees, and watches the libertarian ideas of the eighteenth century find brief fruition in the Revolution, but then vanish into militant imperialism under Napoleon, who in his turn is crushed by the victory of reaction. The young questing warriors, who gravitate round the non-existent knight Agilulfo, find that the fruits of their search crumble or change colour when grasped: their condition of permanent pursuit seems real enough, but the true existence of their quarry is left more problematic. In all three works, Calvino has adopted some of the format of the folk-tales which during these same years he was collecting and editing: he uses as a metaphor for the business of living the image of the single protagonist, whether prince or peasant, trying to do the best he can with a threatening or enigmatic world. But whereas folk-tales have unambiguous and dramatic endings, whether happy or unhappy, Calvino's pessimistic intellect tells him that in the mind and experience of modern man the outcome is less clear-cut. The complementary optimism of the will is found not so much in what the books depict, but more in the very texture of the books themselves – in their elegance, their sharpness, their fun, their determination both to set the reader thinking and to entertain. The existence of such writing is itself a victory over pessimism. As Calvino acknowledges in his essays, it cannot take over the role of political action or produce a solution to the problems, but it can, by example, stimulate us to keep searching and keep trying.

One further aspect of the trilogy *I nostri antenati* has been widely recognized and discussed. In all three novels, in different ways, Calvino has built into his story a projection of his own position as a writer, of his view of writers in society, or even of the physical act of writing and the problematic status of the word on the page. The quality of self-reference is less strong in *Il visconte dimezzato* than in the others; but even here Calvino makes us face the proposition that anyone who is firmly different (in this case different by being incomplete) may see things of which the rest of us are not aware. This seems like a trial run for an idea expressed much more thoroughly and positively in the central narrative image of *Il barone rampante*, a work which has captured the Italian imagination to the extent, eventually, of being accorded the dubious privilege of study as a school set-book. The hero Cosimo takes to the trees in an impulse of childish revolt against his comically appalling family, but once he is up there he rapidly formulates a stance whereby his cry of 'E io non scenderò più!' ('And I shan't ever come down!') becomes the basis of a personal law. Rebellion and eccentricity, in order to be productive, have to be more disciplined and less self-indulgent than the norm against which they react; or, as Calvino later expressed the point in his introduction to the whole trilogy:

> . . . a person voluntarily sets himself a difficult rule, and follows it through to its ultimate consequences, because without this he would not be himself either for himself or for others.
>
> (*Antenati*, xiv)

This, says Calvino, 'has always been my real narrative theme' – he could equally well have said that it has always been his narrative method, to set the rules by which a given artefact must operate and then follow those rules wherever they lead. But the rules of artistic form can be arbitrary, and so indeed is Cosimo's self-imposed law: it needs a strong sense of purpose to bend the arbitrary until it becomes meaningful. Increasingly aware of the dangers of setting himself apart from people (dangers exemplified by other antisocial solitaries who appear in the book), Cosimo works on making his eccentricity useful to society, becoming 'un solitario che non sfuggiva la gente' ('a solitary who did not avoid people', *Antenati*, 249) rather than an escapist. His attitude is summed up in the observation: 'chi vuole guardare bene la terra deve tenersi alla distanza necessaria' ('If you want to look at the world properly, you must stay the right distance away', *Antenati*, 331). He is an image, Calvino commented later, of 'the vocation of the poet, the explorer, the revolutionary' (*Antenati*, xv). The juxtaposition of those three vocations is crucial. Calvino has written into this book of fantasy an image of the writer of fantasy, one who obstinately does things which make no sense and waits for people to see sense in them. But the more practical tasks of the explorer (the researcher? the theorist?) and the revolutionary are fitted to the same pattern and identified in the same image: they all involve going out on a limb, in hope of discovering, creating, proposing what had not seemed possible before.

In *Il cavaliere inesistente*, however, the writer is initially separated from the men and women of action, as a commentator and recorder of their deeds. This brings out, among other things, the problematic relationship between a written text and what it describes. In the fourth chapter it emerges that the narrative of the book, which had so far seemed quite impersonal, is being composed by a nun in a monastery, Sister Teodora. From then on, at intervals, we are aware of Sister Teodora's presence and of her difficulties. Can a cloistered nun really give a proper description of the active world which she does not know? (But the list of experiences which she does know is made sensationally varied.) How much of what she imagines is influenced by irrelevant images in her immediate surroundings, by her current mood, the time of day? What does the writer gain from writing? But most of all, in the eighth and ninth chapters, Sister Teodora questions the very validity of the black words which she writes down on the white page, questions their ability to refer properly to anything in the world outside. In an apparent crisis of confidence, she resorts to drawing pictures of her characters' journeys and of the obstacles they meet, as though visual images were more reliable than words; and she has moments of mesmeric awareness of the unbroken, meaningless texture of paper and ink. Commentators have since seen these moments, quite rightly, as linking up with more recent developments in semiotic criticism, whereby both critics and writers have become aware of the separateness of the word, the literary signifier, from anything which it might signify. In this respect, as in others, Calvino was slightly ahead of his time; but there has been a tendency since (Cannon 1981, ch. II) to attribute to him a rather despairing perception of the gap between words and things, as if this book were proclaiming an impasse and the impossibility of writing anything significant. This, I think, is an interpretation to be resisted. The impasse is perceived by Sister Teodora, but broken by Calvino, as he incorporates her doubts and questions into a significant literary text. The nun's claim that she cannot write, only draw, is comically exploded by the fact that we read verbal descriptions of her drawings (verbal cartoons again) rather than seeing them, and the story is adequately conveyed none the less. The close-up view of the fibre of a blank page may be discouraging, but the world which you were hoping to describe on the page can sometimes appear equally blank and meaningless:

> Ogni cosa si muove nella liscia pagina senza che nulla se ne veda, senza che nulla cambi sulla sua superficie, come in fondo tutto si muove e nullo cambia nella rugosa crosta del mondo, perché c'è solo una distesa della medesima materia, proprio come il foglio su cui scrivo . . .

> (Everything moves on the smooth page without anything being seen, without anything altering on its surface, just as ultimately everything moves and nothing alters on the wrinkled crust of the world, because all that is there is an expanse of the same matter, just like the page on which I write . . .) ·

> *(Antenati,* 82)

In other words, this state of vertigo is not the fault of literature. Words and signs, it is true, have no intrinsic meaning, but nor does the world as a whole – until it is selectively interpreted into words and signs. Statements of this sort become more explicit in later books like *Cosmicomiche* and *Le città invisibili* but they are implicit here too. The impossibility of writing is successfully written about. To watch a story being composed, to be aware of the conscious and arbitrary choices involved, turns out neither to obscure the story nor to make it insignificant. Rather the story becomes doubly interesting – as an event described, and as an artefact which describes it.

As a final *tour de force* in *Il cavaliere inesistente* Calvino decides to reveal that Sister Teodora is the same person as the warrior lady Bradamante, the most confused and dissatisfied of the vigorous questing characters whom Sister Teodora has been describing. This unexpected transformation can be read in a number of ways, but Calvino's own account deserves at least to be considered alongside other interpretations:

I realized meanwhile, as I proceeded, how all the characters in the tale were like one another, moved as they were by the same anxious searchings, and the nun too, her quill pen, my own fountain pen, I myself, we were all the same person, the same thing, the same anxiety, the same dissatisfied quest. As it is the case for a story-teller – *or, I believe, for anyone who is doing anything* – that everything he thinks is transformed into something he does – that is, into storytelling –, I translated this idea into a final narrative twist. I made the storytelling nun and the warrior Bradamante into the same person.

(Antenati, xix, [my emphasis])

Even this is perhaps ambiguous: it could seem to reduce everything in a book, its signifiers and its signifieds, to the enclosed hermetic personality of its author. But it is more consistent with Calvino's approach to assimilate outwards rather than inwards, and to see this as another way of insisting that writing, thinking and acting are ultimately all of a piece.

Calvino's next substantial piece of fiction, *La giornata di uno scrutatore (A Day in the Life of a Scrutineer,* 1963), seemed even at the time to constitute a pause for reflection. It is as though he could not dismiss, in spite of his own arguments, the thought that his highly selective stylization offered views of the world that were too simple. He may have wanted to avoid being engulfed in the 'sea of objectivity' or the 'labyrinth' of his essays, but the world outside in all its complexity was still there whether he surrendered to it or not. So he wrote what amounts to a sustained interior monologue, in which one man's words and concepts try to explore a multi-layered social, political and biological reality—the Cottolengo, a huge institution in Turin for the mentally and physically subnormal, a city within a city which throws up a series of elusive, contradictory reflections about society, about moral values, and about different ways and levels of being human. The observer this time is a Communist Party scrutineer who vets voting procedures in the institution on election day. Amerigo Ormea is the nearest Calvino has ever come to offering an autobiographical protagonist. The psychological inwardness of the book (itself unusual for Calvino) is balanced by the attention paid once again to the elusiveness of words. The same institution, the same human situation, can be described in different and even contradictory ways, depending on the verbal and mental starting point, on the question asked in the first place. It is notable, with hindsight, that there is no suggestion of any absolute truth towards which the mind is feeling. It is taken for granted that the descriptions which the human mind formulates are the only views available, even if the mind itself recognizes them as inadequate. However, it also becomes clear (and it disturbs and confuses Amerigo) that the mind is capable of producing something better, more all-embracing, than the tunnel vision of a single political orthodoxy, however idealistic and well-founded.

What Calvino wrote next was so utterly surprising that it would be better to abandon any attempt to trace a hypothetical train of thought, as we have been doing so far, from one work to another. *Le Cosmicomiche* (*Cosmicomics*, 1965), and the continuation of the same vein in *Ti con zero* (*t zero*, 1967 – entitled *Time and the Hunter* in the English, as opposed to American, edition), constitute truly unclassifiable writing, in that any models which may have contributed to the books are so transformed as to become irrelevant. What we may refer to as the Cosmicomic stories (that is, *Le cosmicomiche* itself and the first two-thirds of *Ti con zero*) are all narrated firmly in the first person as reminiscences of a character named Qfwfq, who moves throughout among other characters whose names are equally poised between the phonetic joke and the mathematical formula. Each story is preceded by a brief neutral account of a scientific theory, usually one relating to a major change in the history of earth or the universe (the consolidation of matter, the first appearance of coloured light, the emergence of amphibian reptiles or birds), but sometimes referring to more abstract analyses of the nature of space and matter (the light-years of distance between galaxies, the curvature of space). Qfwfq steps in and takes up the story in the manner of a garrulous cosmic bore, eager to subordinate everything in the universe to his own experience. For whatever is referred to, Qfwfq was always there when it happened. What kind of being Qfwfq was, during some of these escapades, is far from clear: the language, associations and analogies are obstinately human, but few of the episodes relate to circumstances in which humans could be present. Qfwfq was there, with his whole extended family, when the uniform spread of atomic particles began to harden into true matter; Qfwfq was there (in an alternative and incompatible cosmic theory) when the whole of matter exploded out of an infinitesimal point and was scattered throughout the universe; Qfwfq made a sign in space from the edge of a galaxy, and waited, revolving, for 200 million years to come back to the same place again; Qfwfq was the last dinosaur; Qfwfq was the first mollusc to secrete a spiral shell. Everything is interpreted resolutely in terms of human subjective experience – not only suitable generalized emotions like expectation, disappointment, desire, suspense, fear, but also more contingent and mundane things like irritable family quarrels, the need to show off, and the sudden urge of a blind mollusc to grow a moustache. This is ludicrous and hilarious – the comic in the cosmic – and it can well be seen as a satire on the human desire to reduce the most inappropriate and ungraspable phenomena to our own scale and our own language. Neither God nor an impersonal universe should be made in man's image, though they always are. Readings of the book along these lines (Bernardini Napoletano 1977; Cannon 1981) have found more support in comparisons with the *nouveau roman* of Robbe-Grillet, much discussed in the mid-60s, which insisted that the time had come to dispense with the human-centred novel and with the anthropomorphic universe.

Calvino himself expressed the matter differently. In an interview which he revised and published in 1968 (now in *Una pietra sopra*, 187-8), he said that he had been fully convinced by Robbe-Grillet's arguments, but (characteristically) had been sent by them in the opposite direction. The Cosmicomic stories, he said, are 'a delirium of anthropomorphism, of the impossibility of thinking about the world other than by using human figures, or more particularly human grimaces, human babblings'. The inappropriateness of language in these stories does indeed produce irony and provoke laughter, but it proclaims in the same breath that human language is what we have, and we must make the most of it. What is more, in defiance once again of a discouraging theory, the book actually achieves insights by its far-fetched procedures. The reader can be persuaded, somewhat to his astonishment, that there is a point in having two obsessive gamblers take bets on the chain reaction of universal causes and effects, or in forcing analogies between the exploding energy of the cosmos and the generous desire of Mrs. Ph(i)nk$_0$ to make everyone a plate of spaghetti. In the vein of unlikely analogies, the greatest *tour de force* comes in the *Priscilla* section of *Ti con zero* where Calvino makes Qfwfq tell us what it is like to perform the most elementary act of reproduction, that of a single cell which divides itself into two cells on an inner impulse all its own. The meticulous account of desires, thoughts and existential states at each stage of the process is on the one hand eerily plausible (Calvino, the son of biologists, has done his homework thoroughly), and on the other hand it is twisted to correspond at all points with the different stages of sexual desire, love, self-projection and orgasm which should be the human equivalent. As a result, although we do not believe for a moment that all organisms speak a human language, we are left with an eloquent impression that somewhere there could in theory be a common language which all organisms speak.

In such language, which in sober theory would seem to have no foundation and therefore nothing to say, Calvino manages to say a great deal. There are, for example, some more sophisticated speculations on the nature of signs and of meaning, Calvino showing an exciting ability to translate theories of semiotics into narrative terms. When Qfwfq makes a 'sign' in space, this is the first act of its kind in the whole universe. Consequently there is some trouble in determining in what sense it can be a 'sign': it is not a sign 'of' anything (except perhaps of Qfwfq), and no one can read it because no one knows what a 'sign' is or what sort of code this one belongs to. The same problem arises in another story, when the mollusc Qfwfq creates his spiral shell as a response to, but also as a signal to, a female mollusc. What is the use of a visual message, if there are no eyes in the universe to receive it? The existence of the visual signal in fact creates the need for a response and a reader, so other beings develop eyes in order to see Qfwfq's shell. But what will those eyes read in the shell when they see it? There is, as has been noted (Bernardini Napoletano 1977, 96–106), a possible allegory here of writer, text and reader, and the casual uncontrollable relationship which builds up between them. Here again, however, it can be suggested that to read these passages exclusively as writing about writing is to miss a lot of the point.

These two stories ('Un segno nello spazio', 'A Sign in Space', and 'La spirale', 'The Spiral') embody notions not only of self-expression, but of self-assertion, desire, and the attempt to establish contact with the world. This undifferentiated impulse leads the protagonist to do or make something – in concrete terms the result might be a work of art, but could equally be a house, a new law, a scream of joy or an act of aggression. The product of such action, whether considered as a 'sign' or not, has then changed the world, because the world has to accommodate to its existence. The world's response may be a huge chain reaction, which has very little to do with the self-assertion or self-projection sought by the protagonist. The spiral shell stimulates the development of the optic nerve – but not in Qfwfq, who does not benefit at all. He has triggered a step in evolution, but been left behind by what he has created. In 'Un segno nello spazio', Qfwfq eventually loses his sign completely in a proliferating mass of other signs which respond to his example. These signs expand until they seem to constitute the universe – perhaps Qfwfq has actually created the universe – but the results do not match his casual and modest intentions. The *Priscilla* sequence presents the same pattern in all processes of reproduction, whether asexual or sexual: the urge of self-assertion or desire or both sets a process in motion, but the results are irrelevant to that urge. A similar pattern can be seen in a number of other stories, including 'Tutto in un punto' ('All at one point') already referred to, where Mrs. Ph(i)nk$_o$ sets off the cosmic 'big bang' with her creative urge, produces the universe, but destroys or disperses herself.

Amongst all the interleaved themes of change, evolution, desire and withdrawal, potential and act, which are permutated and played with in the Cosmicomic stories, this pattern is the most recurrent and the one on which the *Priscilla* sequence sets a seal. It springs from the view that the repercussions of any action are too complex for the single mind to grasp, and in this sense it relates to Calvino's steadily diminishing participation in active politics. It is a vision which, of course, could easily inhibit one from action of any sort. But the Cosmicomic stories seem to express a paradoxical confidence that action will continue to be taken, because self-assertive, creative and interpretative instincts are irrepressible. The individual will never achieve what he was trying for, but things will continue to happen because of his attempts. This is a far cry from the tidy confidence of Kim, in the very first novel, that unruly urges can be harnessed to the services of History, and that we know just where History is going; but the unruly urges are still seen to operate, and to help construct a history whose total significance is still larger than the sum of its parts.

Kim was a man of action whose function (as commissar) was to describe and make sense of that action. He had to step back and contemplate the strange relationship of the parts to the whole in a large-scale human phenomenon. The Cosmicomic stories also examine this relationship, though the phenomena they deal with are larger than the merely human. The patterns which they throw up are expressed in stories which in a certain sense are contemplated at a distance, in the very act of narrating them, but where the emphasis is most of all on the dynamic succession of event upon event. Calvino has always seen himself prinicipally as a teller of tales. However, in *Le città invisibili* (*Invisible cities*, 1972) he produced a work of pure contemplation in which nothing happens at all, a book which bears the same relationship to narrative as still photography does to cinema. If, in his narrative, the act of writing provides a kind of contemplation of events, then in this book contemplation is offered, by a reverse process, as a kind of action.

The fictitious cities of the book's title are images of human communities, of composite reality, of the whole bewildering multiplicity of the world in time and space. They are 'invisible' because their essence is beyond grasp, shifting, endlessly reformulated by the mind according to its circumstances, its mental codes, and the question it chooses to ask. What the mind finds in a city may be dictated by its own Memories or Desires (which may be the same thing), or by the Eyes through which it looks; a city may express itself through the Exchanges which take place within it, through Signs variously interpreted or the Name which it is given; it carries the marks of its own Dead and of the Heaven to which they aspired; it can be Tenuous and insubstantial, Continuous and therefore formless, even Hidden. The capital letters are deliberate here, because we have just listed the eleven headings under which cities are examined in the book. Within each verbal category five variant approaches are considered, making each category tend to overlap with others; and the result is fifty-five brief descriptions of individual cities, in which one concept is explored at a time and clothed in imaginative detail. The analysis of reality which all the descriptions represent is by nature disorderly and endless, so any controlling shape must belong to the book as an artefact and not to the inquiry itself. In fact the eleven categories are spread and contained in a tight mathematical pattern, which is pleasing but has no obvious significance, dividing the book into nine chapters. But these frozen pictures also have a human frame which is more informative: all the descriptions of cities are being recounted by the traveller Marco Polo to the Emperor Kublai Khan. The Oriental despot is trying to possess with his mind an Empire which is too large, and he turns to the outsider, the Venetian, to express it for him. Dialogues between Polo and Kublai appear at the beginning and end of each chapter, and they are essential in making more explicit the book's sense of direction. One of the briefer ones, structured like a proverbial piece of folk wisdom, has rightly been singled out (Mengaldo 1975) as central and exemplary:

Marco Polo descrive un ponte, pietra per pietra.

– Ma qual è la pietra che sostiene il ponte? – chiede Kublai
Kan.

– Il ponte non è sostenuto da questa o quella
pietra, – risponde Marco, ma dalla linea dell'arco che esse
formano.

Kublai Kan rimane silenzioso, riflettendo. Poi soggiunge:
Perché mi parli delle pietre? È solo dell'arco che m'importa.

Polo risponde: Senza pietre non c'è arco.

(Marco Polo describes a bridge, stone by stone.

'But which is the block which holds up the bridge?' asks
Kublai Khan.

'The bridge is not held up by any one block,' answers
Marco, 'but by the line of the arch which they form.'

Kublai Khan falls silent, pondering. Then he says: 'Why
do you talk to me about the stones? I'm only concerned with
the arch.'

Polo replies: 'Without stones there is no arch.')

(*Città*, 89)

Le città invisibili continually reflects this oscillation between
the abstract and the concrete in our attempts to come to terms with
the world; and, predictably, it also investigates the language in
which we express our findings. The language, that is, of the whole
mind and not merely of the literary pen – it can consist of words
and verbal concepts, but also of images, associations, man-made
symbols, memories, dreams, numbers or abstract patterns. All of
these form code systems which on analysis seem arbitrary and
without substance, but without which the world becomes certainly
formless and perhaps even in a sense non-existent. Once again the
human mind is faced with the necessity of using the tools it
possesses, provided that it does not invest them with too
absolute a significance. The mass of reality must be grasped by a
perception of systems, and it matters little whether the systems lie
already within reality or are imposed upon it. Thus Kublai Khan at
one point, wearying of what seem fruitless efforts to grapple with
interminable reality, prefers the image of a chess game and its
systems of relationships, even prefers the chess game as such.
(Saussure, in a famous analogy, compared human language itself
to a game of chess; and we are dealing here with the 'grammar' of
perception and existence.) But the extreme abstraction of chess on
its own leads Kublai to an impasse – what, in concrete terms, have
you won or lost when checkmate is reached? An empty black or

white square on the board? A void? Marco Polo rescues the Emperor by turning back from systems to concrete objects. He examines the piece of wood from which the chess square is made, and constructs the necessary existence behind it of a tree, a woodworm, a woodcutter, a forest . . . The pendulum between abstract and concrete must keep on swinging, and not come to rest at either of its equally meaningless poles.

At the very end of the book, Polo and Kublai consider two more polarities: the two cities between which the future must choose, the city as Utopia and the city as Hell. Value-judgements enter the book, to remind us that there is a practical purpose behind our contemplating, exploring, classifying, and that the conclusions which we reach will help bring the future into being. What are we to do, asks Kublai, if the formless all-embracing nightmare city is already beginning to blot out the earth? Marco's answer is perhaps a little sententious by Calvino's usual standards, but this is a book in which statements have to do the work of narrative:

> L'inferno dei viventi non è qualcosa che sarà; se ce n'è uno, è quello che è già qui, l'inferno che abitiamo tutti i giorni, che formiamo stando insieme. Due modi ci sono per non soffrirne. Il primo riesce facile a molti: accettare l'inferno e diventarne parte fino al punto di non vederlo piú. Il secondo è rischioso ed esige attenzione e apprendimento continui: cercare e saper riconoscere chi e che cosa, in mezzo all'inferno, non è inferno, e farlo durare, e dargli spazio.
>
> (*Città*, 170)

> (The hell of the living is not something still to come; if there is one, it is that which is already here, the hell which we live in day by day, which we create by being together. There are two ways of not being hurt by it. The first is what many find easy: to accept hell and become so much a part of it that you no longer see it. The second way is risky and demands constant alertness and skill: to seek out and learn to recognize who and what, in the midst of hell, is not hell, and to make that last, and to give it room.)

In *Le città invisibili* then, as in previous books, an indisputable preoccupation with the written word, a tendency of the writing to be self-referential, is balanced by attributing to literature a function analogous to other activities both intellectual and practical. Discussions about the status of the literary sign tend to have both a literal meaning and a metaphorical one, referring to human action and creativity in general. In his two most recently published works, however, this metaphor seems to lapse: *Il castello dei destini incrociati* (*The Castle of Crossed Destinies*, 1973) is a book about storytelling, and *Se una notte d'inverno un viaggiatore* (*If on a Winter's Night a Traveller*, 1979) is a book about books. In neither case is it easy to perceive the wider applications which have been maintained so far. These two books are pieces of writing whose subject, principally and perhaps exclusively, is writing.

As early as 1967 Calvino showed how seriously he had been taking the theoretical questions raised by modern literary criticism, when he went on a lecture tour with his much-quoted essay 'Cibernetica e fantasmi' ('Cybernetics and Ghosts': now in *Una pietra sopra* 164–181). In this essay he offers a theory of storytelling as a combinatory game, in which a finite number of signs or narrative elements, regulated by a set of rules as to how they may relate, are combined in a series of permutations which for practical purposes may be considered as infinite. The analogy is with human language as a chess game, the notion faced by Kublai Khan in *Le città invisibili*. Calvino characteristically proposes literary language, or the narrative game, as a continual search via new combinations for things which have not been said before, for formulae offered experimentally which then turn out to strike a chord of freshly discovered truth. There are influences here of structuralist approaches, and of the researches into narrative formulae conducted by Vladimir Propp; and Calvino also shows increasing acceptance of avant-garde arguments (Italian and generally European) about the 'open text', about the ultimate freedom of the reader to find in a text whatever the text creates for him, irrespective of what the author intended to put there (cf. Chapter 3; Calvino in fact acknowledged that freedom at least as early as 1960, in the introduction to *I nostri antenati*, xix). These arguments are led round to the reduction of the author's importance in the literary process, and to focussing more exclusively on how the text and the reader interact. If the reader is in any case going to interpret the text in his own way, then (it is argued) the author as an individual is almost eliminated from the picture: his chosen re-development of the existing signs of language and narrative will operate, or fail to operate, in a way which leaves his own aims and motivations far behind. This is the same pattern as was explored, though not specifically in relation to literature, in the Cosmicomic stories. In such a situation Calvino claims, in 'Cibernetica e fantasmi', to find a paradoxical freedom for the author. Released from the responsibilities of a dictator or pedagogue, he can concentrate on sheer craftsmanship, on the effort to get words down on to the page, knowing that in any case the effect on the reader is beyond his control. It could be said that in *Il castello dei destini incrociati* this theory is put into practice, while in *Se una notte d'inverno un viaggiatore* the theory itself and a number of related problems become the subject-matter of fiction.

Il castello began as a purely occasional game. To accompany published reproductions of an exquisite pack of tarot cards, Calvino put together a set of narratives in which the cards act as stages of each story, as symbols variously and hesitantly interpreted. The whole pack is laid out, one story after another, until it forms a dense oblong pattern, across which the different tales can be traced, interleaving neatly with one another, continually re-interpreting the arcane pictures so as to give each card a totally different meaning according to the sequence within which it is 'read'. This game acquired its own fascination, (though for a critical view of it, see Chapter 4, p. 112), and Calvino tried it again with a different tarot pack in the second half of the book entitled *La taverna dei destini incrociati* (*The Tavern of Crossed Destinies*); but the second time the game failed to work out according to its own rigid rules, and the author admits in a concluding note that he published the results as they stand in order finally to rid himself of an obsession. The book has attracted much interest and approval for the way in which it so neatly embodies up-to-date theories. It is curious, however, that the stories in it repeatedly lose their impetus as narrative, and end up not with a firm eventful outcome as in the Cosmicomic stories, but with an abstract theory, attitude or statement of themes. A book which attempts to experiment specifically with narrative dynamics ends up being curiously static, as though the techniques and preoccupations of *Le città invisibili* were overflowing into a book to which they are less appropriate. The most interesting part of the book is openly an essay rather than a story, in which Calvino plays with the twin images of himself, the writer, as man of action and contemplative, as Knight of Swords and Hermit, as St. George and St. Jerome. The alternation, or fusion, personified by Bradamante and Sister Teodora in *Il cavaliere inesistente* still seems to be functioning.

Se una notte d'inverno un viaggiatore is a much more complex achievement and a much more entertaining book. Its subject is the Book, as a creative artefact, as a tool, as an object of desire, as a stimulus, as an irritant, as a piece of merchandise. In conformity with the new emphasis on the reader-text relationship, the protagonist of the book is the Reader, who is addressed for most of the time in the second person, whereas the author or authors are the object of a wild goose chase, untraceable and perhaps non-existent. Faced frustratingly by a series of interrupted first chapters of novels, 'you' the reader embark on a search for a complete text, which brings 'you' successively into contact with the Bookseller, the Female Reader (Ludmilla), the academic Critic, the Author (but is it the right author?), the Non-Reader, and the literary Censor. Over all there dominates the figure of the Forger, one Ermes Marana, who is never seen face to face but seems responsible for the whole endless pursuit, and particularly responsible for the doubts about the identity and existence of real authors. The book seems to culminate with an apotheosis of reading, of its ability to triumph over the most startling defects in writing. Ludmilla the reader defeats the machinations of Marana the forger by being open to any positive stimulus which any text can give her. In the face of such unshakable ability to profit even from the most 'false' of texts, all questions of authenticity become irrelevant, as do philosophic doubts about the objective relationship between the literary sign and the world outside it. In a properly literary happy ending, 'you' the reader marry Ludmilla.

Both *Il castello* and *Se una notte* confirm Calvino's continuing ability to perform the unexpected. The second of the two is complex, thought-provoking and funny – indeed, it shows a happy resurgence of its author's comic vein, by means of which his best insights have usually been deployed. It remains true, however, that both books, in restricting their sights and their subject-matter to the literary process itself, run the risk faced by all self-referential writings, namely that of a certain circularity. What is more, in espousing so openly the view that authors are unimportant and may take a back seat, Calvino is for the first time suggesting a serious break with his previous practice, and renouncing what many would see as the basis of his achievements so far. His decision to embrace fantastic allegory in the early 50s was dictated by a determination to preserve his personal authorial tone, and to salvage 'the attack, the drive, the energy' of Neo-realism in order to continue making some impression on society. Up until *Le città invisibili* his writing maintained an organic development, sometimes complex but always traceable, from those initial principles. Now the claim to an authorial 'voice' is abandoned:

does this mean the abandonment also of the assault on reality conducted by the author's critical mind?

It has been argued (Cannon 1981, 107–109) that in *Se una notte* the renunciation of authorial dominance is only apparent, and that it is implicitly re-asserted by Calvino's effective control of the whole novel as we read it. This seems logically unavoidable: it is, after all, a type of argument which we have offered in these pages in relation to earlier works. It may be felt nevertheless that the 'attack' which has characterized Calvino's work in the past, his special combination of colloquialism, humour and precision are ultimately dependent on his accepting (and, whether he admits it or not, enjoying) full authorial responsibility. In most of his works, along with the artistry, there is a kind of urgency and concern which we are implicitly asked to transfer outside the books and apply to life around us. Thus did Calvino fulfil his reiterated intention that his fiction should open up possibilities, stimulate attitudes, even if it could not propose solutions; and thus were we aware that behind the invention and the nonsense was a voice speaking in response to a world which both author and reader shared. In the last two 'literary' books the urgency is relatively lacking, and the writing responds only to itself. It should be admitted in return that literature too can be something shared by both author and reader, and perhaps Calvino has simply come to accept that a reading public is not quite a general public, and that he is writing for an intellectually oriented minority: 'A book gets written in order to be placed alongside other books, so that it can take its place in a hypothetical bookshelf' (1967, reprinted in *Una pietra sopra*, 159). It is possible to feel that this constitutes a diminishment of his earlier programme, which was to appeal to 'the young person, the worker, the peasant who has found a taste for reading' and to help that person to resist 'terrible reality' ('Il midollo del leone', 1955, now in *Una pietra sopra*, 18). On the other hand, the actual size of Calvino's readership (large as it is, by Italian standards) may have seemed over the years to make that programme unrealistic.

Nobody, in any case, would be rash enough to draw final conclusions about watersheds or the lack of them in Calvino's literary development. To draw any conclusions at all about living, active writers is to offer hostages to fortune, and it is better simply to await with confidence Calvino's next proof of his ability to confound expectations. For those who have found his writing rewarding, the essential image of him remains the one he created for himself, that of the 'solitary who did not avoid people' in *Il barone rampante*. Firmly apart, constantly aware, he takes eclectic note of everything around him, and transforms all theories and models into a fresh contribution unmistakably his own. In order to 'look at the world properly' he stays 'the right distance away' both from the engulfing orthodoxies of mass industrial society and from the more self-conscious counter-orthodoxies which are thrown up as barricades against it. His has always been a perverse, playful, dedicated search for the unsaid, unthought alternative, the one which none of the orthodoxies has yet been able to see.

BIOGRAPHICAL NOTE

Italo Calvino's father was an agronomist, and his mother a botanist. They worked together for many years in Latin America. Calvino was born in Havana, Cuba, in 1923, but the family returned immediately to Italy and Calvino was brought up in San Remo. In 1943–44 he spent some months in a Communist partisan brigade in the Maritime Alps. He stayed in the PCI until 1957, when he resigned following the invasion of Hungary. In 1959 he joined Elio Vittorini in the foundation of *Il Menabò*, a periodical to which he contributed some important essays. *Il Menabò* folded soon after Vittorini's death in 1966. Calvino's participation in political debate dwindled, but his sympathies remained with the left. From 1947 he worked for Einaudi, the publishers, who also published all his own writings. He lived at various times in Rome and Paris. He married in 1964 and had one daughter.

Italo Calvino died suddenly in September 1985.

BIBLIOGRAPHY

PRINCIPAL WORKS

Il sentiero dei nidi di ragno, Einaudi, Turin, 1947; 2nd ed. introduced by the author, 1964; (trans. A. Colquhoun) *The Path to the Nest of Spiders*, Beacon Press, Boston, 1957; repr. Ecco Press, New York, 1976

I racconti, Einaudi, Turin, 1958 (incorporates among other collections *Ultimo viene il corvo*, 1949; *L'entrata in guerra*, 1954; *La speculazione edilizia*, 1957); (trans. A. Colquhoun and P. Wright) *Adam, one afternoon, and other stories*, Collins, London, 1957; Secker & Warburg, London, 1983

I nostri antenati, Einaudi, Turin, 1960 (incorporating *Il visconte dimezzato*, 1952; *Il barone rampante*, 1957; *Il cavaliere inesistente*, 1959); (trans. A. Colquhoun, 1959 and 1962) *Our ancestors*, Pan Books, London, 1980

Marcovaldo, ovvero le stagioni in città, Einaudi, Turin, 1963; (trans. W. Weaver) *Marcovaldo*, Secker & Warburg, London, 1983

La giornata di uno scrutatore (A Day in the Life of a Scrutineer), Einaudi, Turin, 1963; (trans. A. Colquhoun and W. Weaver) *The Watcher, and Other Stories*, Harcourt, New York, 1971

Fiabe italiane, Einaudi, Turin, 1965; (trans. G. Martin) *Italian Folktales*, Harcourt, New York, 1980; Penguin, Harmondsworth, 1982

Le cosmicomiche, Einaudi, Turin, 1965; (trans. W. Weaver) *Cosmicomics*, Harcourt, New York, 1968; Cape, London, 1969; Abacus, London, 1982

Ti con zero, Einaudi, Turin, 1965; (trans. W. Weaver) *t zero*, Harcourt, New York, 1969; *Time and the Hunter*, Cape, London, 1970

Le città invisibili, Einaudi, Turin, 1972; (trans. W. Weaver) *Invisible Cities*, Harcourt, New York, 1974; Secker & Warburg, London, 1974; Pan Books, London, 1979

Il castello dei destini incrociati, Einaudi, Turin, 1973; (trans. W. Weaver) *The Castle of Crossed Destinies*, Harcourt, New York, 1975; Secker & Warburg, London, 1977; Pan Books, London, 1978

Se una notte d'inverno un viaggiatore, Einaudi, Turin, 1979; (trans. W. Weaver) *If on a Winter's Night a Traveller*, Harcourt, New York, 1979; Secker & Warburg, London, 1981; Pan Books, London, 1982

Una pietra sopra, Einaudi, Turin, 1980; contains the great majority of Calvino's essays, including nearly all those quoted in the present study

WORKS CITED

Bernardini Napoletano, F. *I segni nuovi di Italo Calvino*, Bulzoni, Rome, 1977

Calligaris, C. *Italo Calvino*, Mursia, Milan, 1972

Cannon, J. *Italo Calvino, writer and critic*, Longo, Ravenna, 1981

Mengaldo, P. V. 'L'arco e le pietre (*Le città invisibili*)', *La tradizione del Novecento da D'Annunzio a Montale*, Feltrinelli, Milan, 1975, 406–426

FURTHER READING

Almansi, G. 'Il mondo binario di Italo Calvino', *Paragone* 22 (1971), 95–110

Bonura, G. *Invito alla lettura di Calvino*, Mursia, Milan, 1972

De Lauretis, T. 'Narrative discourse in Calvino: Praxis or Poesis?', *PMLA* 90 (1975), 414–25

—, 'Semiotic models: *Invisible Cities*', *Yale Italian Studies* 2 (Winter 1978), 13–37

Heiney, D. 'Calvino and Borges: some implications of fantasy', *Mundus Artium* 2 (1968), 66–76

Illiano, A. 'Per una definizione della vena cosmogonica del Calvino: appunti su *Le Cosmicomiche* e *Ti con zero*', *Italica* 49 (1972), 291–301

Pescio Bottino, G. *Calvino*, La Nuova Italia (Il Castoro), Florence, 1967

Woodhouse, J. R. *Italo Calvino: a reappraisal and an appreciation of the trilogy*, University of Hull, 1968
—, 'Fantasy, alienation and the *Racconti* of Italo Calvino', *Forum for Modern Language Studies* 6 (1970), 399–412

Index